EXTREMISM, COUNTER-TERRORISM
AND POLICING

In loving memory of Abdul Ghafur.

This work is dedicated to Geoff Coliandris, a good friend and excellent colleague who would have contributed his expertise on this subject matter to this text had circumstances allowed.

We would also like to thank our beloved family members Liz, Amel, Hiba, Sobia, Afreen, Asaf and Tasvir.

Extremism, Counter-Terrorism and Policing

Edited by

IMRAN AWAN
Birmingham City University, UK

BRIAN BLAKEMORE
University of South Wales, UK

Routledge
Taylor & Francis Group

LONDON AND NEW YORK

First published 2013 by Ashgate Publishing

Published 2016 by Routledge
2 Park Square, Milton Park, Abingdon, Oxfordshire OX14 4RN
711 Third Avenue, New York, NY 10017, USA

First issued in paperback 2016

Routledge is an imprint of the Taylor & Francis Group, an informa business

British Library Cataloguing in Publication Data
A catalogue record for this book is available from the British Library

The Library of Congress has cataloged the printed edition as follows:
Extremism, counter-terrorism and policing / [edited] by Imran Awan and Brian Blakemore.
    pages cm
 Includes bibliographical references and index.
 ISBN 978-1-4094-5321-5 (hardback : alk. paper)
 1. Radicalism. 2. Extremists. 3. Terrorism--Prevention. 4. Police.
 I. Awan, Imran. II. Blakemore, Brian.
 HN49.R33E984 2013
 303.48'4--dc23

2013000856

ISBN 13: 978-1-138-24877-9 (pbk)
ISBN 13: 978-1-4094-5321-5 (hbk)

Contents

List of Figures and Tables

List of Contributors

Imran Awan is a Senior Lecturer in Criminology at Birmingham City University and has previously held academic posts at the Centre for Police Sciences (University of South Wales) and Wolverhampton University. He has taught on a variety of modules, such as International Policing, Policing Cyber Crime, Terrorism Theory, and Violent Extremism and Terrorism. He has published widely in the area of counter-terrorism, human rights, and policing and recently co-edited the book *Policing Cyber Hate, Cyber Threats and Cyber Terrorism* (Ashgate 2012). In March 2010 he was invited by the Office for Security and Counter-Terrorism to a Prevent Seminar held in London to discuss government policy on how best to prevent violent extremism, and in 2011 took part in a review of UK government counter-terrorism legislation for the Equality and Human Rights Commission. Mr Awan is also a member of the Advisory Committee for the Measuring Anti-Muslim Attacks Project organised by Faith Matters, a non-profit organisation which hopes to show the scale of the problem of Islamophobia and provide support for victims. He is an ambassador for the Make Justice Work Campaign, a Fellow of the Higher Education Academy, and is the Founder and Director of the Ethnic Minority Research Network in Criminology.

Brian Blakemore is Head of the Police Sciences Division at the University of South Wales. He has previous experience on a wide range of academic awards with several academic management positions during his previous 29 years within this institution. He teaches on modules such as Science for Law Enforcement, Crime Investigation, Researching Police Practice and Researching Contemporary Issues. He has published on cognitive processes in investigation, Higher Education for police officers and professionalising the police force, the human rights aspects and investigative effectiveness of the national DNA database, and has co-edited three texts with Professor Colin Rogers on community and partnership working and more recently co-edited the book *Policing Cyber Hate, Cyber Threats and Cyber Terrorism* (Ashgate 2012). Mr Blakemore has also taught on several postgraduate programmes, often distance programmes, with the universities of Bradford, Bristol and Bath and also with the Bristol Management Centre. He is a Vice-Chair of the Higher Education Forum for Learning and Development in Policing and represents this forum on the former National Policing Improvement Agency (NPIA) and now COP HE framework Steering Group.

Jane Prince is a Chartered Psychologist and Principal Lecturer in the School of Psychology at the University of Glamorgan where she is course tutor for two

MSc awards; she has a particular research interest in identity, social identity and the ways in which individuals respond to threats and challenges to their identity positions. She has published on identity threats across the lifespan, identity issues in migration and social identity. Dr Prince's PhD research was on the challenges to identity experienced by policewomen; she has studied in Cardiff, London and Bordeaux and has worked in the UK, France and the Netherlands.

Angharad Saunders is a Senior Lecturer in Human Geography at the University of South Wales. Dr Saunders teaches on a range of modules and fieldwork across all years, alongside supervision of MSc students, and is currently engaged in several funded research projects that utilise participatory methodologies to explore ideas of place and identity. Two of those funded projects are Sounding the Way – a community audio-walk project taking place in Grangetown, Cardiff that is funded by Beacon for Wales – and Cartographies of Neighbourhood, which adopts participatory methods to explore ideas of neighbourhood and crime in Merthyr Tydfil, South Wales.

Huw Smart has been a part-time lecturer with the University of South Wales on the BSc Police Sciences honours degree since 2003. He retired from South Wales Police this year after a 30-year career covering many roles. He has been involved in publishing texts for policing for many years, ranging from police law for recruits and higher ranks examinations to more specific areas such as custody suites.

Patrick Tucker is a Senior Lecturer in Police Sciences at the Centre for Police Sciences at the University of South Wales. He has 30 years' policing experience, which includes Operational Policing Command, Firearms Command, Child Protection and Partnership working. He is currently the second year tutor for the BSc award. Mr Tucker also teaches on the Operational Planning and Investigation, and Strategic Management and Leadership in the Police Service modules of the online Masters programme. Before joining the University of South Wales, he was a police officer for 30 years. In his early career he held posts in uniform patrol, administration, child protection and training. His later career included positions managing crime and disorder partnerships, policy construction and finally BCU command. Mr Tucker has a broad command experience including firearms, major events and the day-to-day command of the capital city of Wales. He retired in 2007 in the rank of Superintendent.

Introduction

This text aims to bring together a diverse range of multidisciplinary ideas to explore the extent of extremism within the present context of society living in a constant state of heightened alert due to the threat of terrorism. The book is multifaceted and covers the origins of extremism and as the new Prevent Strategy 2011 comes into force it provides a crucial link to getting a better understanding of UK government policy and the methods of tackling extremism from a policing and community level. The book will give a policing rationale alongside specific community means of tackling extremist threats, providing key details for policy readers as well as academics. The range, law and definition of extremism will be explored and the present trends and possible future of the forms of extremism and the ability to police extremism are considered. This book is designed to be a 'one stop shop' for all these aspects.

The book begins by examining the meaning of extremism as a definition and the debate over the terminology. It also includes a study of the behaviour and motivations of individuals viewed as extremists. The book will then look at the psychology of potential extremists, the journey into extremism and on to terrorism; national legislation, international treaties and legislation will be critiqued in terms of effectiveness to combat the problems posed by extremism and terrorism, the national strategies proposed by UK and other governments will be reviewed and their effectiveness examined. The final chapter will draw on all the preceding work to discuss and examine the future of policing extremism. This text is not an encyclopaedia but is more than an introduction and references and further reading are provided for the reader. It includes an examination of legal frameworks and legislation regarding extremism and its limitations in an international setting will be analysed. The public perceptions and understanding of other groups within communities is also explored as is policing and the threat of overreaction and working with communities to prevent development into extremism. When the police service seeks 'engagement' with a community and attempts to help build community 'cohesion', there are implicit preconceptions and stereotypes at play, such as notions of heterogeneity, that is that most of the community is similar in its ideals, its ideas and its wants and needs. This book will examine this premise and seek to identify sub-groups within communities that are extreme. The main aim is to give a full understanding of the range of activities that develop extremism and lead to extremist action and terrorism, how such activity forms in our communities and what can be done to try to prevent individuals from becoming extremists and terrorists.

Extremism arises not only from outside an identity grouping, it is also created by those inside as a way of marking out difference and belonging. A range of extremist organisations is described, including but not overly concentrating on Islamist extremism both far right and far left; the relatively new digital populist extremism will also be covered. Lessons that should be learned from the conflict in Northern Ireland are compared to the approaches used presently to combat extremism. The book will look at background areas such as the concept of extremism and how it provides a platform for unlawful action and terrorism, definitions of these terms and analysis of the type of individuals likely to be recruited into activist groups and the methods used to recruit such individuals.

Global forces are dynamic and communities may struggle to remain cohesive within technological and economic change coupled with mass migration. This may cause governments to drift into mass surveillance and other counterproductive policing strategies. In essence, the police and security services need to find 'the balance between the need to maintain order online and the need to enforce the law' (Wakefield and Fleming, 2009: 77). The interactions between networks and modern communications hyperreality, social networking, clicktivism, social control and the surveillance/electronic police state are explored.

Sheldon and Wright state that 'cyber-security has become a national security issue' (2010: 10) that needs to be addressed. Ball and Webster (2003) argue that, following the 9/11 attacks, a massive expansion of security-surveillance capacities around the globe ensued. There was also an accompanying set of legislative powers such as the 'Patriot Act' in the USA which Roy (2004) describes as ushering in an automatic systematic of surveillance with the government using the powers to monitor phones, emails and computer use in general. While technology can aid prevention and detection of extremist cyber activity, there have been notable design flaws, and aspects such as privacy and human rights issues need to be addressed. It can be appreciated that one piece of technology cannot be expected to be the 'silver bullet' of any specific form of crime, and technology is double-edged and the implementation of anti-terrorist surveillance cameras, for example, can alienate the community it is supposed to protect (Awan 2012). The psychology relating to hate, extremism and terrorism is explored as well as an examination of the wider theories that relate to alienation from society, such as social identity theory, social influence, the social identity model of de-individuation effects and selective moral disengagement.

The recruitment of individuals who are likely to become deployable agents ready to commit atrocities for the cause follows well-established patterns and processes and the use of the Internet enables activists to magnify the propaganda effect of their argument and to phish for suitable individuals. The amplification of the propaganda effect online is analysed using the terror management theory. Extremism is a phenomenon exhibiting multiple dimensions, with hate-groups achieving their goals in four main ways: promoting ideology, promoting hatred of other racial or religious groups, exerting control over others and targeting opponents.

The book is also concerned with policing all forms of extremist activity and looks at the processes used by police forces in tackling the extremist threat. In particular case studies will be adopted to examine the level of police response to extremist threats and terrorism-related issues. The level of need for more international cooperation and legislation to combat a global network of activists is explored. Finally, we consider the overall position in relation to policing extremism and extremist activities. However, there are many questions on the best way to prevent and disrupt extremism and ultimately a multi-agency and community co-production may be needed to tackle it successfully. The UK government decided to restructure its Prevent Strategy 2011 in that it aimed to coordinate local and international responses to extremist crimes through coordinated strategies and proactive responses. Whilst this may true in Britain there is a need for a more universal national and international strategy to deal with extremism and this needs to be strengthened.

References

Awan, I. 2012. 'The Impact of Policing British Muslims: A Qualitative Exploration', *Journal of Policing, Intelligence and Counter-terrorism,* 7(1): 22–35.

Ball, K. and Webster, F. (eds). 2003. *The Intensification of Surveillance: Crime, Warfare and Terrorism in the Information Age.* London: Pluto Press.

Broadhurst, R. 2006. 'Developments in the global law enforcement of cyber crime policing', *International Journal of Police Strategies and Management,* 29(3): 408–33.

Casey, E. 2004. *Digital Evidence and Computer Crime: Forensic Science, Computers and the Internet.* San Diego: Academic Press.

EURIM. 2002. The European Information Society Group. *E-crime – A new opportunity of partnership briefing paper.* France: EURIM.

Jewkes, Y. and Yar, M. 2008. 'Policing Cybercrime: Emerging Trends and Future Challenges', in Newburn, T. (ed.) *Handbook of Policing,* (2nd edition). Cullompton: Willan Publishing.

Chapter 1

Extremism, Radicalisation and Terrorism

Imran Awan

Introduction

There is no single pathway towards extremism, violence and acts of terrorism instead there are a range of factors that lead to such incidents. Extremism has become a nebulous term with many different interpretations and definitions of what the term constitutes (Eatwell and Goodwin 2010). In the UK tackling this threat from extremism has led to a wave of counter-terrorism policies and anti-terrorism legislation. Indeed, the term has also resulted in a polarised debate about what the term 'extremism' means amongst academics, policy makers and politicians. For example, Hussain in his book entitled 'the Islamist' argues that extremism as a 'preamble to terrorism' (2007: 278). However, critics argue that the term extremism is far too broad and being converged with problematic associations with words linked to violent acts, such as 'violent extremism'; 'fundamentalism'; 'radicalisation'; 'jihad'; 'Islamism' and 'terrorism' (Davies 2008). Moreover, Eatwell (2006) argues that the term 'cumulative extremism' should be adopted as a means to define extremist threats to UK national security.

The British Government has defined extremism as a 'vocal or active opposition to fundamental British values, including democracy, the rule of law, individual liberty and mutual respect and tolerance of different faiths and beliefs. We also include in our definition of extremism calls for the death of members of our armed forces, whether in this country or overseas' (HM Government 2011: 107).

The problem with such definitions is that they will shift over time and similarly the term extremism will also evolve and change. Indeed, Hillyard (1993) argued that Irish communities in the 1960s were being labelled as extremists and had therefore become a 'suspect' community following the conflict in Northern Ireland. Similarly, Pantazis and Pemberton (2009) have also argued that the post-9/11 political discourse on extremism and the 'war on terror' rhetoric has led to British Muslims becoming the 'new suspect' community. The author agrees with the label that Muslim communities have become the 'new suspect' community and argues that the current Prevent Strategy (2011) reinforces this perception (Awan 2012). Furthermore, the above definitions can be considered as value-laden and subjective and as a result can be problematic when it comes to trying to understand the behaviour and patterns of individuals, groups, and movements described as extremists (Sunstein 2009; Hopkins and Kahani-Hopkins 2009). In 2006 this unprecedented threat from extremism was described by British Prime Minister Tony Blair at the time as:

> the poisonous propaganda of those people that warps and perverts the minds of younger people. it's a very long and deep struggle, but we have to stand up and be counted for what we believe in and take the fight to these people who want to entice young people into something wicked and violent but utterly futile. (*The Guardian* 2006)

Whilst media coverage and debate about extremism has focused on negative stereotypes and associations with people regarded as terrorists, critics argue that many individuals once regarded as extremists are now considered high profile political activists and reformers (Davies 2008). Furthermore, the word extremism in particular has, in the past, been used to describe people such as Mahatma Ghandi, Nelson Mandela, Malcolm X and Dr Martin Luther King, Jr who are now accepted as being pioneers for change and individuals who have made an important contribution towards social activism and social community cohesion. As Hopkins and Kahani-Hopkins (2009: 101) state:

> Dr King sought to re-define the meaning of extremism and moderation so as to re-shape the terms of reference with which his activism was to be judged. Specifically, his contrast between these forms of extremism (love and hate) left no place for moderation or passivity: all right-thinking people must identify with the project of mass activism.

Thus, this pervading debate as to who is and who is not an extremist is rooted in the political versus legal interpretation of extremism and terrorism. The analogy that 'one man's terrorist is another man's freedom fighter' is ample example of the problems when it comes to defining extremism and indeed terrorism. . Despite the conceptual challenges involved in attempting to define the word extremism there is little doubt that some people labelled as extremists have had the capacity to inflict harm and damage upon society in the pursuit of their ideological causes. Thus, the problem for international governments is the need to balance civil liberties whilst also preserving security (Bleich 2010). Grayling (2009) for example argues that the major problem for democracies across the world is the terrorist threat and also how values and liberalisation are protected within communities.

As noted above the label extremism, for some groups and individuals, can become a symbolic feature of the organisation, giving it credence and an opportunity to gather support and voice supporters' opposition or concerns (Chakraborti and Garland 2009). Presently, the UK Government identifies the most serious threat emanating from international terrorism as Al-Qaeda led terrorism, followed by the domestic threat from terrorist groups in Northern Ireland and the threat from far right extremist groups or lone individuals (HM Government 2011).

However, the British Government does recognise that similar extremist ideologies are also considered a threat to UK national security from the violent gang culture depicted in the London riots in the summer of 2011, animal rights extremism, anti-abortionists and anti-capitalist extremism. As discussed above there is no single pathway towards extremism; instead there are a wide range of reasons why someone would hold such views depending on their beliefs, vision, motivations, aims and values. These factors are based on a number of socio-economic, socio-demographic and cultural factors which are linked to issues of identity and self-critique (Davies 2008). Although there are many different forms of extremism this chapter will be focusing upon animal rights extremism, the threat from far right extremism and Islamist extremism.

Defining Extremism?

The UK counter-terrorism strategy CONTEST has four key themes in tackling the threat from terrorism. They are to 'Protect'; 'Pursue'; 'Prepare' and 'Prevent' a terrorist attack. The PREVENT strand of the strategy changes the original phrase of 'violent extremism' to just 'extremism'. According to the Crown Prosecution Service in Britain extremism could include 'glorifying, provocation or the promotion of criminal or terrorist inspired activity' (cited online CPS website 2010). Indeed, the problem with the interpretation of extremism is that the phrase can often be merged with other themes of violent acts. For example, Choudhury (2007) argues that extremism and radicalisation often merge into one uniform principle. He states that; 'Radicalisation requires the communication of extremist ideas' (Choudhury 2007: 22).

However, as noted above, extremism is a vague concept and one that has, by implication, the potential to marginalise and stigmatise a specific community (such as the Muslim community when discussing Islamist extremism) (Spalek 2011). The PREVENT Strategy 2011 does not help shed light on the debate on the meaning of extremism but instead provides further problematic issues of interpretation and analysis. The Citizenship Survey, run by Ipsos MORI on behalf of the Communities Analysis and Migration Division within the Department for Communities and Local Government, found that most people involved in the survey had rejected all forms of violent extremism (Ipsos MORI 2011).

In defining extremism the PREVENT Strategy 2011 has to focus on challenging and understanding what makes someone follow an 'extremist' or a 'radical' way of life and begin a process of engagement with support for those who the government deem at risk of becoming extremists or terrorists. Moreover, there is a need for a wider discourse to further understand not just what the term extremism means but also the increasingly important role technology and the internet is playing, as extremist groups begin to use it as a means to recruit, indoctrinate and radicalise 'vulnerable' individuals (these issues will be discussed in more detail in Chapter 5).

As noted above extremism as a term is so wide that it could cover far right extremism, Islamist extremism and animal rights extremism.

Different Forms of Extremism

Animal Rights Extremism

Counter-terrorism policies in Britain have not made any significant distinctions between different types of acts of terrorism or indeed extremism and as such extremism could be applied to animal rights groups who have used tactics of fear and violence to promote an ideological cause. Moreover, the UK Government has stated that 'Animal rights extremists engaged in these activities should not, therefore, be surprised to find themselves treated as terrorists' (Home Office 2004:10). Hadley (2009: 363) in his article 'Animal Rights Extremism and the Terrorism Question' raises serious questions and issues regarding whether acts of violence from animal rights protestors should be equated with acts of terrorism or extremism. He stated that: 'Perhaps animal rights extremists do not warrant the pejorative label "terrorists" but instead deserve to be known as freedom fighters consistently applying philosophically respectable views.'

Social movements and groups within animal rights organisations such as the Animal Liberation Front argue that their core purpose and moral rationale is to cause disruption of research involving animal testing. However, the problem with such groups and movements is the strong links that can be made with forms of extremism and therefore the goals they aim to achieve can often be undermined by the manner in which they protest thereby taking away the credence of these movements. Hadley (2009: 364) states that: 'A strong association of animal rights with terrorism in the public consciousness could undermine the credibility of the animal rights movement and set the cause of animal protection back decades.'

As noted above, animal rights protest groups have been criticised for the nature of the acts of violence used in their demonstrations. These problems can be manifested in the arguments made by such groups about the merits, morality and ethics of scientific research whereby violence is justified as its use may not be legal but is deemed to be proportionate and fair. Another major issue when labelling particular groups with the words extremism or terrorism is the lack of a universal definition of such terms.

The modern definition of terrorism, for example, has been controversial – the United Nations has not yet accepted a definition of terrorism. Furthermore, not having a universal definition of the word extremism has also led to the media and politicians often portraying terrorists as either dangerous 'Islamists' or 'Jihadists' which evokes images of 'Muslim terrorists' and 'Muslim fundamentalists' dressed in long robes, wearing the 'topi' (hat) and with beards. However, without a universal definition of the words extremism and terrorism it is a dangerous step to begin to label persons and groups based on their faith/religion and indeed this may lead to further resentment and anger amongst minority groups.

The UK definition of terrorism can be found under section 1 of the Terrorism Act 2000 as the use of threat of action where:

- the action falls within subsection 2
- the use or threat is designed to influence the Government or to intimidate the public or a section of the public the use or threat is made for the purpose of advancing a political, religious or ideological cause
- Action falls within this subsection if it
- Involves serious violence against a person
- Involves serious damage to property
- Endangers a person's life other than that of the person committing the action
- Is designed seriously to interfere with or seriously to disrupt an electronic system.

The debate surrounding the word terrorism has been problematic since its inception. For example, in a House of Lords debate surrounding the terminology there was a lack of clarity when it came to defining the word terrorism:

> I can only agree with what was said by both the noble Lord, Lord Goodhart, and the noble Lord, Lord Cope; namely, that there are great difficulties in finding a satisfactory definition. Indeed, I was unable to do so and I suspect that none of us will succeed. As I say, we must do our best but I hope we will not spend too much time on the definition. (Report by Lord Carlile 2006: 4)

Hadley (2009: 367) states that:

> It is not an exaggeration to say that there are as many definitions of terrorism in the literature as there are terrorist attacks in the real world. All of the leading definitions of terrorism, moreover, it is widely acknowledged, have their strengths and weaknesses and are more or less vulnerable to objection by counter-example. This has prompted some recent commentators to eschew attempting to define terrorism; instead they try to show what is distinctive or characteristic about it. (Schmid)

The Threat from Far Right Extremism

As noted earlier, PREVENT 2011 aims to promote integration, cohesion and community safety but as critics argue, failed to tackle the wider issue of far right extremism and instead paved the way for anti-Islamist groups such as the English Defence League (EDL). The UK Government identifies international terrorism, and in particular Al-Qaeda led extremism, as a major threat to UK national security

(HM Government 2011). However, the policy has little depth and substance in relation to the threat from far right extremist ideologies and although far right extremist groups have different aims and goals as compared to terrorist groups such as Al-Qaeda critics argue that they also pose a unique threat to international democracy. For example, groups such as extreme anti-capitalists, anti-abortionists and anti-Semites do not necessarily have the same motives as terrorist groups but could also be a threat (Hadley 2009).

Therefore, PREVENT 2011 has the potential to marginalise a single community, and thereby exacerbate the EDL rhetoric that Islamism is on the rise in Britain and should be combated (Chakraborti and Garland 2009). The case of Anders Breivik highlights how far right extremists can have the same impact as Islamist terrorist groups (Blake and Morris 2011). Breivik, who described himself as a Christian fundamentalist, claimed to have had links with the EDL, following his attacks that killed 77 people.

Although in his interview with Norwegian police he openly expressed his deep anti-Islamist views as a main cause for his actions in actual fact his attacks were not directed at the Muslim community but rather at government policy in relation to the migration of Muslim communities in Europe. However, his ideology seems to display a wider systemic problem with far right extremism and the rise of this phenomenon across Europe. According to a DEMOS report (2011) entitled 'The rise of populism in Europe can be traced through online behaviour' they found that far right extremist groups in Europe were on the rise. The study, which used Facebook group pages and had over 10,000 respondents from 11 countries, found that many participants across Europe held both hard line nationalist and anti-immigration opinions (Bartlett et al. 2011).

Far right extremist groups have been able to gain momentum and support relatively quickly and without too much notice following the mainstream views from politicians, the media and law enforcement agencies which have been focussed on Islamist groups as the major threat to national security (Bartlett et al. 2011). For example, far right groups such as the Progress party in Norway, the Party for Freedom in Holland led by the Dutch far right politician Geert Wilders and the Freedom Party in Austria, have become powerful political parties. Moreover, a report in 2011 by the Domestic Intelligence Agency in Germany found that over 767 people had some sort of affiliation with a far right extremist group (German Intelligence Report 2011).

In contrast the UK Government argues that since there are only 17 people associated with far right extremism (at the time of writing) serving a sentence in Britain for a terrorist offence then such far right extremism is not as serious a threat as Al-Qaeda or similar Islamist terrorist groups. Moreover, the PREVENT Strategy 2011 argues that people involved in far right extremism do not have the same training as those involved in Islamist extremism. The PREVENT Strategy (2011: 15) states that:

people involved in extreme right-wing terrorism have not received the same training, guidance or support as many of those who have engaged with Al Qa'ida or Al Qa'ida-influenced organisations.

Another reason the UK Government argues that far right extremism is a lesser threat than Islamist extremism is because the literature available on far right extremist groups is not as developed in a coherent policy framework. The PREVENT Strategy (2011: 20) argues that:

> Given the small number of relevant cases (and the absence here of extreme right-wing terrorist organisations and formal groups) our understanding of how people become involved in extreme right-wing terrorism is inevitably less developed than it is for terrorism associated with Al Qa'ida.

However the review into PREVENT 2011 also found that a majority (80 per cent) of respondents in the consultation believed that PREVENT should address the wider problems of far right extremism (HM Government 2011). Whilst the UK Government has recognised the threat posed by Islamist terrorist groups and as such banned certain Islamist groups which promote violence, critics argue similar far right groups like the EDL remain operational (the main difference between these groups being the ideologies and motives). For example, the Terrorism Act 2000 created measures that meant certain international terrorist groups would not be able to operate in the UK. (Home Office 2011).

The EDL, since its emergence, has staged a number of controversial demonstrations against Islam and Muslim communities which aim to ignite racial stereotypes and exacerbate conflict between Muslim and non-Muslim groups in the UK. Many of these protests have turned violent with a number of EDL and opposition members being arrested. Although similar protests have occurred with anti-capitalist forms of protests the EDL demonstrations have targeted mainly Muslim communities (Taylor 2010). The EDL website states that:

> If, like us and the many other tens of thousands of decent patriotic people in the country, you are fed up with Islamic Extremism, Islamism and our government's spineless inability to address the issues, then join the world's biggest protest group and help us to make a positive change for the better. (English Defence League website)

Indeed, the English Defence League has become a movement which has used a rally in Denmark to express their opposition to Islam. This rally has been used to work with different far right movements as a means to set up an anti-Islamic alliance across Europe to vent their frustration and anger. Although the rally was small the nature of its aim is a concern for those that promote community cohesion and partnerships. The leader of the EDL, Stephen Lennon, argued that they hoped the movement would be 'the start of a European movement that will continue to grow' (BBC website 2012). Moreover, the problem of such anti-Islamist rhetoric is the increased tensions that it could create between different communities. Goodwin (2012) states that; 'What we are seeing here for the first time in British political history is an anti-Muslim far-right organisation taking the lead in trying to mobilise pan-European opposition to Islam' (BBC website 2012).

As noted above, inevitably, within this climate of protest, the EDL have been quick to focus these protests within Muslim communities as a means to provoke public sentiment. In response similar Islamist groups have emerged in the UK such as 'Muslims Against Crusade' who held counter-demonstrations against the EDL. In May 2011, the Home Secretary, Theresa May, under the Terrorism Act banned the group because of fear that some of their demonstrations could possibly incite more violence.

This process requires a deeper understanding of the socio-economic, racial, ethnic and cultural barriers that exist today between law enforcement agencies and communities which have a lack of trust in the legal, criminal and political system. This may be because communities have a perception of being treated unfairly (Hickman et al. 2010). The long-term effects of such tactics upon young Muslim groups may also lead to them becoming disaffected and isolated as shown by a study by Spalek et al. (2008) which found that police accountability and transparency over their actions was a problem and one reason for tensions between police and community engagement.

Islamist Forms of Extremism

The psychology of an extremist is important and is discussed in more detail in Chapter 4, however, one of the major issues as regards behaviours of an extremist is the association with forms of moderation and extremism (Prus 2005; Reicher and Hopkins 2001). This perception of moderation could be used to describe Dr Martin Luther King, Jr who was also regarded as an extremist in the US at the time. However, although he was isolated and marginalised, conversely this led to a worldwide social movement led by Dr King which gained momentum as a movement for change, peace and equality.

As Hopkins and Kahani-Hopkins (2009: 99) state:

> Dr King was an extremist outsider and they called for those attracted to his project to revert to using the courts to redress the wrongs of segregation. In depicting Dr King in this way, the clergymen were drawing on a long history of thought that celebrates the virtues of moderation.

This sense of moderation and understanding is primarily based upon how individuals regarded as extremists have different viewpoints and interpretations of causes they believe to be legitimate. This exploration of opinions cannot always be measured but they are important social and cultural indicators of patterns of behaviour and attitudes. Hopkins and Kahani-Hopkins (2009:100) argue that:

Extremists are often depicted as people who see the world in simplistic black-and-white terms rather than more nuanced shades of grey. This perspective is well illustrated in work linking extremism to individual deficiencies in cognitive complexity.

Many of the theories which relate to extremism have made associations and links between Muslim groups and what is perceived as religious extremism (Loza, 2007; Schmidt et al. 2005). Indeed, one of the major reasons why people or groups deemed to be extremists hold such views is the notion that these individuals feel a sense of alienation, isolation and despair (Prus 2005). One of the core reasons for this isolation is what some groups or individuals consider unpopular counter-terrorism policing, anti-terror legislation, foreign policies and political values.

This can also have a detrimental effect upon communities regarded as extremists, for example, Briggs et al. (2006: 46) argue that:

> A lazy parlance in which the words "extremist" and "radical" have become interchangeable has meant that any Muslim expressing anything other than unremitting support for the government is under suspicion. Not only does this close down the space for important debates about issues which are causing understandable frustration, but it also means that government tends to speak only to those deemed "moderate" voices or the usual suspects.

The recent threat given by both politicians and the media is that Islamist forms of extremism are at an unprecedented level. This interpretation of extremism has become problematic since it risks labelling an entire community as having extremists within it. As a result many Islamic thinkers and theologians have begun a counter-argument which describes the word extremism as a positive word. For example, Hopkins and Kahani-Hopkins refer to a well-respected Muslim Imam named Ibrahim Mogra who argues that the word extremism should be used in its proper context. Below is a direct quote taken from Ibrahim Mogra as cited in Hopkins and Kahani-Hopkins study (2009: 103):

> "I like to think that I am an extremist and a fundamentalist and I'm doing my very best to become a better fundamentalist and a better extremist." He continued "The use of the word fundamentalist and extremist for me as a person of faith are beautiful words actually [excluded] I like to think that I'm extreme in my love for God, I like to think that I'm extreme in my love for the poor, I like to think that I'm extreme in my love for my family. There's nothing wrong with being an extremist."

This counter-extremist narrative has been also used by others such as Dr Zakir Naik, an expert on comparative religion based in India, and has argued that there is nothing wrong in a Muslim being an extremist so long as it promotes social community cohesion. In a speech delivered in London entitled 'Islam the only Solution' at the Global Peace and Unity Event, Dr Naik stated that:

> I am an extremist as I am extremely kind, extremely loving, extremely peaceful, extremely merciful what's wrong in being an extremist ... can any human bring tell me it's wrong to be extremely honest, to be extremely kind, or wrong to be extremely peaceful, or wrong to be extremely just. (Islam the Only Solution 2009)

Hopkins and Khani-Hopkins (2009) use an interesting examination of the word extremism which they argue has been misinterpreted by some Muslim extremists who are using a direct quote from the Quran which defines the concept of moderation and community cohesion for their own interpretation. They make reference to verse 143 in Surah 2 (Al-Baqarah) (the name of the Surah is translated to mean 'The Cow') which, they argue, has been used by extremist groups and organisations to justify violence. However this reference describes the Muslim community as the *Ummatan wasatan* which has been translated in a number of ways (Mawdudi translation of the Quran 2011).

The verse states: 'And it is thus that we appointed you to be the community of the middle way' (Surah Al-Baqarah: 143). Hopkins and Khani-Hopkins argue that some Muslim extremist groups have been using this verse to pander social discomfort and cause confrontation. However, the authors also state that the correct interpretation of the verse is the depiction of moderation and community cohesion. This view is reinforced by a number of translations and commentaries which include the commentary noted above in Sayyid Abul A'la Mawdudi 'Towards Understanding the Quran' which has been translated and edited by Zafar Ishaq Ansari and argues that the reference to the 'community' means that a group of people are following a path of justice, equality, moderation and balance and that they work and support each other for social progression and community cohesion.

The reference is a good example of how Muslim identities are shaped and the importance of community cohesion which relates to moderation, justice and acting in an equitable manner as highlighted in the Quran. As discussed above, Hopkins and Kahani-Hopkins' (2009) article entitled 'Reconceptualising 'extremism' and 'moderation': From categories of analysis to categories of practice in the construction of collective identity' used a qualitative data analysis which is based on two events where they aimed to assess intergroup relations and group identities by observing four key speakers at different conferences in order to gauge the perceptions and categories of moderation and extremism. Their findings suggested that contemporary Muslim affairs were being discussed in variety of positive social interactions. For example, they refer to a well-known Islamic scholar by the name of Dr Jamal Badawi, whose talk examined a number of social issues with respect to women's rights, justice, equality, human rights and democracy. They state that in the discussion of moderation and extremism Dr Badawi argued for more understanding and mutual commonality: 'Then there is also the question of moderation. Many people say there must be clash: Islam is extreme. It's not.' (Cited in Hopkins and Kahani-Hopkins 2009: 106).

Indeed, in a question-and-answer session with Shabir Ally (an Islamic imam) the authors also found that speakers were discussing moderation and rejecting fundamentalism and extremism. They state that: 'Responding to these questions, another respected scholar on the panel (Shabir Ally) referred back to the above speaker's characterization of the Muslim prototype as "balanced" to clarify the terms of reference for debate. First, he questioned the interchangeable use of the terms fundamentalist and extremist' (Cited in Hopkins and Kahani-Hopkins 2009: 107).

Conclusion

As noted above there are many different interpretations of the word extremism and many different groups regarded as extremists. The UK Government uses the PREVENT Strategy 2011 to deal with extremism and a Home Affairs Select Committee Report into examining the root causes of extremism has found that the UK Government will be expanding its PREVENT portfolio with more projects aimed at understanding how people become radicalised (Commons Select Committee, 2011). It does appear, however, that religious indoctrination of British Muslims is rooted in an ideology that promotes hate, anger and alienation, and ultimately leads to people committing acts of violence, extremism and terrorism (Fanshawe and Sriskandarajah, 2010). Extremism has been defined as behaviour which might include 'glorifying, provocation or the promotion of criminal or terrorist inspired activity' (cited online CPS website 2010). However, the Government viewpoint that Islamist extremism is the main threat to UK national security at best lacks clarity, and potentially leads to a perception that Government policy is being shaped in a subjective manner which may marginalise the communities they consider to be extremists (Lambert 2011). The author agrees with Davies (2008), who argues that the term extremism should cover a wide range of forms and should not be simply viewed as Islamist extremism.

Further Reading

Bartlett, J., Birdwell, J., and King, M. 2010. The edge of violence a radical approach to extremism. *DEMOS*. [Online]. Available at: http://www.demos. co.uk/publications/theedgeofviolence [accessed: 5 December 2011].

Dalgaard-Nielsen, A. 2010. Violent Radicalisation in Europe: What We Know and What We Do Not Know, *Studies in Conflict and Terrorism*, 33(9): 797–814.

Hasan, M. 2011. So Prime Minister, are we to call you an extremist now?, *The Guardian*. [Online]. Available at: http://www.guardian.co.uk/2011/June/09/ cameron-counter-terror-muslims [accessed: 11 July 2011].

Innes, M., Roberts, C., Innes, H., Lowe, T., and Lakhani, S. 2011. *Assessing the Effects of Prevent Policing: A Report to the Association of Chief Police Officers*, Cardiff: Universities' Police Studies Institute.

Slack, J. 2011. 40 UK Universities are now breeding grounds for terror as hard line groups peddle hate on campus, *Mail Online*, Available at: http://www.dailymail.co.uk/news/article.1394625/40-uk-universities-breeding-grounds-terror.html [accessed: 1 July 2011].

References

Awan, I. 2012. 'I am a Muslim not an Extremist': How the Prevent Strategy has constructed a 'Suspect' Community, *Politics & Policy*, 40(6): 1158–85.

Bartlett, J., Birdwell, J., and Littler, M. 2011. *The New Face of Digital Populism: 'The rise of populism in Europe can be traced through online behaviour…'*. [Online]. Available at: http://www.demos.co.uk/files/Demos_OSIPOP_Book-web_03.pdf [accessed: 20 April 2012].

BBC News. 2012. *EDL takes part in far-right European rally in Denmark*. [Online]. Available at: http://www.bbc.co.uk/news/uk-17570464 [accessed: 20 April 2012].

Blake, M., and Morris, N. 2011. Endorsement by mass murderer exposes EDL to fresh scrutiny, *The Independent*. [Online]. Available at: http://www.independent.co.uk/news/uk/crime/endorsement-by-mass-murderer-exposes-edl-to-fresh-scrutiny-2326471.html [accessed: 29 July 2011].

Bleich, E. 2010. Faith and State. British policy responses to 'Islamist' extremism. In R. Eatwell and M.J. Goodwin (eds), *The New Extremism in 21st Century Britain*. London: Routledge, 68–84.

Briggs, R., Fieschi, C., and Lownsbrough, H. 2006. *Bringing it home: Community-based approaches to counter-terrorism*. London: Demos.

Carlile, L. (2006). The Definition of Terrorism. [Online] Available at: http://www.official-documents.gov.uk/document/cm70/7052/7052.pdf [accessed 12 April 2012].

Chakraborti, N., and Garland, J. 2009. *Hate Crime: Impact, Causes and Responses*. London: Sage Publications.

Choudhury, T. 2007. *The Role of Muslim Identity Politics in Radicalisation (a study in progress)* (April), Department for Communities and Local Government: London Communities and Local Government. [Online]. Available at: http://www.communities.gov.uk/documents/communities/pdf/452628.pdf [accessed: 10 June 2010].

Commons Select Committee. 2011. Committee questions Minister on roots of radicalisation. www.parliament.uk. [Online]. Available at: http://www.parliament.uk/business/committees/committees-a-z/commons-select/home-affairs-committee/news/111206-rvr-oral-ev/ [accessed: 10 December 2011].

Communities and Local Government (2010). Citizenship Survey: April-September-England *Cohesion Research Statistical Research* (14). [Online]. Available at: http://www.communities.gov.uk/documents/statistics/pdf/1815799.pdf [accessed 1 July 2011].

Crown Prosecution Service. 2010. *Violent Extremism and Related Criminal Offences.* [Online]. Available at: http://www.cps.gov.uk/publications/prosecution/violent_extremism.html [accessed 2 March 2011].

Davies, L. 2008. *Educating Against Extremism.* Stoke on Trent: Trentham Books.

Eatwell, R. 2006. Community Cohesion and Cumulative Extremism in Contemporary Britain. *The Political Quarterly,* 77(2): 204–216.

Eatwell, R., and Goodwin, M.J. (eds) 2010. *The New Extremism in 21st Century Britain.* London: Routledge.

English Defence League. 2012. Join the English Defence League today and start to make a difference!. Available. http://englishdefenceleague.org/ [accessed: 1 February 2012].

Fanshawe, S., and Sriskandarajah, D., 2010. You Can't Put Me in a Box: Super-Diversity and the End of Identity Politics in Britain. London: Institute for Public Policy Research.

Githens-Mazer, J, and Lambert, R. (2010). Islamophobia and Anti-Muslim Hate Crimes: a London case study, *European Muslim Research Centre.* [Online]. Available at: http://centres.exeter.ac.uk/emrc/publications/IAMHC_revised_11Feb11.pdf [accessed: 19 June 2011].

Grayling, A.C. 2009. *Liberty in the Age of Terror: A Defence of Civil Liberties and Enlightenment Values.* London: Bloomsbury.

German Intelligence Report. 2011. Increase in Left-Wing Extremism Sparks Concern, *Spiegel Online.* [Online]. Available at: http://www.m.spiegel.de/international/germany/a-766865.html [accessed: 10 December 2011].

Hadley, J. 2009. Animal Rights and the Terrorism Question. *Journal of Social Philosophy,* 40(3): 363–78.

Hickman, J., Thomas, L., Silvestri, S., and Nickels, H., 2011. Suspect Communities: Counter-terrorism policy, the press and the impact on Irish and Muslim communities in Britain. [Online]. Available at: http://www.statewatch.org/news/2011/jul/uk-london-met-suspect-communities-findings.pdf [accessed: 9 January 2011].

Hillyard, P. 1993. *Suspect Community: People's Experiences of the Prevention of Terrorism Acts in Britain.* London: Pluto Press.

HM Government. 2011. *PREVENT Strategy* Presented to Parliament by the Prime Minister and the Secretary of State for the Home Department by Command of Her Majesty. [Online]. Available at: http://www.homeoffice.gov.uk/publications/counter-terrorism/prevent/prevent-strategy/prevent-strategy-review?view=Binary [accessed: 12 March 2011].

Home Office 2004. *Animal Welfare and Human Rights: Protecting People from Animal Rights Extremists.* London: Home Office Communications Directorate, July 2004, [Online]. Available at: http://webarchive.nationalarchives.

gov.uk/20080726153624/http://police.homeoffice.gov.uk/publications/
operational-policing/humanrights.pdf [accessed: 27 March 2013].

Home Office. 2011. Proscribed terror groups or organisations. [Online]. Available
at: http://www.homeoffice.gov.uk/publications/counter-terrorism/proscribed-
terror-groups/ [accessed: 3 December 2011].

Hopkins, N., and Kahani-Hopkins, V. 2009. Reconceptualizing 'extremism' and
'moderation': From categories of analysis to categories of practiced in the
construction of collective identity. *British Journal of Social Psychology*, 48:
99–113.

Hussain, E. 2007. *The Islamist*. London: Penguin.

Ipsos MORI (2011). *Race, Faith and Cohesion*. [Online]. Available at: http://
www.ipsosmori-com/researchspecialisms/socialresearch/specareas/
racefaithandcohesion.aspx [accessed: 1 June 2011].

Ipsos MORI. 2011. Community Cohesion and PREVENT: How have Schools
Responded?, Prevent Report DFE RR085; Also see Phillips, C., Tse, D., and
Johnson, F. 2010 Department for Education. [Online]. Available at: http://
www.education.gov.uk/publication/eOrderingDownload/DFE.RR085.pdf
[accessed: 8 July 2011].

Jackson, R. 2011. The Failed Paradigm of Prevent Responding to Prevent 2011,
Muslim Council of Britain. [Online]. Available at: http://www.mcb.org.uk/
comm_details.php?heading_id=121&com_id=2 [accessed: 1 July 2011].

Jarvis, L., and Lister, M. (2011). Values and Stakeholders in the 2011 Prevent
Strategy Responding to Prevent 2011, *Muslim Council of Britain*. [Online].
Available   at: http://www.mcb.org.uk/comm_details.php?heading_
id=121&com_id=2 [accessed 1 July 2011].

Lambert, R. 2011. Neo Conservative Ideology Trumps Academic Research and
Practitioner experience Responding to Prevent 2011, *Muslim Council of
Britain*. Available at: http://www.mcb.org.uk/comm_details.php?heading_
id=121&com_id=2 [accessed 1 January 2011].

Loza, W. 2007. The Psychology of Extremism and Terrorism: A Middle-Eastern
perspective. *Aggression and Violent Behaviour*, 12: 141–55.

Mawdudi, S. (2011). *Towards Understanding the Quran*. Translated and edited by
Zafar Ishaq Ansari. UK Islamic Mission, Dawah Centre, Birmingham (UK).

Mullen, E., Bauman, C.W., and Skitka, L.J. 2003. Avoiding the pitfalls of politicized
psychology. *Analyses of Social Issues and Public Policy*, 3: 171–76.

Pantazis, C., and Pemberton, S. 2009. From the 'Old' to the 'New' Suspect
Community. Examining the Impacts of Recent UK Counter-Terrosist
Legislation. *British Journal of Criminology*, 49(5): 646–66.

Pantazis, C., and Pemberton, S. 2011. Restating the case for the suspect community,
British Journal of Criminology, 51(6): 1054–62.

Prus, R. 2005. Terrorism, tyranny, and religious extremism as collective activity:
Beyond the deviant, psychological and power mystiques. *American Sociologist*,
36: 47–74.

Reicher, S., and Hopkins, N. 2001. Psychology and the end of history: A critique and a proposal for the psychology of social categorisation. *Political Psychology*, 22: 383–407.

Schmidt, C., Joffé, G., and Davar, E. 2005. The Psychology of Political Extremism. *Cambridge Review of International Affairs*, 18: 151–72.

Spalek, B. 2011. A top down approach Responding to Prevent 2011, *Muslim Council of Britai.*, [Online]. Available at: http://www.mcb.org.uk/comm_details.php?heading_id=121&com_id=2 [accessed 1 July 2011].

Spalek, B., El Awa, S., and McDonald, L. (2008). Police-Muslim Engagement and Partnerships for the Purposes of Counter-Terrorism: An Examination, *Arts and Humanities Research Council*. Available at: http://www.religionandsociety. org.uk/uploads/docs/2009_11/1258555474_Spalek_Summary_Report_2008. pdf [Online]. [accessed: 10 April 2010.]

Sunstein, C. 2009. *Going to Extremes: How Like Minds Unite and Divide*. Oxford: Oxford University Press.

The Guardian. 2006. Blair backs MI5 terror warning. [Online]. Available at: http:// www.guardian.co.uk/world/2006/nov/10/terrorism.politics [accessed: 20 April 2012].

Taylor, M., 2010. English Defence League: Inside the violent world of Britain's new far right. *The Guardian*. Friday 28 May 2010. [Online]. Available at: http:// www.guardian.co.uk/uk/2010/may/28/english-defence-league-guardian-investigation [accessed: 1 February 2012].

Zakir, N. 2009. Islam the only Solution, *Global Peace and Unity Event*, London. [Online]. Available at: http://www.youtube.com/watch?v=RbJLbR9VUbY [accessed: 20 April 2012].

Chapter 2

Policing Extremism within a Counter-Terrorism Context

Imran Awan

Introduction

The terrorist attacks that took place in London, Madrid and the United States since the turn of the century have led to a heightened atmosphere and impacted upon international counter-terrorism policies and counter-terrorism policing which, critics argue, have been used disproportionately against minority communities under the guise of protecting 'national security' (Awan and Blakemore 2012). Indeed, this sense of fear and anxiety manifested itself following the start of the London Olympics (2012) as the British police were quick to clamp down on any form of perceived threat. For example, an unsubstantiated claim that cigarette vapour might actually be a bomb led to armed police officers closing down one of the UK's busiest motorways in fear that there may have been a bomb on board a bus (Evans et al. 2012). Pickering et al. (2007: 9) state that:

> As such, in many international jurisdictions counterterrorism policing has often been seen as anathema to individual human rights and as part of the highly contestable argument that when it comes to dealing with the threat of terrorism there is an unavoidable trade-off between individual rights and national security.

Although extremism, as noted in Chapter 1, could cover a wide spectrum including animal rights extremism, Islamist extremism and far right extremism, this chapter will focus on counter-terrorism policing of minority communities and the overall effectiveness of such strategies when combating extremism within a counter-terrorism context. This is because the evidence (discussed below) appears to suggest that many Muslim communities in particular have been maligned both by UK and indeed international government counter-terrorism policies (such as the cases in the US, France and Belgium) and also by the manner in which law enforcement agencies have the potential to abuse their powers. Whilst there are clearly a number of complex terrorist plots that the police are having to deal with daily it does appear that many police forces across England and Wales are increasingly abandoning community policing tactics and using counter-terrorism units to gather intelligence from within communities in order tackle the terrorist threat (for example Project Champion, discussed below).

Whilst this chapter does not intend to downplay the threat posed by terrorist groups and individuals it is clear that counter-terrorism policing does risk alienating and marginalising Muslim communities. This chapter will examine broader international counter-terrorism policing tactics and the overall effectiveness of such strategies when dealing with extremism.

Counter-Terrorism Policing in Britain

In the UK counter-terrorism policing is based upon the Government's counter-terrorism strategy CONTEST and the Prevent, Pursue, Protect and Prepare strands of the strategy. Counter-terrorism policing is also closely informed by the Terrorism and Allied Matters (TAM) group which provides the British police with a framework for countering extremism and terrorist threats. Indeed, the police in Britain are also monitoring extremist material online with the use of a counter-terrorism police referral system which aims to deal with extremist websites and online material that may be of a terrorist nature. The Counter-Terrorism Internet Referral Unit was set up by the Association of Chief Police Officers (ACPO) in March 2011 and uses an anonymous referral system for members of the public who are able to alert the police of any suspicious online material which may incite people to commit a terrorist act (Direct Gov 2011).

An article in the *Independent* in 2012 entitled *Police and MI5 get power to watch you on the web* also suggests that both the UK police and intelligence agencies are to be given wider counter-terrorism powers by the UK Government in the future, in order to monitor suspicious online activities (*The Independent* 2012). Whilst such surveillance has been argued by the UK government as necessary for protecting national security, critics argue that such powers will lead to unnecessary surveillance and cause further resentment amongst communities (Awan 2012).

As a result of such measures there have been incidents revealing that hackers have targeted the police counter-terrorism online unit with sustained attacks aimed at disrupting the system. For example, two people from Birmingham (UK) were arrested by counter-terrorism police officers in 2012 for hacking into an anti-terrorist hotline used by senior police officers that gets the public to inform the police of any suspicious terrorist conversations. Following the Olympic Games in London in 2012 critics have also questioned the police capabilities in tackling extremist threats online from groups who have sympathies with Al-Qaeda led extremist groups and those who are victims of online hate crime (Dodd and Halliday 2012). For example, The Tell MAMA (Measuring Anti Muslim Attacks) project has found that 632 hate incidents of anti-Muslim nature were reported to the project since March 2012 and 74 per cent of those crimes were online hate incidents (Tell MAMA website 2013).

Thus a key theme of UK counter-terrorism policing has been to work with the Association of Chief Police Officers (ACPO) alongside the Counter-Terrorism Command within the Metropolitan Police Service, who are tasked with developing a number of counter-terrorism police units across the UK. The role of these units is to assess the risk from extremist groups/individuals and terrorism whilst also developing strategies that help prevent and disrupt terrorist attacks in Britain. Most of these groups are based in regional areas such as the West Midlands, West Yorkshire, Greater Manchester and London. The level of expertise within these groups is diverse and includes those who are trained in providing specialist advice on counter-terrorism issues. ACPO notes that: 'As a whole, the network has a wide range of experts including but not limited to skilled detectives, financial investigators, community contact teams, intelligence analysts, forensic specialists and high-tech investigators' (ACPO website).

Although in theory all forms of extremism, including gang culture, animal rights extremism and anti-capitalist extremists, are monitored by counter-terrorism policing units, in practice these units have been used mainly in communities where there is a perceived high risk of sustained extremism. It is this method of counter-terrorism policing which has caused most controversy and alienated Muslim communities in the UK (Awan 2011). The police have also been given wider powers by counter-terrorism legislation which have been enacted by the UK Government in order to combat the extremist threat. The broad scope of these powers is highlighted under s57 and s58 of the Terrorism Act 2000 which allow a police officer to detain someone who they believe has possession of terrorist material which might be used for a terrorist purpose. For example, three people were arrested under s57 of the Terrorism Act following a flight from Oman for having documents that could be used for a terrorist purpose (*The Guardian* 2012). Moreover, s44 of the Terrorism Act 2000 initially allowed the police the power to stop and search anyone without reasonable suspicion. However, following a recent European Court of Human Rights judgement the power has been amended so as to include reasonable suspicion.

Counter-Terrorism Police Operations

A number of controversial counter-terrorism police raids at the same time have risked alienating and stigmatising Muslim communities. For example, in 2008 counter-terrorism police officers took part in a number of raids across Liverpool and Manchester in pursuit of 12 individuals they suspected had been planning to commit a terrorist attack. Indeed, the manner in which the arrests were made led to the independent reviewer of anti-terrorism legislation at the time, Lord Carlile, openly criticising police officers for failing to take legal advice before the arrests. Furthermore, all 12 suspects were released without charge leading to more speculation about the role of counter-terrorism policing and intelligence-led techniques of gathering evidence by the police. Lord Carlile stated that: 'My main criticism is the police should have consulted the CPS terrorism experts, there are several of them, for their expert advice in relation to areas of law and other material available' (*The Guardian* 2009).

Similarly, Pickering et al. (2007: 57) state that:

> Previous mention has been made of the negative impacts on police–community
> relations in the United Kingdom of the extensive use of 'stop and search' powers
> against young people from minority ethnic communities. Likewise high-profile
> raids on Muslims based on inaccurate intelligence have also had an adverse
> effect on police–community relations.

Although Lord Carlile did argue that in exceptional circumstances (such as the above) some of the men should have been arrested based on the evidence (in particular email conversations) it does suggest a wider problem within the police service of adequate training of counter-terrorism police officers when conducting such high profile operations and also reveals how the police need to have a broader understanding of cultural issues and sensitivities within such communities where counter-terrorism police operations are viewed in a negative light (Awan 2012).

Indeed, one way to improve counter-terrorism policing operations is to work with local communities and inform them of what terrorist operations might be taking place. Although police forces might question the issue of sensitive material being used within such an open forum this could give the community the opportunity to engage with police in a more meaningful and constructive manner. As Pickering et al. (2007:58) state: 'Sharing intelligence on police counter-terrorism activities is an important component in building trust with communities.'

Another example of a controversial counter-terrorism police raid took place in 2006 and involved counter-terrorism officers taking part in dawn raids in Forest Gate in London in the UK. In this particular operation London Metropolitan Police used counter-terrorism police officers to force entry into the home of two Muslim brothers (Mohammed Abdul Kahar and Abul Koyair) and led to one of the brothers being shot by a police officer. Despite the arrests both brothers were released without charge and a number of serious questions remained unanswered about the poor intelligence, the role of counter-terrorism policing, the profiling of innocent people and the use of firearms in such operations.

'In particular, many members of the community felt that the seriousness of the allegations—the production of high-impact terrorist weapons—effectively tarnished the reputations of all Muslims' (Pickering et al. 2007: 104).

The problem with incidents such as the above is the potential for such acts to become tools for extremist groups to target and prey upon vulnerable individuals and this potential remains problematic. Pickering et al. (2007: 104) state that:

> Forest Gate episode provided a publicity coup for extremist groups in Britain,
> who continue to use the incident as a key part in their efforts to recruit from
> within disaffected pockets of British society, despite a substantial effort by the
> Metropolitan Police to repair relations with the local community.

Another problem for the police has been the role and management of counter-terrorism policies and procedures. For example, the UK Home Affairs Select Committee argued that the National Crime Agency should be given the role of wider strategic counter-terrorism operations. Following the Police Reform and Social Responsibility Bill, a number of reforms have been recommended, such as the creation of Police and Crime Commissioners (which are now in operation), which, it is argued, would allow greater collaboration between forces in dealing with counter-terrorism policing. Keith Vaz, the Chairman of the Home Affairs Committee stated that:

> The police perform a difficult and dangerous task on behalf of the public and the continuing uncertainty about the future of many of the bodies involved in policing has the potential to be very damaging. (BBC website 2011)

Counter-Terrorism Policing and Communities

A report published by Monash University in 2007 entitled 'Counter-terrorism policing and culturally diverse communities' provides a unique picture of counter-terrorism policing in Australia and highlights the problematic nature of transnational counter-terrorism policing. The study involved over 50 interviews with Victoria police between April and September 2005 and used online surveys of over 541 participants in 2006; 18 of the interviewees were with specialist units directly engaged with counter-terrorism issues. The findings suggest that the Victoria police force have had to work hard in building trust with local communities because of the role of counter-terrorism police officers. The report also found that whilst Victoria police were benefiting from the Australian Government's investment in the promotion of social cohesion and diversity, they were also under pressure to monitor people within Muslim communities who were deemed to be extremists.

It appears that one of the major problems for the Victoria police was being able to adopt forms of community policing into their counter-terrorism policing agenda. This may have been because of anti-terrorism legislation enacted in Australia such as the the Security Legislation Amendment (Terrorism) Act 2002 and the Anti-Terrorism Act (No. 2) 2005. Similarly in the UK, anti-terrorism laws, such as the Terrorism Act 2000, the Prevention of Terrorism Act 2005, the Terrorism Act 2006 and the Counter-Terrorism Act 2008 aim to prevent and prosecute people for acts of terrorism and extremism. Interestingly, the study found that many police officers from Victoria felt the counter-terrorism legislation had made their jobs more difficult.

Furthermore, they found that almost half of police officers in Victoria did not have adequate training in counter-terrorism related issues. Clearly, the problem with counter-terrorism policing is that it can be viewed as a responsive tactic as opposed to a real preventative or community-orientated policing model. Indeed, the study also found that the Muslim community prior to the counter-terrorism policing programme did have a good relationship with Victoria police, however, this was put under strain by counter-terrorism policing and anti-terrorism legislation.

In the UK counter-terrorism policing has been justified as a necessary tool to combat and deal with the terrorist threat. For example, Lord Stevens, the former Commissioner of the Metropolitan Police, controversially argued that:

> I'm a white, 62-year-old, suit wearing ex-cop—I fly often, but do I really fit the profile of a suicide bomber? ... Of course there'll be instant squealings that this is racism. It's exactly the same as recognising that, during the Northern Ireland troubles that left thousands dead, the IRA were totally based in the Catholic community and the UVF in the Protestant. (Cited in the Report by Pickering et al. 2007: 53)

Innes (2006) argues for a British police force that focuses on community intelligence and the neighbourhood policing model as a means to engage with communities and build trust. A problem with counter-terrorism policing operations is the risk that they could lead to the social exclusion of communities and as such prove difficult for police gathering evidence and building the necessary trust from local communities.

Furthermore, in the United States intelligence-led policing models have been adopted as a mechanism to tackle the extremist threat. Clarke and Newman (2007) in their article 'Police and the Prevention of Terrorism' cite the example of the New York Police force using over 1,000 police officers tackling the terrorist threat. Clarke and Newman (2007), however, argue that although intelligence-led policing does play a role in combating the extremist threats faced in the US, transnational police forces require police commanders and police leaders to have a more pro-active plan for targeting extremist individuals within local communities. They are keen to suggest that the police need to first identify who might be vulnerable to becoming an extremist and then to work with various stakeholders in countering extremist threats. They state that: 'For each target, police must think clearly about the kind of attack that is most likely and, by trying to think like a terrorist, consider how the attack would be undertaken and which specific vulnerabilities would be exploited' (Clarke and Newman 2007: 17–18).

Moreover, they state that police officers are required to have better training in regard to counter-terrorism operations and also in relation to crime prevention:

> the plan should be adequately resourced and each division should ensure that the responsible officers are properly trained in crime prevention and security procedures. The divisional plans should be reviewed by central command to ensure that boundary issues of omission or overlap are addressed. Clarke and Newman (2007: 18)

Racial Profiling in the United States

One of the concerns about counter-terrorism policing is the use of profiling based on a person's religion, ethnicity, gender, age and culture. Such tactics have led to Muslim communities being opposed to counter-terrorism policing and inevitably risked alienating them. Another problem with the issue of profiling is the statistical data that reveals profiling has disproportionately targeted Muslim communities. As a result law enforcement agencies must ensure that their intelligence is credible and that any arrests they make comply with human rights and legal protocols. Pickering et al. (2007) state that in Australia racial profiling is linked to anti-terrorism laws. Indeed, one of the major concerns about racial profiling has also been the substantial evidence (which will be discussed below) that shows anti-terrorism legislation has given the police the use of blanket stop-and-search powers.

Whilst in the UK Muslim communities have been described as the 'new suspect' community, in the US the debate has also shifted towards how counter-terrorism policing/policies and racial profiling have led to US Arab/Muslim communities being viewed as a 'new suspect community'. The American Civil Liberties Union argues that:

> The Obama administration has inherited a shameful legacy of racial profiling codified in official FBI guidelines and a notorious registration program that treats Arabs and Muslims as suspects and denies them the presumption of innocence and equal protection under the law. (American Civil Liberties Union 2009: 9)

In the US profiling has not just targeted Muslim communities; evidence suggests that a number of police raids have also disproportionately targeted immigrant communities from Latin America. The senator of New Jersey, Robert Menendez, stated that: 'The legitimate desire to get control over our borders has too often turned into a witch-hunt against Hispanic Americans and other people of color' (Menendez 2008. Cited in the American Civil Liberties Union Report 2009: 10).

Indeed, in a comprehensive report based on the work of the American Civil Liberties Union and the Rights Working Group which analysed the issue of racial profiling in the US they found that:

> Since September 11, our nation has engaged in a policy of institutionalized racial and ethnic profiling ... If Dr. Martin Luther King Jr. were alive today ... he would tell us we must not allow the horrific acts of terror our nation has endured to slowly and subversively destroy the foundation of our democracy (US Representative John Conyers Cited in the American Civil Liberties Union Report 2009: 11).

President Barack Obama's election to office led to an optimistic viewpoint that racial profiling would end. Obama's presidency campaign, however, which included strong sentiment and indeed slogans against racial profiling, has done little to change the counter-terrorism landscape. In the US like the UK and Australia, however, counter-terrorism legislation such as the Anti-Terrorism and Effective Death Penalty Act 1996; the Financial Anti-Terrorism Act 2001; the US Patriot Act 2001 and the Terrorist Bombings Convention Implementation Act 2001 has also contributed towards an image of racial profiling.

The FBI has also used controversial tactics of surveillance, interrogation, border stop-and-search, airline profiling, the creation of US 'no-fly lists' and the NSEERS (special registration) program. The problem for law enforcement agencies in the US is that this allows them and the police to use wide powers which inevitably have the potential to profile innocent people. As the ACLU states:

> Indeed, data and anecdotal information from across the country reveal that racial minorities continue to be unfairly victimized when authorities investigate, stop, frisk, or search them based upon subjective identity-based characteristics rather than identifiable evidence of illegal activity. (American Civil Liberties Union Report 2009: 12)

In the US a number of law enforcement agencies are responsible for protecting citizens from terrorism and extremist threats, such as the Department of Homeland Security; Immigration and Customs Enforcement agency; the Border Enforcement Security Task Force and the Delegation of Immigration Authority. The ACLA report refers to how the US immigration policy has become heavy handed under the guise of combating terrorism to deport many innocent Muslim suspects. (American Civil Liberties Union Report 2009: 29).

The recent European Court of Human Rights ruling allowing the extradition of four men being held in British prisons (including Babar Ahmed) to the US is also a sign that US counter-terrorism policies and policing extremism has become a transnational issue. For example, 'Operation Front Line', which was designed to 'detect, deter and disrupt terror operations', has been criticised because of the impact it has had upon Muslim communities in America. The programme revealed damning evidence suggesting that the police were using counter-terrorism raids as a means to arrest and detain people unlawfully. Moreover, data from the US Department of Homeland Security revealed that 79 per cent of people investigated for a terrorist offence had come from immigrant Muslim communities. The report also found that people from immigrant communities were 1,280 times more likely to be arrested and stopped than individuals from another country. More worryingly, the statistics showed that none of the people arrested were being charged with a terrorist related offence (American Civil Liberties Union Report 2009).

FBI Relationship with Muslim Communities

One of the core problems with counter-terrorism efforts in the US is the relationship between intelligence services such as the FBI and Muslim communities following the global 'war on terror'. The perception that Muslim communities have become a 'new suspect' community is a real concern.

For example, the FBI have used a number of informants as a means to tackle extremism in America and in 2009 used controversial tactics to infiltrate a number of mosques in California, with the use of hidden cameras, informants and other covert surveillance tools which recorded conversations within the mosques. Similarly, in the UK the police have been criticised for their counter-terrorism operations within mosques with the use of surveillance, as shown by the case of Greater Manchester Police, who used undercover officers to gather intelligence within mosques (Bano 2011).

The problem with such tactics is that they can lead to poor police–community relations and can have a counter-productive effect when working with local communities. Counter-terrorism policing can also have a detrimental effect upon community policing as it could possibly lead to suspicion from within those communities, whose members may decide not to attend mosques for fear that they are being watched and listened to. The ACLA report states that:

> Local residents report that the surveillance has caused them to avoid the mosques and pray at home, avoid making charitable contributions – a fundamental tenet of the Muslim faith – and refrain from having conversations about political issues such as U.S. foreign policy. (American Civil Liberties Union Report 2009: 32)

One of the most controversial counter-terrorism tactics used by the FBI has been profiling of people at airports. This often has led to the questioning of members of minority communities, in particular concerning issues about their faith, ideologies and political opinions. The ACLA findings include a number of interviews with Muslim participants who reported that their personal information and computes were being searched. Such tactics can have a counter-productive effect often leading to a humiliating and degrading experience for those being stopped and searched.

Moreover, the problem with these tactics is that they can lead to the unnecessary stop-and-search of people who are innocent yet deemed to be a threat because they fit a certain profile. This was demonstrated by the case of Raed Jarrar who successfully challenged JetBlue Airways on the basis that they had discriminated against him because of a T-shirt he had worn with the words 'We will not be Silent'. He argued his treatment by the airline officials had amounted to profiling and racial discrimination:

> Jarrar, an Iraqi-born architect, was treated differently from all other passengers waiting to board his JetBlue flight at John F. Kennedy Airport when the

defendants made it clear that he would not be permitted to board until he covered his t-shirt. JetBlue again singled Jarrar out for differential treatment when it moved him from his seat in the third row to the back of the airplane. (American Civil Liberties Union Report 2009: 38)

Moreover, in 2006 the Council on American–Islamic Relations argued that they had seen a number of Muslim communities complain about incidents of racial discrimination at US airports because of the treatment they had received. Another problem that has emerged as a result of counter-terrorism strategies at airports is the issue of religious covering, as Muslim women who wear the *hijab* (head covering) have argued they have faced issues of racial discrimination. This has become an issue of contention and is discussed in more detail in Chapter 5.

Terrorism Arrests and Outcomes

The United Nations Committee on the Elimination of Racial Discrimination has argued that anti-terrorism legislation and counter-terrorism policing does risk targeting only Muslim communities. In the UK, following the damning critique of racial profiling, stop-and-search powers have been amended in order to ensure more proportionality: 'The disproportionate use of these powers against minority youth has been a cause of antagonism between police and young men from these communities' (Pickering et al. 2007: 54).

As noted previously, the UK Government has enacted counter-terrorism legislation which has given the police wider powers of stop and search, pre-charge detention and collecting, and downloading material that may be deemed to be useful for a terrorist purpose. One of the more contentious pieces of legislation that has been reformed following the UK Government's review of counter-terrorism legislation is the police use of stop-and-search powers (HM Government 2011). Section 44 of the Terrorism Act 2000 allowed the police to stop and search anyone without the need for 'reasonable suspicion', provided the powers were authorised by a senior police officer and confirmed by the Home Secretary. A broad power of this type was deeply worrying as, in essence, it potentially gave the police the ability to abuse their position and in many cases, inevitably stop and search innocent people.

Fenwick and Choudhury's (2011) research which examined the impact of counter-terrorism legislation upon Muslim and non-Muslim families found that 283 terrorism-related arrests have been made by the police but not a single person has been convicted of an s44 stop and search offence and 19 per cent of those searched were Asian or Asian British (HM Government, 2011: 16; Fenwick and Choudhury, 2011). Fenwick and Choudhury (2011) state that:

Among Muslim participants, the strongest negative feelings arose from perceptions that individuals were being stopped because of their religion or race

... the absence of the need for the police to provide any reason for stopping a person, combined with individual experiences and accounts of stops from friends and family, led most Muslim participants to feel that they are stopped because of their ethnicity or religion. (2010: 34)

In the UK data also reveals that at the end of September 2011 there were 153 persons arrested for terrorism-related offences compared with 133 in the previous 12 months and in total, 2,050 persons have been arrested for terrorism-related offences since 11 September 2001. Whilst 39 per cent of people arrested were charged, only 59 per cent of these charges were terrorism related. From the 33 people charged with terrorism-related offences in this period, only five were convicted of a terrorism-related offence (at the time of writing) (Home Office Statistical Bulletin 2011a).

Furthermore, statistics from the Home Office reveal that, of those people arrested under s44 of the Terrorism Act 2000, at the end of September 2010 there were 8,819 people who defined themselves as Asian/Asian British Pakistani; 4,498 Black/Black British; 1,021 Mixed; 1,957 Chinese and 3,224 who did not answer (Home Office Statistical Bulletin 2011b). Huq et al. (2011) in their article 'Mechanisms for Eliciting Cooperation in Counter-Terrorism Policing: Evidence from the United Kingdom' used a case study which examined the effects of counter-terrorism policing tactics on public cooperation amongst Muslim communities in London. The study, which adopted a random-sample survey of 300 closed and fixed-response telephone interviews conducted in Greater London's Muslim community in February and March 2010, found that cooperation between the police and community was low.

Conclusion

Whilst the UK Government has argued that engaging with Muslim communities is crucial to tackling extremism, the above set of empirical case studies and data suggests that law enforcement powers of stop-and-search and racial profiling have led to poor police–community relations. Furthermore, an independent report conducted by Thames Valley Police which examined the police use of covert surveillance cameras in the UK in predominately Muslim areas concluded that there was a lack of consistency with the police actions and in particular an element of trust was missing resulting in a lack of 'transparency' (Thornton, 2010: 48–9). Kelling and Bratton (2006) argue that local police forces need to play a crucial role in tackling extremism and terrorism, however, they state that: 'Counter-terrorism has to be woven into the everyday workings of every department. It should be included on the agenda of every meeting, and this new role must be imparted to officers on the street so that terrorism prevention becomes part of their everyday thinking' (Kelling and Bratton, 2006: 6).

Although Kelling and Bratton (2006) argue that local police officers who have a presence in communities are the most effective people in gathering intelligence, in some areas their presence could be viewed with hostility. They state that: 'They are in a better position to know responsible leaders in the Islamic and Arabic communities and can reach out to them for information or help in developing informants' (Kelling and Bratton, 2006: 1). Whilst this, in theory, may be the case with the use of police officers patrolling local areas in order to reassure communities, this does not necessarily build trust and could allow communities to be viewed with suspicion and create antagonism between local communities and the police.

Further Reading

Body-Gendrot, S. 2008. Muslims: Citizenship, Security and Social Justice in France. *International Journal of Law, Crime and Justice*, 36(4): 247–56.

Brodeur, J. 1983. High Policing and Low Policing: Remarks about the Policing of Political Activities. *Social Problems*, 30(5): 507–20.

Douglas, S., and Atherton, S. 2007. To Serve and Protect? The Experiences of Policing in the Community of Young People from Black and Other Ethnic Minority Groups. *British Journal of Criminology.* 47(5): 746–63.

Lowe, T., and Innes, M. 2008. Countering Terror: Violent Radicalisation and Situational Intelligence. *Prison Service Journal,* 179: 3–10.

Pickering, S., McCulloch, J., and Wright-Neville, D. 2008. *Counter-Terrorism Policing: Community, Cohesion and Security.* New York: Springer.

Spalek, B. 2010 Community Policing, Trust, and Muslim Communities in Relation to New Terrorism. *Politics & Policy.* Vol. 38(4): 789–815.

Spalek, B., El Awa, S., and McDonald, L. 2008. Police–Muslim Engagement and Partnerships for the Purposes of Counter-Terrorism: An Examination. *Arts and Humanities Research Council.* Available at: ttp://www.religionandsociety.org.uk/uploads/docs/2009_11/1258555474_Spalek_Summary_Report_2008.pdf [Online] [accessed: 10 April 2010].

Spalek, B., and Lambert, R. 2008. Muslim Communities, Counter-Terrorism and De-Radicalisation: A Reflective Approach to Engagement. *International Journal of Law, Crime and Justice,* 36(4): 257–70.

Vertigans, S. 2010. British Muslims and the UK government's 'war on terror' within: evidence of a clash of civilizations or emergent de-civilizing processes? *The British Journal of Sociology,* 61(1).

References

American Civil Liberties Union. 2009. The Persistence of Racial and Ethnic Profiling in the United States. A Follow-up report to the U.N. Committee on the Elimination of Racial Discrimination. [Online]. Available at: http://www.

aclu.org/human-rights_racial-justice/persistence-racial-and-ethnic-profiling-united-states [accessed: 20 April 2012].

Association of Chief Police Officers Website. Terrorism and Allied Matters. [Online]. Available at: http://www.acpo.police.uk/ACPOBusinessAreas/TerrorismandAlliedMatters.aspx [accessed: 20 April 2012].

Awan, I. 2011. A Lesson in How Not to Spy upon Your Community. *Criminal Justice Matters*, Special Issue, Myths and Criminal Justice, 83(1): 10–11.

Awan, I. 2012. Prevent Agenda and the Doctrine of Fear in the Muslim Community. Arches Quarterly: Terrorism and Counter-terrorism Spotlight on Strategies, 5(9): 63–7.

Awan, I., and Blakemore, B. 2012. Policing Cyber Hate, Cyber Threats and Cyber Terrorism. Farnham: Ashgate.

Bano, R. 2011. Community rift over undercover police in mosques. BBC News. [Online]. Available at: http://www.bbc.co.uk/news/uk-england-15840339 [accessed: 25 July 2012].

BBC website. 2011. Met Police counter-terrorism role should end, MPs say. [Online]. Available at: http://www.bbc.co.uk/news/uk-15029166 [accessed: 22 April 2012].

Clarke, R., and Newman, G. 2007. Police and the Prevention of Terrorism. *Policing: A Journal of Policy and Practice*, 1(1): 9–20.

Direct Gov. 2011. Reporting Extremism and Terrorism. [Online]. Available at: http://www.direct.gov.uk/en/CrimeJusticeAndTheLaw/Counterterrorism/DG_183993 [accessed: 20 May 2011].

Dodd, V., and Halliday, J. 2012. Teenagers arrested over anti-terrorist hotline hacking. *The Guardian*. [Online]. Available at: http://www.guardian.co.uk/uk/2012/apr/12/met-police-anti-terrorism-hotline [accessed: 21 April 2012].

Evans, M., Whitehead, T., and Britten, N. 2012. Fake cigarette triggers major M6 anti-terror incident. *The Telegraph*. [Online]. Available at: http://www.telegraph.co.uk/news/uknews/terrorism-in-the-uk/9377941/Fake-cigarette-triggers-major-M6-anti-terror-incident.html [accessed: 25 July 2012].

Fenwick, H., and Choudhury, T. 2011. The impact of counter-terrorism measures on Muslim communities. Equality and Human Rights Commission Research Report 72, [Online]. Available at: http://www.equalityhumanrights.com/uploaded_files/research/counter-terrorism_research_report_72.pdf [accessed: 20 June 2011].

The Guardian. 2012. Three arrested at Heathrow on suspicion of terrorism. [Online]. Available at: http://www.guardian.co.uk/uk/2012/apr/20/three-arrested-heathrow-suspicion-terrorism [accessed: 25 July 2012].

Hickman, M., and Wright, O. 2012. Police and MI5 get power to watch you on the web, *The Independent*. 2012. [Online]. Available at: http://www.independent.co.uk/news/uk/home-news/police-and-mi5-get-power-to-watch-you-on-theweb-7606788.html [accessed: 21 April 2012].

HM Government. 2011. 'PREVENT Strategy'. Presented to Parliament by the Prime Minister and the Secretary of State for the Home Department by Command of Her Majesty. [Online]. Available at: http://www.homeoffice.gov.

uk/publications/counter-terrorism/prevent/prevent-strategy/prevent-strategy-review?view=Binary [accessed: 14 June 2011].

Home Office Statistical Bulletin. 2011a. Operation of police powers under the Terrorism Act 2000 and subsequent legislation: Arrests, outcomes and stops and searches Quarterly update to September 2011. Great Britain. (22 March 2012) HOSB 04/12. [Online]. Available at: http://www.homeoffice.gov.uk/publications/science-research-statistics/research-statistics/counter-terrorism-statistics/hosb0412/hosb0412?view=Binary [accessed: 21 April 2012].

Home Office Statistical Bulletin. 2011b. Data tables – Operation of police powers under the Terrorism Act 2000 and subsequent legislation: Arrests, outcomes and stops and searches Quarterly update to September 2011. Great Britain. (Microsoft Excel File). [Online]. Available at: http://www.homeoffice.gov.uk/publications/science-research-statistics/research-statistics/counter-terrorism-statistics/hosb0412/ [accessed: 21 April 2012].

Huq, A., Tyler, T., and Schulofer, S., 2011. Mechanisms for Eliciting Cooperation in Counter-Terrorism Policing: Evidence from the United Kingdom *University of Chicago, Public Law Working Paper No. 340, NYU School of Law, Public Law Research Paper No. 11–12*

Innes, M. 2006. Policing Uncertainty: Countering Terror through Community Intelligence and Democratic Policing. Annals of APSS 605 (May):1–20.

Kelling G.L., and Bratton W.J. 2006. *Policing Terrorism.* New York*: Manhattan Institute* (Civic Bulletin 43)*.*

Laville. S. 2009. Counter-terror police 'failed to seek legal advice before arrests'. *The Guardian* (24 November 2009). [Online]. Available at: http://www.guardian.co.uk/uk/2009/nov/24/counter-terrorism-police-legal-advice [accessed: 21 April 2012].

Pickering, S., Wright-Neville, D., McCulloch, J., and Lentini, P., 2007. Counter-terrorism policing and culturally diverse communities (Final Report). Australian Research Council Linkage Project. [Online]. Available at: http://artsonline.monash.edu.au/criminology/news-and-events/counterterrorreport-07.pdf [accessed: 10 May 2011].

Press Release, Senator Robert Menendez (D-NJ), Immigration Raids and Detentions: Sen. Menendez Makes Major Speech on Senate Floor (11 June 2008). [Online]. Available at: http://menendez.senate.gov/newsroom/record.cfm?id=299036 [accessed: 10 April 2012].

Tell MAMA (Measuring Anti Muslim Attacks).2013. MAMA Project, [Online] Available at: http://tellmamauk.org/ [accessed: 22 March 2013].

Thornton, S. 2010, Project Champion Review, [Online] Available at: www.west-midlands.police.uk/ latest-news/docs/Champion_Review_FINAL_30_09_10.pdf. [accessed: 10 March 2010].

Chapter 3

Combating Extremism
through Community Policing

Patrick Tucker

When John Alderson wrote about 'Community Policing' he identified the need for the police to work with the communities that they policed (Alderson 1979) and community policing has continued to work towards that goal. The current terms used describe policing as needing to 'engage' with communities and so promote 'cohesion'. Both terms can be found in strategy documents of local and national government and public service agencies, including the police. While the term 'community policing' is still used and the relationship between 'communities' and the police is still discussed, a newer term, 'neighbourhood policing' is now more widely used in the United Kingdom. The two terms define two different, interlinked concepts. Neighbourhood policing is essentially geographically based and its delivery bound by territorial and political boundaries, the term acknowledges that several communities may exist within a geographical area. Community policing is the delivery style that relies on the police understanding and responding to each different community within a geographical neighbourhood.

For neighbourhood policing to achieve engagement and cohesion it must operate with an understanding of all the communities that exist within its geographically-bound operational area, including their different cultures and how they interact. Neighbourhood policing teams will be responsible for delivering community policing to many distinct communities within the geographical neighbourhood that they police. With a deeper understanding of the communities they police practitioners may be able to identify what is moderate and safe and that which is 'normal' within a particular community and so establish a baseline by which the extreme and dangerous can be identified and measured. This chapter will examine the concepts of 'community', 'community policing' and 'neighbourhood policing' and how they interact. Imran Awan explores the concept of extremism in Chapter 1 of this book, this chapter will explore how extremism is measured and judged to be 'extreme' in the context of operational neighbourhood and community policing. The chapter will explore whether community policing is capable of combating extremism in operational practice, and how that might be done.

Community policing appeals to many sections of society because its perceived adherence to 'traditional policing methods', including uniform patrol and community engagement, is often seen as benign. Community policing is the service that some sections of some communities ask for and what politicians often promise those same sections of those communities. To some extent it has become accepted as 'good' policing to the point that:

> The police have long worked on the assumption that the service you want is local, visible, accessible, familiar, accountable, friendly. (Blair 2005: speech)

These characteristics of service are widely accepted as being present in community policing. The chapter will further consider 'community policing' and 'neighbourhood policing', considering in more depth why the terminology has changed. Consideration will be given to community policing and its relationship with those whom it polices, with politicians and with the democratic processes based on geographically defined electoral wards. Are the geographically and politically co-terminus neighbourhood police the best way of providing police services to communities that are less and less bound by geographical and political boundaries and more by identity and electronic communication? Does the democratic political system of the UK underpin engagement and cohesion or could it be working against those ideals? If it is true that, 'national security depends on neighbourhood security' (Blair 2005:speech), then how should community policing be set up if it is to effectively engage with complex neighbourhoods and so combat extremism that uses so many other mediums to exist, communicate and radicalise?

The identity of individuals and of communities and some understanding of how those identities are arrived at needs to be contemplated before consideration is given to the concept of community or neighbourhood policing. A starting point might be:

> Sociologically, the concept of community implies a group of people with a common history, common beliefs and understandings, a sense of themselves as "us" and outsiders as "them", and often, but not always, a shared territory. (Klockars 2005: 449)

The growth of a diverse society, prompted and supported by government policies, has led to the identification and promulgation of many recognised, separate communities, all of which are expected to co-exist in peaceful harmony. Recent government policy has seen diversity as something to be valued and respected and also something that adds value and strength to society. This growth of recognition and valuing of diversity has led to a situation where communities with distinct identities have to accommodate and tolerate the identity of other distinct and separate communities. Within those distinct identities will be concepts of what is 'right' or 'moral' and what is 'wrong' or 'immoral', and there may be differences that are important, unique identifying features of communities; those differences can provide points of friction between communities within neighbourhoods.

Overarching democratic political systems depend upon a majority to empower the individuals within that group. Through the democratic process the rights of the individual are recognised and protected but at the same time minorities within a democratic society can have their rights compromised because the majority have a direct and powerful influence on public policy (Calhoun 1994). Through the democratic process the majority set what is legitimate and so may marginalise minority community views and standards:

> We have a diverse body of ideas about how various categories of people – communities, classes, elites, ethnicities, genders – come to share a sense of collective identity and, through perceptions of interests common to individual members of their category, begin to tackle problems of collective action. (Mennell 1994: 175)

Coupled with this growth of separate community identities and their promotion as a concept of value to society as a whole, legislation and political development within Europe and the wider world has led to fundamental changes to society. Since Alderson wrote his book in 1979, political and legal development, coupled with far greater personal mobility facilitated by better, quicker and more available transport, added a new complexity to society and the communities within it. In 1995 the implementation of the Schengen Agreement led to a lowering of national frontiers within the European Community and to much freer movement of people between nations. The movement of people between nations has led to the spread of different cultures, beliefs, languages and ideas into different countries, in some cases new and distinct communities have been established in different locations.

Each of these new communities has a complexity of its own but when added to the diverse, multi-cultural mix of the resident population, the interactions between the different cultures add a new and delicate complication. Where the professed foundation of community policing is 'engagement' with 'representation' at a level that influences the delivery of police services, the very complexity of the communities and their interactions can interfere with and obstruct the level of engagement needed to establish that idealised objective even within the relatively small territory that a local neighbourhood policing team might be responsible for.

The democratic political process seeks to engage the electorate on one level but in order to facilitate the direct engagement of communities in policing, other mechanisms may also be in place. Those mechanisms may also involve a way of holding the police to account. In the United Kingdom those systems are currently changing to one involving directly elected Police and Crime Commissioners (PCC), the aim of this is to make the police more directly accountable to the public, however, that accountability and influence needs to be considered in the light of the previous limitations of democracy representing minorities that have been briefly discussed above. At an operational level many community policing systems use a structure of meetings, where there is an interface between the police and the communities, so that problems can be identified, discussed and hopefully addressed. Attendance at those meetings may be numerically low and can be dominated by specific small sectors of a community, who might disproportionately influence the provision of service. In parts of Chicago, for instance, there was a disproportionate representation of middle-class residents at police meetings; the same study found that:

> Beat meetings do a better job of representing already established stakeholders in the community than they do at integrating marginalised groups. (Skogan 2004:73)

The use of beat meetings is only one tool of engagement and consultation that police services use, alongside these meetings will be specialist community intelligence systems, minority support units and public protection units working to construct a full picture of the communities within a particular neighbourhood, however:

> Simply identifying the communities that make up a particular locality will be an ever-changing target. In addition there is the notion of "hard to reach" groups – those that are either hard to identify or those that are resistant to dialogue with the police. (Clement 2006: 106)

The engagement of and consultation with communities is a difficult and continuing task, it requires constant review and assessment in order to keep step with the 'ever-changing target' (Clement 2006). By keeping step, police services will be better able to provide the policing that communities need and other public services will likewise be able to provide the services and responses that are appropriate to the needs of particular neighbourhoods. Linked to and intertwined with the issues of understanding specific communities and how they might function and influence within a neighbourhood, are the broader political systems and how they might influence the way a community is engaged or marginalised. Even if those communities and issues are identified and the links and influences defined, allowing effective policing strategies and tactics to be designed and implemented, one of the key barriers to engagement and true community policing may continue to exist:

> All the good work that can, and is being done at a local level to boost community cohesion is threatened by a climate where access to services is limited for some and increasingly segregated for others. Poverty and deprivation almost certainly remain the single biggest barriers to cohesion, and talk of increased choice is meaningless for our most excluded communities. (Johnson 2008: 8)

The police service role involves dealing with the outcomes of government policy, and while policing can engage with communities and structure its policies, tactics and services to reflect community demands, policing services are at the wrong end of the process to combat the underlying inequalities existing in modern societies. Policing is therefore always likely be dealing with the consequences of inequality, as well as perhaps contributing to those inequalities through the way policing services are delivered at the frontline.

Neighbourhood policing and the officers who deliver it have to have some understanding of the communities, their interactions and cultures if they are to be able to deliver the service that each community and individual expects and is entitled to. In addition to being able to tailor their services to the needs of communities, an awareness and understanding of those communities allows neighbourhood officers to build confidence in the police and also to make some judgments about what is 'normal' and moderate, and therefore what is 'abnormal' and extreme. Where indicators of extremism are identified by this 'local knowledge' neighbourhood officers will be required to work to the needs of the state, by obtaining community intelligence and ensuring it reaches the department or agency that uses it in order to neutralise what is judged by the state to be 'extreme'. Neighbourhood policing engages with communities in order to fulfil differing functions; including providing suitable services, and to watch and observe communities on behalf of the state. Some communities may see 'police' as being an arm of a state, which they perceive to be repressing their rights and their norms. For many arriving in a new country to start a new life the police will be 'the first point of contact with the cold realism of the state' (Blair, 2005). These conflicting roles of community policing can make engagement difficult.

Communities, extremism and extreme communities have always existed and are likely to continue to exist. Therefore the existence of terrorism is likely to continue:

> One of the depressing lessons of the history of terrorism is that is always likely to be with us. (English 2009: 120)

How extremism is judged and what is judged to be extreme continues to change as societies and communities change and interact. The adage, 'Today's terrorist is tomorrow's freedom fighter' encapsulates the difficulty of judging and defining extremism. This situation is further complicated by the fact that each different community will have its own measures of extremism and what it judges to be a reasonable reaction to that perceived concept of extremism. These many different communities exist in different mediums; they exist within geographical neighbourhoods, as interest groups, as political parties, as religious communities, as ethnic groupings, as business communities and many more. They also exist and are bound together in the virtual world of communication communities. Cultural and societal changes have been matched by technological changes in communication that have accelerated the growth and development of the concept of the 'global village'. For neighbourhood policing this has expanded the neighbourhood from a purely geographical territory into the virtual world.

While it may be correct that, 'Neighbourhood officers who have been appropriately trained and have a sense of what is normal and out of place in a specific neighbourhood context, may be well placed to detect the subtle signals of extremist activity' (Innes et al. 2007:10), neighbourhood policing needs to somehow acknowledge the new technological environment that overlaps their geographic delivery system. What is it that neighbourhood policing teams should be seeking to deliver and how can they do it? The role of the geographically-based neighbourhood team continues to be important but the interface between the 'real geographic' neighbourhood and the 'virtual' electronic communities poses difficult operational problems and decisions, including fundamental questions about community intelligence, its source, how it is analysed, how it is communicated and to whom. There are communities that are separate and isolated from other communities but most communities are linked with others and many overlap. Many individuals will be members of and engaged with more than one community.

Internet and computer communication and the development of the 'global village' where communities are not bound by or identified by geographical boundaries, pose particular problems for service deliverers, including the police. Most public services are set up to deliver services within a geographically-bound area. Schools have defined catchment areas, hospitals serve geographical or national areas, and the method of democratic representation is based on geographical electoral wards; the way services are funded may be based in taxes that are levied on specific geographical areas. Divisions defined by an arbitrary political boundary may not follow the realities of the 'community' that exists on the boundary of those two administrations. As previously discussed, community policing in England and Wales has more recently been termed 'neighbourhood policing' and is a service that is set up to deliver service to geographically-defined areas, acknowledging that there may be multiple communities within a geographical neighbourhood. Even prior to the growth of internet communications to its present and still-developing scope and speed, the realisation that political and service delivery boundaries do not always follow the 'real boundaries' of a community was known. Political history shows that where boundaries and frontiers have been decided by politicians it can lead to conflicts and warfare, because those boundaries do not reflect the reality of communities.

Virtual communities do exist and are recognised and often identified as those united by shared interests or needs. The development and recognition of 'virtual communities' further complicates the task of achieving engagement and community cohesion. The growth of different communities through the medium of the internet has forced businesses to reassess how they reach markets, and service agencies how they reach clients. In the arena of extremism and how it is combated it has forced the government and therefore the intelligence and policing services to reassess how they deal with communities. Acknowledgement of traditional communities is still present but now the internet is also acknowledged and seen as an area requiring specific action:

> There should be no "ungoverned spaces" in which extremism is allowed to
> flourish without firm challenge and, where appropriate, by legal intervention.
> (HM Government 2011: 3.39)

Neighbourhood policing may need to develop beyond its current geographical boundaries and consider how new communication and IT systems can assist in combating extremism:

> For instance, by linking all the parts of society into a "networked neighbourhood" we have the potential to allow everyone to contribute to national security by crowding out the opportunity for minorities to create chaos and terror. They become "first responders" in the same way as they willingly volunteer for fire fighting and R.N.L.I lifeboat crews. (Lamb and Williams 2012)

In 1979 John Alderson identified that:

> where in one single police station area there may be two or more ethnic minorities with disparate cultures and attitudes towards the law, religion and custom, difficulties might face the police particularly where minority cultures are not represented in the force. (Alderson 1979: 26)

Alderson's perceptive comment was based on a simpler situation than the situation that currently exists and continues to develop in its complexity. Alderson further stated:

> One of the most important concepts for the police to remember is that the law is lacking in power if it does not have the general backing of the public; or to put it another way, the police in using their law-enforcing powers will generally be effective with public support and generally less effective without it. (Alderson 1979: 11)

It is important that we consider and try to describe differences within those communities, and also important that policing is delivered with those differences in mind. The difference in the attitudes of the young and old within communities is not new and not exclusive to any particular community, and it is important that police officers acknowledge those differences and police to minimise the negative effects that might grow from those differences. In fairly recent British history inappropriate, illegal, or just plain insensitive stop-and-search tactics have led to alienation of whole communities, communities who become united against 'injustice'. More recent research has found that:

> Younger males from Asian backgrounds were significantly more negative in their views than older age groups. (Innes et al. 2007: 4)

Innes also found that:

> Young Muslim men were significantly more likely to report being stopped by the police than were their white counterparts. The combination of high collective

efficacy and low trust in the police inhibits the willingness to pass community
intelligence about a range of problems and issues. (Innes et al. 2007: 4)

This similarity of difference, that is a difference that is present across
many communities and one that causes police services significant problems in
engagement, is even more important within communities where extremism
might be present. Disaffected youth is a fertile recruiting ground for extremist
organisations of any political or religious persuasion. Comparisons may be drawn
here between the recruiting styles of Nationalist parties and extreme religious
organisations through history and across nations (Awan and Blakemore 2012). It is
for this reason that neighbourhood policing in particular must deliver its services
sensitively, fairly and evenly. If that can be achieved and trust engendered then
extremism will find the recruiting ground less receptive and the police will find the
flow of community intelligence growing.

The police services continue to rely on being able to engender trust as an
underpinning principle of successful community and neighbourhood policing.
Although the concept is clear and logical, it has become a much more difficult
concept to deliver in a neighbourhood that often contains far more than the 'two
or more ethnic minorities' that Alderson was describing in the 1970s. Within the
religions of these new communities there are further divisions and sects, with
further differences that need to be understood. This increase in the number of
communities, their complexity and the speed of their development, makes the
engendering of trust even more difficult. Where new communities arrive from
areas where relationships between the police and the community may have been
overtly repressive and the role of the police overtly driven by the needs of the
state, the work of developing and engendering trust will be a difficult and fragile
process.

During the discussion of the concepts of community, neighbourhood and
identity, some of the facets of neighbourhood policing have been touched on
but in order to understand how this particular policing method might combat
extremism, more detailed and focussed consideration of the strategy and tactics of
neighbourhood policing are needed.

The terminology of community policing has changed as the concept has
developed. Prior to Alderson's 1979 work, community policing was known by
a number of terms including 'area policing' or 'home beat' policing, depending
on the force providing that service, these various terms were superseded by
the nationally-accepted term 'community policing'. Recently that term has
been superseded by 'neighbourhood policing'. The term 'community policing'
differs from area, home beat and neighbourhood as it refers to a concept that is
not restricted by geographic boundaries. The concept of 'community' has been
discussed above but draws on many different facets for its boundaries and identity.
The term 'neighbourhood policing' acknowledges a realisation that geographically-
defined policing structures must deliver services to many separate communities
that exist within one neighbourhood. There has been a plethora of guidance and

reports that have defined and reviewed what 'neighbourhood policing' is and how it should operate. In 2006 Centrex[1] published 'Practice advice on professionalising the business of neighbourhood policing' on behalf of the Association of Chief Police Officers, other government publications included a green paper, 'From the neighbourhood to the national: policing our communities together' (Home Office 2008), which laid out how neighbourhood policing might be structured and also examined structures of accountability and engagement.

'From the neighbourhood to the national' examined where neighbourhood policing sat in relation to national policing structures and how it linked with and supported the national protective services. In practice neighbourhood policing service delivery depends on the existence of geographically-defined service areas policed by teams of officers but may deal with communities and issues that extend outside those boundaries. The strength of neighbourhood policing should be that its practitioners understand and know their 'patch'. Neighbourhood police officers are expected to know who their key community contacts are and are also expected to know their key problems, and should then work in local partnerships to deliver effective local solutions. This focus on the 'local' may be further reinforced by contacts with local politicians, whose political success can depend on their ability to provide solutions to problems identified by those engaged in the local democratic process. Neighbourhood policing is often described using its frontline, traditional tactical identity. Those who value this form of policing talk of the reassurance of the uniformed beat officer who stops and talks to residents and community members; very few people describe the importance of the strategic mission and how that mission can be achieved. Neighbourhood policing is referred to in nostalgic terms by members of the community who, in general, are those old enough to remember *Dixon of Dock Green*.[2] These may also be the people who have a disproportionate influence on policing at the neighbourhood level. They are the people who attend police/community meetings and who decide, or strongly influence, the local policing priorities of the area. They are the people who contact local politicians to obtain action on problems and who know how to contact the police and how to use the local political structures in order to influence policing and other service delivery. The power and influence of these traditional stakeholders is very difficult to manage and moderate because of their effectiveness and willingness to use the communication channels they are familiar with. This adherence to a perceived benign, traditional, visible and desired form of policing is also linked into the political rhetoric of police numbers. As cutbacks in the funding of public services in the United Kingdom lead to reductions in police staffing politicians issue statements about the public wanting to see the police on the beat, and how important police numbers are to maintaining feelings of community safety and reducing crime.

---

1   Central Police Training and Development Authority later superseded by N.P.I.A.

2   A television drama programme following the work of the idealised traditional Sergeant Dixon (1955–76)

I know Cleveland Police Authority's Acting Chief Constable is working hard to ensure neighbourhood policing is maintained but it is inevitable that this will suffer. I also have real concerns around the loss of Police Community Support Officers who do such a great job and whose work is greatly appreciated by the public.

We recognise savings need to be made, but the Government has doubled Labour's cuts to police funding, and made the steepest cuts in the first two years. That's not an attack on waste, that's an attack on the police.

As these cuts begin to hit home, it is our local communities that will suffer. (all Cunningham 2012)

Tom slams Tory-led cuts to frontline police. (Blenkinsop 2012)

These statements reflect a regularly occurring rhetoric between opposition and governing political parties in the United Kingdom. The provision of uniformed police patrol, preferably on foot, is presented as highly desirable. The statements reflect what some communities desire and the fact that the increasing of police numbers is seen as a political vote winner. This type of statement often refers to uniformed patrol and so serves to reinforce the sanctity of neighbourhood policing, which is so closely identified with uniform patrol.

This adherence to a perceived 'traditional' form of policing does not acknowledge the specialist areas that have developed to support it and allow it to deliver service in increasingly complex neighbourhoods. As the recognition of separate communities and their identities has been encouraged by recent government policies, and that in turn has led to the emphasis of 'difference', so police services have sought to understand these differences and adapt their tactics accordingly. Police services have set up 'Diversity Units' or 'Minority Support Units' who specialise in understanding the complex communities within a policing area; part of that that understanding will include how traditions, religion and customs may interact with police service delivery, and how those differences may influence what members of that specific community may need to meet their specific requirements, in order to conform with their traditions, religion and customs. This concentration on understanding the 'differences' between communities within a neighbourhood might detract from the identification of 'similarities' in needs and expectations. In the similarities might lie the key to engagement and community coherence:

Rather than appeal to people as part of an ethnic group, we should look to identities that cross barriers – parents, patients, library users, sports fans. Interaction in these fields breaks down barriers and creates cohesion. It is therefore imperative that the choice agenda does not seek to divide parents into different groups or limit the opportunities for that interaction. (Johnson 2008: 8)

By concentrating on the similarities of communities and their shared needs and expectations, policing can help to establish 'engagement and cohesion'. Actions and services that respond to shared needs underline the similarities and shared social capital within a neighbourhood:

> A signal crimes analysis of insecurity drivers in the Muslim communities studied suggested three key signal crimes: drugs problems; burglary; hate crime. The latter may be especially important in supporting a sense of local injustice, which is a potent factor in disposing some individuals to radicalisation. (Innes et al. 2007: 3)

Innes's work focused upon the Muslim community in particular but the principles referred to, dentifying the 'common ground' that united different communities within a neighbourhood, will bear further examination. Drugs and burglary are seen as important signal crimes in many areas and have been identified as such in Crime Reduction Partnership crime assessments across the United Kingdom. While the fear of hate crime has been heightened amongst Muslim communities following actual and feared reprisals for terrorist atrocities, hate crime is not exclusive to Muslim communities. The definition of 'hate crime' is wide but includes hate crimes directed at race, religion, sexual orientation, disability and age and these issues are present in most communities to some extent. The wide-ranging impact that hate crime has on policing is acknowledged by the Association of Chief Police Officers, where it falls in the specific business area of equality, diversity and human rights, which has a nominated lead officer (A.C.P.O. 2012).

The important similarities of need in separate but sometimes intertwined communities offer a starting point on which to build engagement and cohesion. The many differences and identities of communities in a neighbourhood will make service provision more complicated but by concentrating on the similarities of need and the attitude to specific types of signal crime, the police may be able to build confidence in their ability to protect the community. These similarities are reflected and reinforced by research indicating that some minority communities hold the strongest feelings of 'Britishness', despite also maintaining separate community loyalties (Nandi and Platt 2012).

Confidence in the police is an important part of the effort to combat extremism and should not be underestimated, a point reinforced in the 'PREVENT' strategy aimed at combating extremism in the United Kingdom:

> It is clearly essential that *Prevent* policing develops community trust. (H.M. Government 2011: 11.30)

Community confidence is needed if there is to be a flow of 'community intelligence' to the police through the channels offered by neighbourhood policing. The services offered by the police need to be sensitive to community need and that will include effective solutions to the problems identified by the stakeholders of a community. Sensitivity alone may not build confidence, communities need effective policing and that might be best achieved by concentrating on addressing those problems identified as common to communities within a given neighbourhood:

> Information will only be forthcoming if the community has confidence in the police service or other agencies seeking community help. (Harfield 2008: 80)

While the perception of neighbourhood policing might be benign and traditional with its connotations of cohesion, legitimacy, openness and visibility, when it comes to the gathering of community intelligence it has a different role that is more covert. As well as this intelligence function effective neighbourhood policing involves a level of enforcement which will include the use of powers including arrest, stop-and-search and entry of homes:

> the modern movement toward what is currently called "community policing" is best understood as the latest in a fairly long tradition of circumlocutions whose purpose is to conceal, mystify, and legitimate police distribution of non-negotiably coercive force. (Klockars 2005: 443)

This clash between the overt, covert and enforcement aspects of a policing method that is portrayed as open, engaging, assuring and benign can cause problems when it comes to building community trust. It might be said that the police only wish to engage and assure in order to obtain intelligence on sections of communities that the state and the police perceive to be extreme, in order to neutralise that threat. This, however, is a basic problem faced by society and its institutions and:

> Understood in this light, the police are not fundamentally and irreconcilably offensive in their means to the core cultural aspiration of modern society, but an ever present reminder that all of these noble institutions, which should make it possible for citizens to live in non-violent relations with one another and with the state, often come up very short. (Klockars 2005: 443)

The long view of terrorism and its roots, presented by Richard English (English 2009), gives an historical perspective, often centred around Irish extremist activity and its development from bullet to negotiation, he proposes a model that offers a number of guiding principles for dealing with extremism and the terrorist:

> 'We are going to have to learn to live with terrorism as part of our political reality'
> 'Ultimately the best way to remove the terrorist symptom is to address the political source, if that is feasible'
> 'Intelligence is the most vital element is successful counter-terrorism'.
> 'Respect orthodox legal frameworks and adhere to the democratically established rule of law'. (English 2009: 120, 123, 131, 133)

These four principles, of the seven that English proposes, are of particular relevance to neighbourhood policing and how it might help in combating extremism. British policing has lived with extremism and terrorism for many years, the face and source of that extremism has changed but the problems of policing it and identifying its proponents remain. The importance of intelligence has already been addressed, as has the problem of trying to engender trust when that trust can be perceived as being established in order to extract information from communities about the source of extremism and who those extremists might be. However, when research (Nandi 2012) is showing minority communities adhering to ideals and values of Britishness, which include Human Rights, democracy and openness, it is important that policing and neighbourhood policing in particular adhere to and express those values through the actions it takes and the service it delivers.

This could be seen as a 'political' element of policing; the police service must show reasonableness and fairness at every turn, as that will be an intrinsic part of addressing the 'political source' of the growth of extremism. The 'political' aspect of policing is difficult to balance with operational policing independence. As referred to earlier, for neighbourhood policing to engage with communities contact with local politicians is needed but difficulties arise if officers are associated with particular politicians, political parties, or other political groupings. The introduction of elected Police and Crime Commissioners in England and Wales has brought politics closer to policing as many candidates are sponsored by specific political parties, yet engagement by the police in this process is proscribed by law and discouraged by the Home Office. Dame Helen Ghosh, Permanent Secretary at the Home Office, is reported in *The Times* as stating, 'that any intervention *(by chief officers)* might breach electoral law or police regulations' (O'Neill et al. 2012).

Neighbourhood policing relies on close contacts with its communities and with the representatives of those communities, many of those representatives are likely to be 'political' in one guise or another, be they elected councillors or people lobbying for interest groups. The reality of neighbourhood policing is that it involves political decisions, decisions taken at all levels, from Constable upwards through every rank to the Chief Constable, indeed it is important that neighbourhood police officers are both political and politically aware:

> The real problem in policing today is more often to find ways of putting politics into policing than it is to find ways of taking it out. (Klockars 2005: 446)

This delicate line between being operationally non-political and independent but politically astute and presenting the values and ideals of a society are important roles for neighbourhood policing, particularly in how it helps to combat extremism.

Neighbourhood policing is important to combating extremism, because of its representative and symbolic power. Neighbourhood policing is often portrayed as benign and simple policing, it is presented as 'traditional' British policing, encapsulated by visions of the idealised world of *Dixon of Dock Green*. The reality is that neighbourhood policing must reach out to its separate communities and protect each of them; if it manages to do this it will help to project the values of the greater society in which it is based. The strategic ideals of Human Rights, Diversity and Freedom, can be effectively portrayed and translated into operational tactics through neighbourhood policing and so reinforce the shared needs and cohesion of neighbourhoods.

Understanding the differences between communities within a neighbourhood is important but what is more important is an understanding of what the consequences of those differences may be. In terms of policing, difference is often linked to vulnerability. Understanding why and how vulnerability is accentuated by difference will lead to effective tactics that protect vulnerable groups that will build trust and therefore lead to the provision of effective community intelligence. Innes points out:

> The construction of security in Muslim communities compared with white respondents, those living in Muslim communities perceived their environments as less threatening. This resilience is attributable to higher levels of social capital which manifest in the form of apparently robust collective efficacy. The downside of this is it contributes to something of an insular, inward looking cultural disposition within some areas and amongst some groups. (Innes et al. 2007: 3)

Governments at national and local level and the police seek to support strong community identity but strong community identity and self-reliance can lead to insularity and where such insularity exists, perhaps accentuated by issues of poverty and feelings of neglect, the police can be seen as one of the agents that are perpetuating that injustice. In that circumstance community intelligence is unlikely to be provided and an environment in which extremism can thrive may be cultivated. Neighbourhood policing can combat extremism by ensuring that, through its actions, the state is presented as reasonable and fair; it can do this by being effective at solving problems that are identified by communities, understanding and acting on the shared needs of neighbourhoods whilst recognising the differences between the communities within that neighbourhood.

One of the difficulties for policing and neighbourhood policing in particular is implementing a neighbourhood policing strategy that acknowledges and addresses the very different issues and resource demands of virtual and geographical communities. What is seen as effective policing by one community within a neighbourhood can be seen as repression by another community in the same neighbourhood. How engagement is achieved across all communities is the problem that neighbourhood policing faces but by ensuring that officers deliver services in line with human rights principles, fairness and equality, and in particular by identifying and addressing the common needs and problems of separate communities, engagement will be more easily achieved and confidence more easily established. If that occurs, more intelligence should be available and the results of that engagement will promote cohesion and combat extremism.

Further Reading

Bettison, Sir N. (2009). Preventing Violent Extremism—A Police Response. *Policing*, 3(2): 129–38.

Innes, M. (2005). Why 'soft' policing is hard: on the curious development of reassurance policing, how it became neighbourhood policing and what this signifies about the politics of police reform. *Journal of Community & Applied Social Psychology,* 15(3): 156–69 May/June 2005.

Maguire, M., and John, T. (2006): Intelligence Led Policing, Managerialism and Community Engagement: Competing Priorities and the Role of the National Intelligence Model in the UK, *Policing and Society: An International Journal of Research and Policy*, 16(1): 67–85

Savage, S.P, (2007). Neighbourhood Policing and the Reinvention of the Constable. *Policing*, 1(2): 203–13.

References

ACPO2012 www.acpo.police.uk/ACPOBusinessAreas/Equalitydiversityand humanrights.aspx [accessed: 10 July 2012].

Alderson, J. 1979. *Policing freedom: a commentary on the dilemmas of policing in Western democracies*. Plymouth: Macdonald and Evans.

Awan, I., and Blakemore, B. 2012. *Policing Cyber Hate, Cyber Threats and Cyber Terrorism*. Farnham: Ashgate.

Blair, I. 2005. What kind of police service do we want? Dimbleby Lecture 2005 (cited in McClaughlin 2007) Full text at http://news.bbc.co.uk/1/hi/uk/4443386.stm.

Blenkinsop, T. 2012 Website of Tom Blenkinsop Labour MP, Middlesbrough South and East Cleveland, http://tomblenkinsop.com/ [accessed: 9 July 2012].

Briggs, R., Fieschi, C., and Lownsbrough, H., 2006. Bringing it Home, Community-based approaches to counter-terrorism. Demos and online at www.demos.co.uk

Calhoun, C. 1994. Social Theory and the Politics of Identity. In Craig Calhoun (ed.), *Social Theory and the Politics of Identity*. Oxford: Blackwell

Cantle, T. 2008. Parallel lives – the development of community cohesion. In Nick Johnson (ed.), *Citizen, Cohesion and Solidarity*. London: Smith Institute

Centrex 2006. Practice guidance on professionalising the business of neighbourhood policing. Association of Chief Police Officers. Wyboston: National Centre for Policing Excellence.

Clement, P. 2006. Policing a diverse society. Oxford, New York: Oxford University Press

Cunningham, A. 2012. Website of Alex Cunningham Labour MP Stockton North, http://www.alexcunninghammp.com/2012/07/alex-mp-slams-tory-led-governments-cuts-to-police-numbers/ [accessed: 9 July 2012].

English, R. 2009. Terrorism – How to Respond. Oxford, New York: Oxford University Press.

Harfield, C. and Hartfield, K. 2008. *Intelligence Investigation, Community and Partnership*. New York: Oxford University Press.

HM Government. 2011. Prevent Strategy. Stationery Office. Available at www. homeoffice.gov.uk/.../prevent/prevent-strategy/prevent-strategy [accessed: 25 March 2013].

Home Office. 2008. From the neighbourhood to the national: policing our communities together. also at www.official-documents.gov.uk/document/ cm74/7448/7448.pdf [accessed: 6 August 2012].

Innes, M., Roberts, C., Lowe, T., and Abbot, L. 2007. Hearts and minds and ears and ears. Cardiff: Cardiff University 2007.

Johnson, N. 2008. Citizenship, Cohesion and Solidarity.The Smith Institute 2008

Klockars, C.B. 2005. The rhetoric of community policing. In T. Newburn (ed.), *Policing Key Readings*. Collumpton, Devon: Willan.

Lamb, G., and Williams, R. 2011. A nation of cyber-activists can keep the peace. *The Times* 1 November 2011.

McLaughlin, E. 2007. *The New Policing*. London: Sage.

Mennell, S. 1994. The formation of We-images: a process theory. In C. Calhoun (ed.), *Social Theory and the Politics of Identity*. Oxford: Blackwell Publishing.

Nandi, A., and Platt, L.s (2012) https://www.iser.essex.ac.uk/2012/06/30/ethnic-minorities-living-in-the-uk-feel-more-british-than-white-britons [accessed: 9 August 2012].

O'Neill, S., Hamilton, F., and Ford, R. 2012. Police chiefs cautioned over commissioner elections, *The Times*, 2 July 2012.

Skogan, L.G. 2004. *Community Policing (Can it work?)*. Belmont, CA: Thomas Wadsworth.

Chapter 4
Psychology of Extremism

Jane Prince

This chapter explores the ways in which psychology can explain the etiology of extremist behaviour and extremist thought, the power of extremist views and the challenge posed by extremism to those seeking ways to counter it. The Oxford Dictionary (1980) defines an extremist as 'one who goes to extremes or who holds extremist opinions or advocates extremist measures'. As a definition this is tautologous and not particularly enlightening; as the 21st century progresses we are more in need of a definition which explains both the origins and maintenance of extremism and, hopefully, a definition of the word which includes ways of developing a means to counter it. Definitions of extremism have been problematic in the psychological literature too; extremism is seen as being more than the holding of extreme negative attitudes towards a particular group, it also involves an attempt to operationalise those attitudes either by actions of the extremist him/herself or vicariously through targeted others.

An extremist may be motivated to engage in behaviours which demonstrate his belief system or may encourage others so to do, via propaganda or face-to-face encouragement. The distinction between attitudes and behaviour has been an object of study for psychologists for nearly 80 years since the work of LaPiere (1934) on prejudiced attitudes towards certain groups and actual behaviour towards those disliked groups showed that for the general population the holding of hostile attitudes towards a member of another group did not usually lead to hostile actions. The difference between a person holding prejudiced views and an extremist may be seen to be the willingness of the extremist to act so as to fulfil goals in line with his belief system and where those beliefs lie outside of the ordinary. It is a state rather than a trait; the extremist view has a core characteristic which is the belief that the in-group is absolutely correct in its views, that the in-group holds a position of moral superiority and that all outsiders are engaged (whether explicitly and consciously or not) in behaviours for which the aim is to destabilise the in-group.

Identity

It is probably useful at this stage to consider the ways in which psychology has explained processes of identity development and identity conflict. Identity has been approached through a number of perspectives, which have encompassed views of identity understood with respect to social group membership (Tajfel 1981), as knowledge of self through engagement and communication with others (Mead 1934), a construction historically situated and emerging from social and cultural processes (Gergen and Gergen 1987) and a set of socially produced rules acquired by the person (Harré, 1983).

Breakwell (1986) suggested that identity can perhaps best be understood as a dynamic or rather as a product (continually changing) of a dynamic between the set of current social contexts within which an individual is placed (including relationships, cultural rules, norms and values) and the individual's own history. Gergen and Gergen (1987) suggest that identity formation is guided by three principles: continuity across time and situation, distinctiveness or uniqueness for the person, and feelings of self-esteem or personal worth. Thus identity can be seen as a consequence of a series of unconscious and conscious conflicts and resolution of these, between existing self and the requirements of a particular situation. Not only is identity an outcome of actions it *directs* actions; in search of continuity, self-value and distinctiveness the individual makes decisions and undertakes acts. In the specific context of a possible challenge to identity, actions will be taken to reduce challenge in some way (Breakwell 1986).

For extremists it is argued that the guiding principle for their identities is located in their adherence to a powerful and clearly defined belief system. This definition includes a clear understanding of what it is not (as well as what it is) and incorporates a wholehearted intolerance of those who do not share these beliefs. Social Identity Theory can be used to explain the psychological processes involved

In social identity theory (Tajfel and Turner 1986), a social identity is a person's knowledge that he or she belongs to a social category or group. A social group is a set of individuals who hold a common social identification or view themselves as members of the same social category. Through a social comparison process, persons who are similar to the self are categorized with the self and are labelled the in-group; persons who differ from the self are categorized as the out-group. In early work, social identity included the emotional, evaluative, and other psychological correlates of in-group classification (Turner et al. 1987). Later researchers often separated the self-categorization component from the self-esteem (evaluative) and commitment (psychological) components in order to empirically investigate the relationships among them.

The two important processes involved in social identity formation, namely self-categorization and social comparison, produce different consequences (Hogg and Abrams 1988). The consequence of *self-categorization* is an accentuation of the perceived similarities between the self and other in-group members, and an accentuation of the perceived differences between the self and out-group members. This accentuation occurs for all the attitudes, beliefs and values, affective reactions, behavioural norms, styles of speech and other properties that are believed to be correlated with the relevant intergroup categorization. It is the self-categorization process which creates the group-based identity of the extremist. The consequence of the *social comparison* process is the selective application of the accentuation effect, primarily to those dimensions that will result in self-enhancing outcomes for the self. Specifically, one's self-esteem is enhanced by evaluating the in-group and the out-group on dimensions that lead the in-group to be judged positively and the out-group to be judged negatively. Thus it is through social comparison processes that an extremist can identify 'inequity' and the justification of actions which might reduce or eliminate the inequity.

As Hogg and Abrams (1988) make clear, the social categories in which individuals place themselves are parts of a structured society and exist only in relation to other contrasting categories (for example, old vs. young); each has more or less power, prestige, status, and so on. Further, the social categories precede individuals; people are born into an already structured society. Each person, over the course of his or her personal history, is a member of a unique combination of social categories; therefore the set of social identities making up that person's self-concept is unique. Nonetheless it is the broad social identity of the individual which will allow him to make comparisons with other groups which allow perceptions of injustice to be felt and hence legitimises attempts to counteract these. The injustice might be perceived as being directed to a group of individuals or to the core of a belief system (political, social or religious); for example animal rights extremists may believe that the harm done to animals through their being used in medical research justifies the placing of a bomb in the home or office of a research scientist regardless of possible harm to colleagues or family of that scientist.

One of the consequences of strong in-group identification is a loss of feelings of personal responsibility and a concomitant willingness to engage in progressively aggressive actions if the in-group is perceived as being at threat from an out-group (Battegay 1996).

Individual Psychological Factors

The psychology of the extremist has not been particularly well-researched in part because the term itself inevitably defines an 'other' who may not be available for or amenable to being an object of research. Steinberg (1998) suggests that hostility to others is rooted in a poor attachment in childhood (Bowlby 1989). Bowlby's work indicated the importance of a secure and loving relationship with a parent/carer in early childhood for a psychologically healthy adult life; Steinberg suggested that a deprived attachment experience could lead to behaviour which attempts to secure feelings of worth through power or the admiration of others. Thus extremism serves as an outlet for emotions arising from insecurity and loss. If this is the case then the emergence of extremism in those which have been raised in conditions where children routinely experience emotional trauma as a consequence of civil disturbance, war, etc. should not surprise us. Salvendy (1999a) has identified such development in children who lived through the Balkan wars in the 1990s.

Battegay (1996) suggests that as a reaction to feelings of low self-worth, such individuals overly identify with any group which offers them recognition and power; moreover the loss of personal relationships leads to a generalised internalised view or all 'others' (non in-group members) as being bad and hence allows the individual to devalue and demonise them and legitimises aggression and cruelty. Salvendy (1999b) notes that since holding negative views of others allows aggressive and cruel actions to take place without invoking the normal guilt responses, effectively bypassing any mental conflict, then the extremist can create for his or herself an absolute and very personal view of what is right and good and with it, a total certainly also of what is evil and bad, which view then becomes part of the individual's identity.

Laor, Yannay-Shimi, Wolmer and Khoury (2010) propose a 'trauma' model for explaining the development of extremism which integrates the social identity approach with an element of the underpinning concept of emotional insecurity implicit in the explanations proposed by Battegay and by Steinberg. They studied the ideological zeal of people from different groups in Israel – Israeli-Jewish adults, university students, West Bank settlers and left-wing activists. They took measures including basic demographic information as well as information on religious identity, political identification and the effect (if any) of the holocaust on their family. They also measured political activism using a purposely designed scale, self-transcendence, political attitudes, attitudes to conflict and perceptions of political threat (the extent to which worries about political threats, such as the return of Israeli land to Palestinians, worried the participants on a daily basis). Their findings indicated that those occupying politically extreme positions (right-wing) displayed more self-transcendence, (losing their sense of who they were 'in the moment' and in so being removing themselves from specific socially-normed moral imperatives); this group consisted mainly of participants living on the West Bank with the Intifada an ongoing experience. Extremists on the right scored more highly than those on the left on perceived threat to national identity and continued existence while those left-extremist scored more highly on perceptions of threats to moral integrity.

Laor et al. argued that right-wing extremists differenced from left-wing extremists in this sample in their 'chosen trauma'; the right extremists focused on the historical experience as victims (the holocaust) and on threats to existence and national identity while the left-extremists focused on the threat to their moral integrity and in so doing over-identified with the victimiser (both historically and currently) and in fearing becoming one sought actions which could prevent this in their relationship with the State of Israel. In this group their family experience of the holocaust led to identification with the current victims, the Palestinians. In so doing they perceived themselves as potentially regaining the moral high ground by empathising with and acting on behalf of the victims.

A key finding was that all extreme groups felt themselves and their values to be more under threat than did non-extremists. This research is of interest because of the insight it gives into the formation of extremist identities. Both left and right in this study used values which they felt to be core to their ethnic and national identity to elevate their views to occupy a moral high ground; it is also the case that experience of trauma and threat to the very existence of the identified-with in-group may lead to the development of extremist affiliations and identities.

The material summarised above suggests that the development of extremism may be inevitable; if it is the case that trauma and lack of appropriate attachment figures and role-models can prefigure the development of extremism we may conclude that in certain regions of the world (indeed, if not in all countries), there exists groups of people for whom the emergence of an extremist identity can be predicted. In situations in which a group of people perceives that that group has in the past experienced trauma and is at risk either physically or psychologically, then members of that group may respond by developing extremist ways of viewing the world.

Steinberg, Brooks and Remtulla (2003) studied the contexts in which extremist ideas developed and the factors which led to such ideas being acted out, whether as focused hate crimes or more general acts of terrorism. They noted the classifications of hate-crimes into three main groupings – those which were motivated primarily by 'thrill-seeking', whereby the enactors, mainly young males, were motivated by boredom and by a desire to appear strong and manly; 'reactionists', whose main motive was directed at protecting limited resources and privileges from outsiders (interesting in the light of the research by Laor et al. discussed above,); and those referred to as 'mission offenders' (Levin and McDevitt 1993), who have a belief that their thoughts and actions are logical and appropriate and legitimised by the authority of some higher being or belief system and standing in the eyes of the perpetrators as focused appropriately on the eradication of some group of inferior beings.

In contrast to the findings of Laor et al., however, Steinberg et al. (2003) found that there was not necessarily a direct concern about the threat to the economic, psychological or physical well-being of the in-group which acted as a trigger to extremist actions. Their extremists were neither poorer economically nor more pessimistic than non-extremists – what was found was a common factor of fear of the 'other' an existential crisis relating to anxiety and fear of groups whose customs, history, values and culture were different. They suggested that those who developed extremist views and behaviours had failed to develop the internalised moral system which enables adolescents and adults to comprehend the enormity of the potential consequences for others of their actions; they fail to inhibit hostile thoughts and indeed may take pleasure in anticipating the downfall or some 'other'. Psychoanalytic theory also stresses the importance of a secure, loving and boundary-setting environment in allowing young people to cope with the normal anxieties and fears of adolescence.

Without such supports young people may project their own fears and uncertainties about their identity onto others – even groups with which they have no contact or experience (Young-Bruehl 1996). The resulting constellation of hostility bordering on anger and indignation at the perceived faults of the other group (which faults will mirror the positive attributes ascribed to the personal in-group) is the most immediately effective way for the person to deal with his own identity fears. A group of like-minded people, whether personal acquaintances or people met via internet sites, act as a substitute for the support lacking in his immediate environment, validate his chosen 'identity' with its concomitant values and play the role of an external superego guiding and justifying his thoughts and actions within the ethics, morals and logic of the extremist group.

Beck (1999) takes a different stance; his work has focused on the cognitive element of extremist behaviours and views problematic behaviours and beliefs as having their origins in faulty thought processes. The extremist views his own behaviour as morally correct and appropriate and those of his out-group, potential victims of his antagonism, as responsible for any negative experiences they might have. The sense of vulnerability (awareness that not everyone tings and acts within the same righteous and moral code as does he) may be reflected in his becoming overly sensitive to any social interactions, whether experienced directly face-to-face, via electronic media or vicariously, which might hint at disparagement or an attempt to dominate his way of thinking. Effectively he sees his thoughts as being 'facts'; he finds it impossible to question his beliefs or even to consider them in any reflective sense – they are factual and enduring and correct. Any challenge to his belief system is morally wrong and factually wrong; primarily he is driven to see himself and other members of his in-group as victims and all others as perpetrators of victimisation.

In some ways there are similarities between the ways of thinking of extremists and that of those who are diagnosed with depression or with paranoia (Beck 1999); people suffering from depression characteristically feel that they have no control over what happens to them and feel to an extent powerless. Beck's therapeutic approach is about facilitating a reshaping of their faulty cognitions to deal with their depression. Those suffering from paranoia perceive themselves to have been betrayed, believe that another person is responsible for betrayal and that they deserve to be punished for that. However, it would be over-simplistic to draw an analogy between an extremist and someone suffering from a diagnosable medical condition. In the context of a human history in which dissenters from the dominant political ideology have been imprisoned in psychiatric hospitals and their dissent 'treated' (or contained) as a psychological one (here we all think of the treatment of dissenters in the Soviet Union but such responses are neither unique nor confined to the past) it is important that we are not sloppy either in our choice of terminology nor our understanding of the behaviour under focus. It is not necessarily helpful to view the extremist as psychologically sick; what matters is to understand the antecedents of extremist thoughts and consider how their development can be prevented.

McGregor, Nash, Mann and Phills (2010) conducted a series of studies which focused on the development of extremist thoughts as a means to reducing anxiety. They argued that reactive approach motivation serves to provide an alternative focus for anxieties which then become damped down by the changed goal focus. They note that in animals under conditions of anxiety and stress, displacement behaviours are observed. These are behaviours which serve no direct purpose in terms of reducing anxiety and can actually be harmful to the animal as in the case of anxious dogs that lick themselves so fiercely that skin lesions are produced. The function of the behaviours seems to be simply to distract. McGregor et al. argue for a similar phenomenon in humans and propose that this reactive approach motivation (RAM) can explain the development of extremist thoughts and behaviours.

The experience of anxiety of necessity incorporates an element of uncertainty; the core of anxiety is the unpredictability of the future which is how it differs from fear which is threat-focused and from panic where there is no internal conflict as to the nature of threat. This distinction is the core of the neuropsychology of anxiety. The potential for anxiety is particularly strong in a situation of approach-avoidance conflict (where there is motivation to engage in a behaviour but where engagement brings about a concomitant threat) but is also the case for approach-approach (conflict between equally enticing or compelling alternatives) as these in any case are potentially approach-avoidance in that one alternative implies the frustration of alternative goals. In situations of such motivational uncertainty the septo-hippocampal system in the brain responds with anxiety, with inhibition of goals relating to the focus of the motivation and a general negative bias towards all goals. These responses are adaptive if they result in drawing back for the contexts which render uncertainty to the individuals goals (and hence lead to anxiety) and allow engagement with more reasonable and less threatening but still viable alternatives. It is known for example (Gray and McNaughton 2000) that lesions in the septo-hippocampal system lead to animals and humans losing their ability to remove themselves from conflicting-goal situations.

For any person it is obvious that it is more difficult to disengage from important goals than it is for more trivial ones and hence important goals are more likely to produce anxiety.

When a person is feeling anxious he experienced an increase in vigilance round the threat; this allows him to flee should that be necessary but also allows him to identify a realistic alternative route to achieve a goal (not necessarily the same as the original goal). This ability – to identify and focus on an alternative goal when the original goal is producing feelings of anxiety and threat – is adaptive in that it can lead to alternative goal achievement. McGregor et al. argue that it is also palliative; RAM directed towards any compelling ideal or goal state may be rewarding for the individual because it protects the individual form anxiety and hence may be engaged simply in order to alleviate negative emotions without regard for long-term outcomes. They call this 'motivational tunnel vision' and argue that this explains why, in anxiety-provoking situations, there is such a strong association between general well-being plus lessened reactivity to risky stimuli and the neural markers of approach motivation.

If we consider the earlier consideration of factors in the social environment which have been identified as being associated with the development of extremist thinking and behaviours we can identify a constellation of factors associated with risk of anxiety – insecurity in early attachment relationships, low self-esteem and perception of self-efficacy, a perception that either the individual or their in-group has been victimised in the past, allegiance to an identifiable in-group and hostility to all out-group members (whom the individual may never have actually encountered in a face-to-face situation) – each of which explains a route through which the development of extremism may be facilitated. These routes are not prescriptive, inevitablenor , indeed, exclusive but they serve to explain processes which might explain the development of extremism and possibly to identify routes to its prevention.

According to Carver and Scheier (1998) ideals are abstract goals and the mere fact of reflecting on ideals can activate the neurological pattern which characterises approach motivation. Their power lies in the fact that they are long-established cognitive structures which are relatively immune to short or medium term frustrations and can easily be considered, elaborated and hypothetically acted-on within the privacy of one's own mind or imagination. Conflicts in the present are known to trigger flights into fantasy or unreal hopes and plans. Thus extremist ideals may be self-perpetuating and self-elaborating given that they serve an anxiety-reducing function in times of threat. The threat may be physical or psychological or emotional – the elaboration of ideals will serve to lessen the impact of that threat. McGregor, Zanna, Holmes and Spencer (2001) found that when threats were simulated in experimental conditions participants did indeed react to these dilemmas and uncertainties by adhering to idealistic values, personal projects and identities and reported a strong urge to find some higher purpose to their existence.

Allport (1943), one of the leading figures of 20th-century psychology, noted that humans could cope with frustration in drive states if they could find some kind of success, no matter how unrelated to the original drive these might be; these successes he noted tended to be related to super-ordinate motives such as integrity, meaning and symbolic immortality. Any attractive outcome which can relatively easily be achieved is appealing in the face of goal conflict as it would restore a clarity of motivation while at the same time relieve anxious uncertainty. The super-ordinate goals identified by Allport will guide more concrete goals and activities – hence throwing oneself with enthusiasm into one's idealistic projects is an effective way to deal with anxiety. The empirical findings of Nash, McGregor and Prentice (2011) supported the view that threats to important goals can cause anxiety and ideological extremism.

Ideals and Principles: Impact on Extremist Behaviours

Ginges, Atran, Sachdeva and Medin (2011) provide an overview of what they describes a 'very limited' research into the psychology of extremism. They note that the assumption of a rational model of decision-making (that people make decisions based on known probabilities of specific outcomes and cost of achieving this) has failed to explain extremism as manifested in the 21st century. In particular they criticise psychology for a failure to understand how sacred ideals and values, as well concepts of identity and group salience lead people to act in terms of principles rather than cost-benefit analysis when the two approaches conflict.

Atran (2010) reports on a series of studies he carried out with Islamic fighters in Sulawesi; in one interview he reports a participant as saying (in response to a question as to whether God would be better pleased the more of the enemy were killed) that if a fighters intentions were 'pure' (that is serving God's interests rather than the individuals own agenda) it mattered not how many or few were killed, or even if the fighter only killed himself. It is the collective (god-serving) benefit which is important rather than any individual benefit or outcome; given that, any rational decision-maker would opt to freeload on the collective activities of others! Internalisation of group identities and values makes such a strategy untenable; commitment to ideology leads to a willingness to forgo or delay personal incentives – it may even be the case that the delay of reward until after death is acceptable. This does not only apply to religious extremists but also to political extremists who view the possibility of an ideal state being achieved, even after their own demise, is a sufficient if vicarious goal.

Rai and Fiske (2011) argue that any understanding of extremist violent behaviour will fail if it fails to engage with the person's moral commitment to an in-group, ideology and the values and principles associated with group identity can negate any effect of individual-level motivation. People with extreme views make choices – not on the basis of choosing to do something which will lead to a specific outcome but on the basis of a moral imperative and while driven by moral reasoning. This has echoes of the Kantian approach which proposes that 'sacred' values represent a moral imperative which means that people will act in a certain way because that way is the right and moral thing to do.

While the concept of 'sacred values may have its origins in the religious, core secular belief systems such as belief in reciprocity, fairness and even a collective identity (Ginges et al. 2011) such as demands for 'justice for my people' can be seen as sacred values and behaviour based on these values do follow a logic of moral appropriateness if not of logical reasoning. It is the case that these values are bound into both personal and collective identities and it is transgression by others against these values, particularly the group identity values, which lead to acting out extremist values.

One of the psychological consequences of adhering to such a value system is the strong and negative emotions experienced by a person who transgresses them – feelings of guilt, shame and anxiety accompany the transgression. Hence decisions made in relation to these values by those who hold to strong extremist views are rarely made using traditional utility-based reasoning – indeed it may be seen as shameful to even consider logic when making decisions. Hence the comment reported by Atran (2010) above; it is the moral underpinning to an act rather than the act itself which determines God's judgement of an individual.

Youth and Vulnerability to Extremism

Zubok and Chuprov (2010) note that young people are particularly vulnerable to developing extremist thoughts because of the psychological conflicts experienced in adolescence and early adulthood. While their focus is on young people in Russia their ideas resonate with those watching the large presence of young people in the emergence of extremism in western Europe (for example the resurgence of fascist groups in historically liberal countries such as the Scandinavian countries, the Netherlands and Belgium) as well as in political and religious extremist groups in Africa and Asia. They argue that young people face specific challenges in contemporary society including age discrimination in relation to work and any benefits, access to good housing and a lack of opportunity for their spiritual (in a non-religious sense) development. They describe an existential crisis for the young that is exacerbated by current economic and social forces; they are required to be 'independent' yet there are few jobs and no housing other than a continuation of residence with parents. If they cannot gain employment and rely on benefits they are demonised as scroungers. Their social positions are marginalised and uncertain and they are hence attracted to subcultures which offer them a positive identity denied them by the dominant culture. Because of their developmental status they are responsive to emotional appeals, their marginalisation leads them to deviate from accepted norms and to identify with those of a subculture.

These subcultures range from political groupings including violent right-wing political groups, musical subcultures and punk-anarchist subcultures. It is the first and the last groups which are perceived to pose a threat to the Russian political system, exemplified perhaps in the Russian judicial systems response to the punk-anarchist female band Pussy Riot, three of whose members were jailed for two years for singing anti-Putin songs in a Moscow cathedral (BBC, August 2012). I will consider the consequences of punitive responses to extremist behaviour as an effective method for countering extremism below.

The young are more likely to be economically disadvantaged than older groups (Burgoon 2006) and poverty can cause suffering which fuels social and political extremism whether because the individual young person feels relatively deprived and scapegoating another group or another country can fuel extremist beliefs. An empirical study of individuals in Northern Ireland cited by Burgoon showed more support for political violence and extremism amongst the unemployed, the young and the poorer citizens.

Steinburg, Brooks and Remtulla's study into the manifestation of extremism as hate crimes in the USA identified young people as being disproportionally represented amongst offenders. They viewed hate crimes as a manifestation of extremist views, with the perpetrator focusing on the victim not as an individual but merely as a representative of the disliked out-groups (as defined by ethnicity, religion, gender orientation etc.). Extremist offenders were more likely to be young and male with the majority of hate-crimes being committed by men in their late teens and early twenties with under 18s committing about a quarter of all hate offences.

The extremist views underpinning the offences are often based on a perception that these views are the norm for their social group; young people because of their emotional development discussed earlier in the chapter are particularly vulnerable to group influences particularly where they lack a strong attachment figure in the home. The researchers also suggest that young people today lack the means to meet basic and profound human needs such as the need for a positive identity, a sense of having control over and being effective within their lives and connection to a place in a broader society. They suggest that while many young extremists are economically deprived this is not the case for all but what they do share is an existential crisis of identity and their place in the world.

Extremism through Computer Mediated Communication (CMC)

While there have been several reports of intentional deception using the web (for example Ellison, Heino and Gibbs 2006, Feldman 2000, Campbell, Fletcher and Greenhill 2009) there is little research evidence for the specific importance of anonymous communication in developing extremist views. While many of the extremists' hate-sites do use anonymous or rather pseudonym-based posting this is primarily to avoid identification by outsiders rather than to pretend to potential recruits that a person is what they are not. It is the power of CMC to induce a group-based identity rather than the potential for deceit which underpins the importance of the world-wide-web in facilitating extremism. Here there are two main factors in play, firstly the enhancement of social-norm factors and secondly the impact of a de-individuating environment on moral responsibility of the individual. De-individuating environments are known (Prince 2012) to have an impact on the influence of group-derived social attitudes such as social stereotypes and prejudice; this is related to a reinforcement of the meaning of a group identity to the individual (raising its salience) and justifying negative consequences of the extremist behaviour or words on out-group members, the eventual victims of extremist behaviours, as de-individuating qualities of CMC focus the attention of extremists away from any individual variation in thought, action or affect and towards the significance of meaningful social identities held in common whether positively regarded (in-groups) or disliked (out-groups).

CMC raises the influence of social norm factors within a communicating 'group' and also enhances the perceived differences between groups as self-categorisation theory (Tajfel and Turner 1987) would predict in that the meaningfulness of group identity is a consequence of a comparison of some sort, however unconscious, with a relevant out-group. As the relevance of the social identity is enhanced then identification with the group increases, particularly the case when *who an individual actually is* can be hidden from other group members. Thus online group members' affiliations with the group, its goals, its values and its methods are enhanced in the conditions of quasi-anonymity which operate in online extremist talk-boards and chat-rooms.

It might seem common sense to assume that the absence of other group members (in the anonymous conditions of CMC) would mean that no group identity could develop and hence there would be no potential for a development of group norms and the associate influence they would have. However, Postmes, Spears and Lea (1999) propose that the condition of anonymity conferred on members of a CMC group leads to group members becoming MORE responsive to the group and more likely to assimilate group values and norms. They argue that situations where groups do not meet face-to-face provide exactly the conditions predicted to maximise social influence exerted by social norms and social identities. Indeed if anonymity increases the significance of a group for its members then it would be expected that people would report higher group identification in anonymous situations such as CMC mediated groups.

Postmes and his colleagues conducted a series of experimental studies (for example Postmes et al. 2001) in which specific group norms were activated in a group and then that group was asked to discuss an issue and reach a solution via CMC. There were two conditions; in the first one, group members were completely anonymous (identified by a number) and in the second condition a still photo of the participant was used to represent the person communicating (so eventually all members of the group would be known to all others by their image). The induced social norm which had been induced in the group prior to the start of the experiment had a great impact on both the decision outcome and the quality and quantity of social interactions between group members when group members were anonymous but not when they were identifiable by pictures. The effect was to heighten the salience and influence of the induced norm. Anonymous groups are more task-oriented than are groups where individual members are identifiable. If anonymity increases the significance of that group for its members then it would be expected that people would report higher group identification in the anonymous situation.

Thus CMC not only allows extremists to communicate without the need for risky or expensive travel or meeting as an identifiable group which may raise the suspicions of security or police services but the medium actually facilitates the cementing of a common bond of purpose, values and ethics amongst its members.

Conclusion: Implications for Countering Extremism

It would appear to be unlikely that relying on giving exemplary sentences to individuals convicted of crimes relating to extremism or killing suspected extremists through 'targeted' bombings will deter other extremists from acting out their ideals. The evidence is that punishments handed out to convicted extremists serve to valorise others; Ginges et al. (2011) note that one of the factors helping the Taliban in Afghanistan is the use by NATO and the USA of strategic air strikes and remote-control Drone bombing of suspected extremist shelters as, rather than lessening the appeal of extremist ideology, each death inspires more young people to take up arms against the Allies. They argue 'We speculate that the lesson for understanding violent extremism, at least in the long run, is that the most important measure may be to provide alternative hopes and heroes that speak to people's – especially young people's – yearning for moral significance' (Ginges, Attran, Sachdeva and Medin 2011, p. 515).

One thing we can note from this is that, while rational models of decision-making focus on immediate reward or certain future outcomes, where behaviour is driven by an ideology or 'sacred value' then primary concerns are often about either maintaining a tradition, be that a cultural value or religious belief, for posterity or a desire for some state which transcends the material world and is a dream of what ought to be rather than what is. In either case attempts to eradicate extremisms by punishing or taking aggressive anticipatory measures is unlikely to stop the extremist. It is important to identify the underlying values in any conflict; what may appear to be a conflict of religious ideals and beliefs may actually be a reflection of some more subtle distinction built around feelings of existential threat or a conflict between other goals not as easily expressed as the goals of extremist ideology. It is important to recognise also the changing nature of dynamics within and between groups; the relationship between the United States and the Taliban is very different in 2012 to what it was in 2002 and both relationships are even more different to that which existed in the 1980s. Possibly a clearer example is that of the relationship between the American colonies and Britain; the initial rebellion against British rule was fuelled in part by heavy taxation which the colonists felt was a violation of the 'no taxation without representation' code.

By the time the British rulers, not the most politically astute group, had understood the nature of the rebellion and withdrawn all the heavy taxes leaving only a token tax it was too late; the colonists had fully internalised as moral the right of being able to determine their own future and rejected all rule from a colonial power. The threat to the values held by the in-group was so great and so immoral that extremist action was justified in order to overcome it. Values become most meaningful when challenged (much the same way we only understand the value of water when it is in short supply) and threats to values and beliefs are most obvious when a different moral/value community is engaged.

How is the group moral value engaged? Active engagement with family, friends or fellow travellers is a key to predicting who will carry out extremist acts (Ginges et al. 2011). While the 7/7 bombers in London in 2005 would in all likelihood have been exposed to extremist material in the mosque and in other places, they appear to have indoctrinated themselves through personal contact and group bonding exercises similar to outward bound courses – white water rafting, etc. It is known that for young adult males the presence of a peer group increases risk-taking behaviour (Gardner and Steinberg 2005). Risky shift makes it likely that group discussion will lead opinion (and related decisions about actions) to be oriented to the extreme (Zimbardo 2008).

If it is the nature of a group which influences extremism (rather than personal characteristics of individuals) then it is not psychological profiling but a better understanding of the group and an investment into understanding better how 'sacred causes' and associated moral beliefs are created by inequalities and injustices which will defeat extremism. Burgoon (2006) gives an overview of the issues faced by those who wish to counter extremis in an article which summarises empirical research and theoretical arguments; the core of his thesis is that there is a need for social welfare provision on both domestic and international fronts to counter the extremist threat. His ideas fit well with the suggestion that impoverished childhood experiences, with a lack of a secure parenting regime and poor access to resources, is a predictor of later amenability to extremist ideas (see above). He argues that the evidence suggests there is less extremism enacted both in the home country and trans-nationally by the citizens of countries which provide a secure welfare base – health, education, housing and nutrition – for its people.

This resonates with the arguments of Strenberg et al. concerning the evolution of extremist thoughts and their manifestation in young people as being triggered, at least in part, by a feeling of alienation from the social world; marginalised in the employment marketed and unable to manifest their own value system they are vulnerable to extremist values. They argue for social and educational intervention to prevent the development of extremist thought. Nash et al. (2011) and McGregor et al. (2010) take a more global perspective on extremist thoughts and their manifestation in action in their accounts of the psychological basis of extremist thought lying in Reactive Approach Motivation which serves to reduce anxiety and threat, particularly to an ideal or a value system as well as existential threat.

It is a truism that words carry meanings and other connotations of judgement and that our use of words reflect our own meaning systems and ideals; to understand extremism and to counter it requires psychologists to remove themselves from their own personal, social and political views as to what constitutes extremism and to be reflective researchers in the context of our own value systems. We need to develop theories which provide a robust explanation for and prediction of extremism, as well as means of countering and diminishing the part it plays in a global community in the 21st century.

Further Reading

Atran, S. (2010). *Talking to the Enemy: Faith, Brotherhood and the (Un)making of Terrorists*. New York: HarperCollins.

Hogg, M., and Blaylock, D. (2011). *Extremism and the Psychology of Uncertainty*. New York: Wiley.

Zimbardo, P. (2008). *The Lucifer Effect: Understanding How Good People Turn to Evil*. New York: Random House.

References

Allport, G. (1943). The Ego in Contemporary Psychology. *Psychological Review*, 50: 451–578.

Altran, S. (2010). *Talking to the Enemy: Faith, Brotherhood and the (Un)making of Terrorists*. New York: HarperCollins.

Battegay, R. (1996). Group Leaders: Charisma and possible dangers in religious congregations, political movements. *International Journal of Psychotherapy*, 1: 35–43.

BBC News. Pussy Riot jailed for two years for hooliganism. Online at http://www.bbc.co.uk/news/world-europe-19297373 [accessed: 28 August 2012].

Beck, A. (1999). *Prisoners of Hate: the Cognitive Basis of Anger, Hostility and Violence*. New York: HarperCollins.

Bowlby, J. (1969). *Attachment: Attachment and Loss*. Vol. I. London: Hogarth.

Breakwell, G. (1986). *Coping with Threatened Identities*. London: Routledge.

Burgoon, B. (2006). On Welfare and Terror. *Journal of Conflict Resolution*, 50(2): 176–203

Campbell, J., Fletcher, G., and Greenhill, A. 2009. Conflict and identity shape shifting in an on-line financial community. *Information Systems Journal*, 19(5): 461–78.

Carver, C., and Scheier, M. (1998). *On the Self-regulation of Behavior*. New York: Cambridge University Press.

Ellison, N., Heino, R., and Gibbs, J. (2006). Managing Impressions Online: Self-presentation processes in the Online Dating Environment. *Journal of Computer-Mediated Communication*, 11(2): 415–41.

Feldman, M. (2000). Munchausen by Internet: detection of factitious illness and crisis on the internet, *Southern Medical Journal,* 93: 669–72.

Gardner, M., and Steinberg, L. (2005). Peer Influence on Risk taking, Risk preference and risky decision making in adolescence and adulthood: an experimental study. *Developmental Psychology*, 41(4): 625–35.

Gergen, K., and Gergen, M. (1987) Narrative and the self as relationship. *Advances in Experimental Social Psychology*, 21: 17–36.

Ginges, J., Atran, S. Sachdeva, S., and Medin, D. (2011) Psychology out of the Laboratory: the challenge of violent extremism. *American Psychologist,* 66(6): 507–519.

Gray, J., and McNaughton, N. (2000) *The Neuropsychology of Anxiety: An Enquiry into the Functions of the Septo-Hippocampal System*. New York: Oxford University Press.

Harré, R. (1983). *Personal Being*. Oxford: Blackwell.

Hogg, M., and Abrams, D. (*1988*). *Social Identifications: A Social Psychology of Intergroup Relations and Group Processes*. London: Routledge.

Joinson, A. (2003). *Understanding the Psychology of Internet Behaviour*. Basingstoke: Palgrave Macmillan.

Laor, N., Yanay-Shani, A., Wolmer, L., and Khoury, O. A trauma-like model of political extremism: psycho-political fault lines in Israel. Annals of the New York Academy of Sciences 1208: 24–31.

LaPiere, R.T. (1934). Attitudes vs. Actions. *Social Forces*, 13: 230–70.

Levin, J., and McDevitt, J. (1993). *Hate Crimes: The Rising Tide of Bigotry and Bloodshed.* New York: Plenum Press.

McGregor, I., Nash, K., Mann, N., and Phills, C. (2010). Anxious Uncertainty and Reactive Approach Motivation. *Journal of Personality and Social Psychology*, 99(1): 133–47.

McGregor, I., Zanna, M., Holmes, J., and Spencer, S. (2001). Compensatory conviction in the face of personal uncertainty: going to extremes and being oneself. *Journal of Personality and Social Psychology*, 80: 472–88.

Mead, G.H. (1934). *Mind, Self and Society*. Chicago: University of Chicago Press.

Nash, K., McGregor, I., and Prentice, M. (2010). Threat and Defence as Goal Regulation: From Implicit Goal Conflict to Anxious Uncertainty, Reactive Approach Motivation and Ideological Extremism. *Journal of Personality and Social Psychology*, 101(6): 1291–301.

Postmes, T., Spears, R., and Lea, M. (1999). Social Identity, Normative Content and 'Deindividuation' in Computer-mediated Groups. In N. Ellemers, R. Spears, and B. Doosje (eds), *Social Identity: An Introduction*. Oxford: Blackwell.

Prince, J. (2012). Psychological aspects of cyber hate and cyber terrorism. In I. Awan and B. Blakemore (eds), *Policing Cyber Hate, Cyber Threats and Cyber Terrorism*. (2012). Farnham: Ashgate.

Rai, T., and Fiske, A. (2011). Moral psychology in relationship regulation: moral motives for unity, hierarchy, equality and proportionality. *Psychological Review*, 118: 57–75.

Salvendy, J. (1999a). The dynamics of prejudice in Central Europe. International *Journal of Psychotherapy*, 4(2):145–59.

Salvendy, J. (1999b). Ethnocultural considerations in group psychotherapy. *International Journal of Group Psychotherapy*, 49(4): 429–64.

Shorter Oxford Dictionary (1980) Vol. 1, Oxford: Oxford University Press.

Steinberg, A., Brooks, J., and Remtulla, T. (2003). Youth hate crimes; identification, prevention and intervention. *American Journal of Psychiatry*, 160(5): 979–89.

Steinberg, P. (1998). Attachment and object relations in formulation and psychotherapy. Annals of the Royal College of Physicians and Surgeons of Canada, 31: 19–22.

Tajfel, H. (1981). *Human Groups and Social Categories*. Cambridge: Cambridge University Press.

Tajfel, H., and Turner, J.C. (1986). The social identity theory of inter-group behavior. In S. Worchel and L.W. Austin (eds), *Psychology of Intergroup Relations*. Chicago: Nelson-Hall.

Turner, J.C., Hogg, M.A., Oakes, P.J., Reicher, S.D., and Wetherell, M.S. (1987). *Rediscovering the Social Group: A Self-categorization Theory*. Oxford: Blackwell.

Young-Bruehl, E. (1996). *The Anatomy of Prejudice*. Cambridge, Mass.: Harvard University Press.

Zubok, I., and Chuprov, V. (2010) The Nature and Characteristics of Youthful Extremism. *Russian Education and Society*, 52(1): 45–68.

Zimbardo, P. (2008). *The Lucifer Effect: Understanding How Good People Turn to Evil*. New York: Random House.

Chapter 5

International Strategies for Preventing Extremism and Terrorism

Imran Awan

Introduction

Following an international security conference held in Munich in 2011 there were a number of serious questions raised about how to prevent extremism (Cameron 2011). Former American President George W. Bush stated that: 'No group or nation should mistake America's intentions: We will not rest until terrorist groups of global reach have been found, have been stopped, and have been defeated.' (President George W. Bush, 6 November 2001. Cited in the National Strategy for Combating Terrorism 2003: 1). This chapter will examine the effectiveness of international strategies when it comes to tackling extremism and the threat from far right groups, including an examination of both the UK and US counter-terrorism policies which have been criticised for being ill-defined and reactionary (Githens-Mazer and Lambert 2010).

The European Union have defined a terrorist offence as including murder and hijacking which could be used to intimidate a population or destabilize a country's political system. In 2005 the EU also created a strategy which focused on four main strands of counter-terrorism (Prevent, Protect, Pursue, and Respond). Furthermore, the European Commission in 2007 also created the 'Check the Web' project, which aimed to tackle and monitor online extremist material. The EU has been working with Member States to create a broader strategy that tackles extremism through an initiative known as the 'workstreams' project, which uses integration programmes with Muslim imams (religious scholars) to help spot the signs of extremism and at the same time improve imams' language and citizenship skills. Archick et al. (2011:1) state that: 'Successive U.S. administrations and Members of Congress have welcomed European initiatives to promote better integration of Muslims and curtail Islamist extremism in the hopes that such efforts will ultimately help prevent future terrorist incidents.'

Prior to the 9/11 attacks a number of European countries appeared to have adopted a 'laissez faire' attitude when it came to dealing with extremism. However, following numerous terrorist plots, including British Muslims planning to detonate liquid explosives on airliners to the United States, and in 2011 a terrorist attack at Germany's Frankfurt airport, a number of serious questions about the threat from home-grown terrorism and the nature of far right extremism had become more crystallised. As a result the UK, the US and a number of its close allies (France, Germany, the Netherlands and Spain), have been working together in multi-faceted programmes that aim to eradicate the extremist threat.

The European Response to Extremism

France

Al-Qaeda has been responsible for a number of terrorist attacks in France, such as a 2009 suicide bombing at the French Embassy and a more recent attack in 2012 where Mohammed Merah was involved in a suicide mission which led to the death of four people (BBC News 2012). In France the threat level has been heightened regarding Al-Qaeda and as a result the French government has enacted a number of controversial counter-terrorism policies and legislation that risk alienating the vast majority of law abiding French Muslim communities. Indeed, a number of socio-demographic and socio-economic factors, such as poor education, high unemployment rates, and dissatisfaction from political parties, have led to many French Muslims being underrepresented.

Whilst the above factors could be used as a tool to measure Muslim issues and concerns within French society, opinion polls also seemed to indicate that communities in France are also worried about what they perceive as 'Islamist' extremism. For example, Archick et al. (2011: 11) refer to a survey conducted on behalf of *LeMonde, fr* in December 2010 which found that almost 68 per cent of French people believe that Muslims have not integrated into society and over 42 per cent of those surveyed argued that Muslim communities were seen as a 'threat' to French national security. Moreover, in 2003 the French Council of the Muslim Faith was used as an organisation that would work with French Muslims at helping integrate them into society. Archick et al. (2011:12) note that:

> Observers viewed the government-led founding of the CFCM as an attempt to
> reduce foreign influence on France's Muslim population and to thereby promote
> a French brand of Islam that is not in conflict with the values of the republic.

Through the use of the CFCM the French government has provided funding streams that aim to target Muslim imams to play a more active role in working with Muslim communities at grassroots level. Former French President Nicolas Sarkozy provided a narrative on getting Muslims to integrate into French society through French language courses and citizenship programmes. However, this rhetoric inevitably has a subliminal message of tackling extremism but appeared to be more a political motive from Sarkozy that would appeal to the French conservatives. Critics therefore argue that the French government used these hardline approaches as a means to create support among conservative voters following a 2012 public campaign from the far-right group (Marine Le Pen).

Some of these counter-terrorism strategies in France have included the law which banned the wearing of the full face veil in public. The ban includes Muslim women who wear the *burqa* (a covering of the face, hands and full body). It imposed a €130 fine on any person seen wearing the *burqa* in a public place. Similar bans against people wearing religious clothing in a public place have also been imposed in countries such as Belgium and Italy. Inevitably, cases now will arise where people continue to wear the *burqa* despite the threat of being fined, based on religious grounds. For example, in 2011 two women who were fined for wearing a full face veil in a public area in Paris (Chrisafis 2011). Similar counter-terrorism efforts in France have caused controversy where tactics such as 'over-policing', surveillance, stop and search and wiretapping of Muslim suspects as a means to prevent a terrorist attack, have been used.

Archick et al. (2011:14) state that:

> The anti-terror magistrate's prosecutors have greater authority than other French prosecutors to order wiretaps and surveillance, and they may order preventive detention of suspects for up to six days without filing a charge.

Germany

Germany, like France, has also been working through integration and community cohesion programmes such as the National Integration Plan which focuses on the improvement of language and equal opportunities. Indeed, Germany has used a number of policies that try to integrate and promote Muslim imams and as such provide training and language courses for them. However, as one of the world's leading economies Germany has also suffered in the economic downturn, leading to poor unemployment and high deprivation of many Muslim communities:

> Many Germans see Muslims as refusing to accept German norms and values and as wanting to stay apart from the majority population. German attitudes toward Muslim communities, though rooted in differences in culture and values, also have been exacerbated by persistent social and economic problems facing the country as a whole. (Archick 2011: 16)

Germany has also been targeted by terrorists who have planned and plotted major attacks. For example, in 2010 a number of German suspects linked to the Islamic Jihad Union were arrested and prevented from carrying out a terrorist attack. Whilst there have been these reported incidents there has also been an anti-Islamist sentiment against Muslim communities within Germany. For example, in 2009, Marwa el-Sherbini – nicknamed the 'martyr of the head scarf' – was stabbed to death in court following a case against her neighbour who had called her a terrorist (*The Guardian* 2009). Similarly, although not linked, the head of the German domestic intelligence agency was forced to resign following revelations that three people from the National Socialist Movement were suspected of killing eight people of Turkish origin between 2000 and 2006. The group's founders, Uwe Böehnhardt and Uwe Mundlos committed suicide whilst the third suspect, Beate Zschaepe, eventually turned herself in. Despite Germany setting up a centre that attempts to work with national agencies in tackling far-right extremism critics argue that the unit had been too busy tackling only 'Islamist' extremism and therefore have neglected the threat posed by far right groups (Guardian Press Association 2012).

Indeed, groups within Germany linked to the far right, which have become commonly known as the 'Free forces', are attracting new crowds, enhancing their influence with the use of social media by recruiting from the middle class and students. Similar to other far right groups the 'Free forces' main aims are constructed in a main rejection of the German states multicultural strategy. It does appear that German nationalists are also playing upon the disaffection from the Euro-zone crises and wider economic issues as a means to increasingly becoming sympathetic to the anti-immigrant agenda nurtured by far right extremist groups.

Germany has also adopted anti-terrorism legislation and policies that aim to protect Germany against extremist groups and 'lone wolf' terrorists through the Federal Office of Criminal Investigation (a group who are tasked with anti-terrorism operations and are responsible for conducting terrorist investigations and the prevention of terrorist attacks). The legislation has also banned a number of groups regarded as extremists, such as Hizb-ut-Tahrir.

The Netherlands

The Netherlands National Counter-terrorism Coordinator's Office has ranked the current terrorist threat as 'limited' (at the time of writing). In the Netherlands the Dutch ambassador to the US, however, has raised further questions about Al-Qaeda being able to recruit vulnerable young Dutch Muslims to fight with extremists, in particular across Somalia and Afghanistan. Indeed, in 2009 the Dutch Ambassador to the US, Renee Jones-Bos, argued that the Netherlands would be able to cope with the terrorist threat through 'preventative' techniques. Whilst this policy is used to tackle extremism the strategy also aims to use integration methods and tactics as a means to work better with Muslim communities and help identify triggers for extremism and radicalisation.

Policy in the Netherlands also focuses on extremism within prisons and schools, and the use of the Internet as a tool for extremism and radicalisation and as such policy focuses here on monitoring websites and terrorist-related material. In addition, the Dutch government has enacted counter-terrorism legislation such as the Crimes of Terrorism Act 2004 which attempts to define terrorism and extremism. The other major problem within the Netherlands has been the rise of far right groups such as the Freedom Party, which was discussed in more detail in Chapter 2.

Spain

Spain has also been the subject of terrorist attacks and witnessed firsthand the threat from extremist groups and organisations. The most prominent attacks were conducted in 2004 following the train bombings in Madrid which killed over 192 people. In Spain the counter-terrorism model has been multi-faceted using a global approach to tackling extremist groups. Similar to other European countries discussed above Spain has been struggling with high levels of unemployment and poverty, which has led to resentment against minority communities such as Muslims, who are deemed to be the 'problem'. Archick (2011: 28) states that:

> Some analysts assert that Muslims in Spain typically experience prejudice based as much on their poverty as on their religious or national identity.

Spain has adopted a penal code which creates a number of offences that relate to extremism and terrorism. However, the offences within this section have been criticised for the broad nature of the powers available to police officers in Spain such as the creation of offences that deal with recruitment, indoctrination and glorifying or encouraging terrorism. Spain has also taken steps to strengthen monitoring of extremist activity in prisons.

The UK Context

The UK counter-terrorism strategy is enshrined in its CONTEST strategy which aims to reduce the risk to the UK from international terrorism. However, part of such counter-terrorism policies in Britain has led to an erosion of trust between Muslim communities and law enforcement agencies (Awan 2011). Furthermore, critics argue, that PREVENT (see below) is driven by state-led policies, embedded within vague and ambiguous local initiatives that lack both clarity and detail and in effect get Muslim communities to act as 'informants' (Lambert 2008; 2011; Spalek 2010). Fenwick and Choudhury (2011) argue that; 'Counter-terrorism measures are contributing to a wider sense among Muslims that they are being treated as a "suspect community" and targeted by authorities simply because of their religion.' (Fenwick and Choudhury 2011: 11).

The UK PREVENT Strategy 2011 has three main purposes; firstly, to tackle the ideological causes and challenges of terrorism; secondly preventing people from being drawn into terrorist related acts and finally promoting partnerships between institutions working together to tackle the risk of extremism (HM Government 2011). The PREVENT Strategy 2011 has been criticised for the unsystematic way in which government funding had been allocated. Fenwick and Choudhury's (2011) study explored the issues of both Muslims and non-Muslims across Britain and the impact of counter-terrorism legislation upon Muslim families and revealed how British Muslims regarded the funding of PREVENT initiatives as a major concern. They state that 'There was also concern about the lack of focus and clarity around the nature and scope of the programme' (Fenwick and Choudhury 2011: 15).

Similarly, in March 2010, the House of Commons Select Committee for Communities and Local Government Report into PREVENT stated that; 'much Prevent money has been wasted on unfocused or irrelevant projects, as a result either of misunderstanding of Prevent or of a lack of willingness and capacity of local organisations to deliver' (House of Commons 2010: 61)

The broader literature suggests that Muslims in the UK feel that law enforcement agencies (such as the police) have begun to use a campaign of surveillance against Muslim communities. Thus, one of the debates about the new PREVENT Strategy 2011 is the manner in which it is becoming labelled as an agenda for 'spying' upon communities. For example, Project Champion, an initiative which involved the police using covert and overt surveillance cameras in predominately Muslim areas of Birmingham (in the UK), was criticised for breaching human rights legislation (Awan 2011; Innes et al 2011).

Overall, the PREVENT Strategy 2011 aims to eradicate and prevent extremism through the identification of extremists by tackling the 'root' causes of that ideology (that is, the radicalisation process, which is where people support extremism and, in some cases, join terrorist groups) (Gregory 2010; Ferguson and Hussey 2010; Campbell and Connolly 2008; Brittain 2009; Hillyard 1993). According to the British Home Secretary, Theresa May, the previous PREVENT policy was flawed because it failed to identify the threat of extremism. She states that; 'It failed to confront the extremist ideology at the heart of the threat we face; and in trying to reach those at risk of radicalisation, funding sometimes even reached the very extremist organisations that Prevent should have been confronting' (*Daily Telegraph* 2011).

However, the Home Secretary does fail to identify what the term 'extremism' means and her speech does have the potential to create a fear element within the public arena, thus leading to more discriminatory acts against law-abiding Muslim citizens who are viewed as extremists.

United States Policy on Preventing Violent Extremism

The US National Security Strategy (2010) states that:

> Several recent incidences of violent extremists in the United States who are committed to fighting here and abroad have underscored the threat to the United States and our interests posed by individuals radicalized at home. Our best defenses against this threat are well informed and equipped families, local communities, and institutions. The Federal Government will invest in intelligence to understand this threat and expand community engagement and development programs to empower local communities. (Cited in Empowering Local Communities to Prevent Violent Extremism 2011: 1).

Indeed, the US President, Barack Obama, has stated that:

> As extremists try to inspire acts of violence within our borders, we are responding with the strength of our communities, with the respect for the rule of law, and with the conviction that Muslim Americans are part of our American family. (President Barack Obama, State of the Union, January 2011. Cited in Empowering Local Communities to Prevent Violent Extremism 2011: 3).

The US policy on tackling violent extremism is incorporated in the 'Empowering Local Communities' publication which uses an agenda that works with understanding how people become violent extremists and then begins to tackle the process of radicalisation. The strategy's main focus is getting local communities to work in a partnership with law enforcement agencies and intelligence agencies who also have a crucial role to play when it comes to combating extremists. The US policy on preventing violent extremism and empowering local communities states that: 'Law enforcement plays an essential role in keeping us safe, but so too does engagement and partnership with communities' (Empowering Local Communities to Prevent Violent Extremism 2011: 2).

The Obama Administration definition of extremism is:

> "Violent extremism" to refer to ideologies, secular or religious, that support or encourage ideologically motivated-violence to further political goals. According to the Administration, supporters of "[violent extremist] groups and their associated ideologies come from different socioeconomic backgrounds, ethnic and religious communities, and areas of the country, making it difficult to predict where violent extremist narratives will resonate". (Empowering Local Communities to Prevent Violent Extremism 2011:1).

As noted above, the US administration, similar to the UK government, argues that local communities must play a pivotal role in identifying would be extremists from within their communities. The problem with this approach is that law enforcement agencies such as the police are required to be working within communities in building trust and at the same time combating extremism. For example, a number of intelligence-led police operations, within local communities have involved the disproportionate use of stop and search powers and police surveillance. The US policy on preventing extremism states that:

> The best defenses against violent extremist ideologies are well-informed and equipped families, local communities, and local institutions. Their awareness of the threat and willingness to work with one another and government is part of our long history of community-based initiatives and partnerships dealing with a range of public safety challenges. (Empowering Local Communities to Prevent Violent Extremism 2011: 2–3)

Another problem with tackling extremism has been attempting to define the term (as discussed in Chapter 1) and understanding the extremism and radicalisation process. The US policy on preventing extremism describes a number of socio-economic factors that need to be taken into account when tackling extremist individuals or organisations. US policy states that:

'While we can and must prioritize our efforts, our approach should be enduring and flexible enough to address a variety of current and possible future threats. Individuals from a broad array of communities and walks of life in the United States have been radicalized to support or commit acts of ideologically-inspired violence' (Empowering Local Communities to Prevent Violent Extremism 2011: 2).

US policy in this area also raises important issues as regards the potential threat to US national security from Al-Qaeda led extremism and its affiliates. This threat could now be intensified following the death of Osama bin Laden and in particular could have serious consequences that relate to home-grown threats to the US. As a result the risk is that new Al-Qaeda actors will emerge with influence and charismatic appeal that would allow them to indoctrinate and recruit vulnerable US citizens capable of committing acts of terrorism on American soil. The US policy states that: 'The past several years have seen increased numbers of American citizens or residents inspired by al-Qa'ida's ideology and involved in terrorism' (Empowering Local Communities to Prevent Violent Extremism 2011: 2).

Indeed, recent examples highlight how US citizens have plotted to commit acts of terrorism, for example, Faisal Shehzad, who attempted to plant a bomb in Times Square and the failed attempt to bomb a Detroit-bound airliner. As a result of such tactics the US administration has begun a process whereby they are using a screening policy for all flights to the US. Moreover, one of the key areas for the US PREVENT Strategy is an attempt to build trust between local communities and law enforcement agencies. Whilst the US PREVENT policy identifies Al-Qaeda led extremists as the main threat to US national security it does not provide any clear or conclusive evidence on how law enforcement agencies should build trust and empower communities to voice their opinions and grievances.

Clearly, law enforcement agencies require a multi-faceted approach which has them build police-community relations through community workshops, meeting community representatives and young people in order to build trust and relationships. The problem at the moment is that both in the US and the UK there are problematic relationships between the Muslim community and the police where Muslims are being viewed as 'suspects' and possibly feel alienated and maligned by tactics of racial profiling by law enforcement agencies:

Communities are best placed to recognize and confront the threat because violent extremists are targeting their children, families, and neighbors. Rather than blame particular communities, it is essential that we find ways to help them protect themselves. (Empowering Local Communities to Prevent Violent Extremism 2011: 3)

Tackling forms of extremism requires community-based projects which get local communities to work in a partnership with law enforcement agencies. Therefore adopting community policing is vital to ensure communities are informed about policing operations and are able to work together in a productive manner. As stated above, this type of partnership would require collaborative work with communities. Currently, the US Departments of Justice and Homeland Security has also created a new 'Building Communities of Trust' initiative which aims to get local US communities and law enforcement agencies to work together in community-based projects that aim to rebuild trust.

One of the most important aspects of this initiative is the use of focus groups and interviews with community members in order to empower them to express their opinions and concerns. It is anticipated that the use of such an open forum within communities would allow the US government to respond and act accordingly to the concerns and attitudes of local communities and at the same time help build trust. As discussed in Chapter 1, extremism can include a wide range of forms and US policy on challenging extremism is not confined to 'Islamist' forms of extremism and therefore the policy cites extremism as also being related to gang culture, school shootings, drugs and hate crimes.

Extremism and US Gang Culture

The US Department of Justice has used the 'comprehensive gang model' as a means to work with local communities in identifying individuals with affiliations in gangs and uses local community-based educational projects that can prevent people joining gangs. Such strategies aim to prevent extremism within gang culture and are explored in more detail in Chapter 6.

> Local community organizations and government offices responsible for addressing gangs—police, schools, probation officers, youth agencies, grassroots organizations, government, and others—help identify causes, recommend appropriate responses, and select activities for local implementation, supported by integrated Federal, state, and local resources to incorporate state-of-the-art practices in gang prevention, intervention, and suppression. (Empowering Local Communities to Prevent Violent Extremism 2011: 4)

In the US the fatal shooting of a number of children in schools has also led to questions about the threat from extremists who target schools. As such the departments of Education, Justice, and Health and Human Services have used the Safe Schools and Healthy Students initiative to create a number of multi-faceted programmes within schools that discuss the dangers of guns, extremists, and violent acts in schools. This initiative was taken in order for local communities and schools to work together in partnership approaches:

> the Initiative has resulted in fewer students experiencing or witnessing violence, increased school safety, and an overall decrease in violence in communities where the program is active. (Empowering Local Communities to Prevent Violent Extremism 2011: 4)

US Partnerships and Communities

Community work at preventing violent extremism in the US has used open forums, online discussions and email correspondence as a means to reach 'hard-to-reach' community groups. This system can also help inform US policy on preventing violent extremism and allows information to be shared and provides an opportunity for feedback. The US policy on preventing extremism states that:

> We also reach out to communities directly to answer questions and provide information and guidance, offering opportunities for communities to provide valuable suggestions about how government can be more effective and responsive in addressing their concerns. (Empowering Local Communities to Prevent Violent Extremism 2011: 5)

The US policy on preventing extremism therefore provides a more holistic approach towards tackling the terrorist and extremist threat. Therefore the importance of using community approaches means that the US government can use a wide range of approaches to work with local communities, partners and stakeholders in building partnerships and gathering information:

> We must ensure that in our efforts to support community-based partnerships to counter violent extremism, we remain engaged in the full range of community concerns and interests, and do not narrowly build relationships around national security issues alone. (Empowering Local Communities to Prevent Violent Extremism 2011: 5)

As noted above, US policy on preventing extremism uses engagement tools as a means to work with communities and includes sharing information between agencies as to the possible risk of people within certain communities being radicalised. The strategy focuses on community feedback as a mechanism to shape US government policy in this area and finally, working with community-based organisations in order to understand the causes of radicalisation. US policy also attempts to be proactive and not reactive towards the threat of extremism by constantly evolving new policy.

Furthermore, US policy is concerned with working with a number of partners across the international community who aim to transfer and share experiences that can help inform best practice. For example, the US Federal Government has been involved in creating training programmes that provide a broad curriculum that can be used by prison staff, law enforcement agencies and local communities across the international community.

United States National Security Counter-Terrorism Strategy 2011

The US National Counter-terrorism Strategy merges key aims of the US PREVENT policy into a universal policy. The US policy in this area aims to challenge such extremist ideologies. For example, the US PREVENT policy states that: 'There is no single profile of an al-Qa'ida-inspired terrorist, but extensive investigations and research show that they all believe: (1) the United States is out to destroy Islam; and (2) this justifies violence against Americans' (Empowering Local Communities to Prevent Violent Extremism 2011: 6–7).

Interestingly, both Al-Qaeda and US policy on tacking extremism argue that they are promoting religious freedom. In particular this has led to a propaganda campaign by both sides that attempt to appeal to the outside world. Indeed this narrative has also led to many US Muslim communities feeling that they are being targeted because of their faith, religion and ethnicity. The US PREVENT policy is quick to dismiss such links. The strategy notes that:

> As the President has stated repeatedly, the United States is not, and never will be, at war with Islam. Islam is part of America, a country that cherishes the active participation of all its citizens, regardless of background and belief (Empowering Local Communities to Prevent Violent Extremism 2011: 7)

While policy is aimed at combating extremist ideologies it also is being used as a means to protect people's civil liberties and preserve human rights. The US PREVENT Strategy states that: 'We must do everything in our power to protect the American people from violent extremism while protecting the civil rights and civil liberties of every American' (Empowering Local Communities to Prevent Violent Extremism 2011: 7).

The US National Security and Counter-terrorism Strategy 2011 cites the death of Osama bin Laden as being a major achievement in tackling extremism. Historically, the US rhetoric in tackling extremism has been historically rooted in a philosophy of a 'war' against Al-Qaeda. This is something that US President Barack Obama has argued is a narrative that needs to be amended. The NSC notes that:

> The United States deliberately uses the word "war" to describe our relentless campaign against al-Qa'ida. However, this Administration has made it clear that

we are not at war with the tactic of terrorism or the religion of Islam (National Strategy for Counterterrorism 2011: 2)

The US national security strategy for tackling terrorism sets out a number of overreaching principles which include protecting; preventing; eliminating; disrupting, dismantling, and defeating Al-Qaeda led extremism. The strategy implies that Al-Qaeda is the major threat to US national security yet at the same time, as noted in Chapter 2, it potentially risks alienating people from minority communities who may have been targeted by counter-terrorism legislation, counter-terrorism policies and counter-terrorism policing.

Another problem for such policies is the current theological debates that surround extremism, Islam and terrorism. US policy in this area argues that a counter-extremist narrative must be deployed and used by religious leaders from the Islamic faith as a means to portray Islam in a positive image and one that does not promote global jihad. According to the US PREVENT policy these misinterpretations of Islam can be used as a recruitment tool for extremists to indoctrinate vulnerable Muslim communities towards acts of violence. The problem for the US and its partners is a global recruitment push by Al-Qaeda which means that Al-Qaeda can become a more sophisticated transnational organisation who are able to mobilise a wide range of groups from as far as the Middle East, Africa and Asia. Thus the issue with regard to protecting US citizens through counter-terrorism policies is justified by the US administration as a necessary tool.

As noted previously, the US national security strategy on countering terrorism argues that the policy is based upon the promotion of US values and building community trust through partnership work. Within this charter of human rights US policy argues that intelligence-led operations remain a key tool in gathering evidence and tackling the extremist threat. However, the problem with such policies, as shown in Chapter 2, is the tactics used in order to gather intelligence such as interrogation techniques used by the FBI and heavy-handed policing. The NSC states that:

> The successful prosecution of terrorists will continue to play a critical role in U.S.CT efforts, enabling the United States to disrupt and deter terrorist activity; gather intelligence from those lawfully held in U.S. custody; dismantle organizations by incarcerating key members and operatives; and gain a measure of justice by prosecuting those who have plotted or participated in attacks. (National Strategy for Counterterrorism 2011: 6)

The US national counter-terrorism strategy has also been controversial because of the manner in which its extradition agreements with the UK have been used. Indeed, following a recent ECHR ruling that a number of terrorist suspects in Britain are to be transferred to the US to face trial over terrorist offences committed in Britain, there are further questions about the manner in which the US counters extremism and terrorism. As a result, US policy argues that the best way to tackle the wider terrorist threat from extremists requires an international and regional approach:

> The United States is committed to strengthening the global CT architecture in a manner that complements and reinforces the CT work of existing multilateral bodies. (National Strategy for Counterterrorism 2011: 7)

Conclusion

Muslim communities, both in the UK and US, have increasingly been asked about issues of national identity. The problem with such a nuanced approach is that it could potentially lead to discrimination and unfair treatment by counter-terrorism policies and operations (Mahmood 2004). Preventing extremism requires a multi-faceted approach which uses international agreements between governments that should work together in aiming to tackle the terrorist and extremist threat. It appears that different countries as shown above are adopting similar policies in preventing extremism to the UK. However, they must now ensure that they do not infringe upon people's basic human rights and civil liberties in implementing some of the principles that could be deemed disproportionate.

Further Reading

Casciani, D. 2009. Nursery visited by counter-terrorism police officer, *BBC News* [Online]. Available at: http://www.news.bbc.co.uk/1/hi/uk/8408305.stm [accessed: 8 July 2011].

Centre Burschette. 2009. *Report on the conference on Public Private Dialogue to fight online illegal activity* (27 November 2009) [Online]. Available at: http://www.edri.org/files/Report_first_conference.pdf [accessed: 8 July 2011].

Change Institute. 2009. *Understanding Muslim Ethnic Communities,* London: Department for Communities and Local Government.

Choudhury, T. 2007. *The Role of Muslim Identity Politics in Radicalisation (a study in progress) (*April), Department for Communities and Local Government: London Communities and Local Government [Online]. Available at: http://www.communities.gov.uk/documents/communities/pdf/452628.pdf [accessed: 10 June 2010].

Communities and Local Government. 2010. Citizenship Survey: April-September-England *Cohesion Research Statistical Research* (14) [Online]. Available at: http://www.communities.gov.uk/documents/statistics/pdf/1815799.pdf [accessed: 1 July 2011].

Daily Telegraph. 2011. *Universities complacent over Islamic radicals, Theresa May warns* [Online]. Available at: http://www.telegraph.co.uk/news/uknews/

terrorism-in-the-uk/8558499/Universities-complacent-over-Islamic-radicals-Theresa-May-warns.html [accessed: 3 July 2011].

Dalgaard-Nielsen, A. 2010. Violent Radicalisation in Europe: What We Know and What We Do Not Know, *Studies in Conflict and Terrorism*, 33(9): 797–814.

Department for Business, Innovation, University and Skills. 2007. *Promoting Good Campus Relations, Fostering Shared Values and Preventing Violent Extremism in Universities and Higher Education Colleges* [Online]., Available at: http://www.bis.gov.uk/assets/biscore/corporate/migratedD/ec_groups/22-07-HE_on [accessed: 10 July 2011].

References

Archick, K., Belkin, P., Blanchard, C., Ek, C., and Mix, D. 2011. Muslims in Europe: Promoting Integration and Countering Extremism, September 7, *Congressional Research Service*. [Online]. Available at: www.crs.gov [accessed: 25 April 2012].

Awan, I. 2011. Terror in the Eye of the Beholder: The Spy cam Saga: Counter-terrorism or Counter-productive, *The Howard Journal of Criminal Justice*, 50(2): 199–202.

BBC News. 2012. France shootings: Toulouse gunman killed by sniper. 22 March 2012. [Online]. Available at: http://www.bbc.co.uk/news/world-europe-17473207 [accessed: 1 May 2012].

Brittain, V. 2009. Besieged in Britain, *Race & Class*, 50(3): 1–29.

Campbell, C., and Connolly, I. 2008. A Model for the 'War against Terrorism'? Military Intervention in Northern Ireland and the 1970 Falls Curfew, *Journal of Law and Society*, 33(3): 341.

Cameron, D. 2011. PM's speech at Munich Conference, *No10.gov.uk* [Online]. Available at: http://www.number10.gov.uk/news/speeches-and-transcripts/2011/02/pms-speech-at-munich-security-conference-60293 [accessed: 2 July 2011].

Carlile, L. 2011. Sixth Report of the Independent Reviewer pursuant to s14(3) of the Prevention of Terrorism Act 2005 [Online] Available at: http://www.statewatch.org/news/2011/feb/uk-counter-terrorism-lord-carlile-sixth-report.pdf [accessed 3 July 2011].

Carlile, L. 2011. Report to the Home Secretary of Independent Oversight of Prevent Review and Strategy [online] Available at: http://www.homeoffice.gov.uk/publications/counter-terrorism/prevent/prevent-strategy/lord-carlile-report?view=Binary [accessed 15 July 2011].

Chrisafis, A. 2011. French veil ban: First woman fined for wearing niqab. *The Guardian*. Tuesday 12 April. [Online]. Available at: http://www.guardian.co.uk/world/2011/apr/12/french-veil-ban-woman-niqab-fined [accessed: 9 May 2012].

Crown Prosecution Service. 2010. *Violent Extremism and Related Criminal Offences,* [Online]. Available at: http://www.cps.gov.uk/publications/prosecution/violent_extremism.html [accessed 2 March 2011].

Department for Communities and Local Government. 2007. *Preventing Violent Extremism Pathfinder Fund: guidance note for government offices and local authorities in England*, (February). [Online]. Available at: http://www.communities.gov.uk/documents/communities/pdf/320330.pdf [accessed: 12 July 2011].

Direct Gov. 2011. Reporting Extremism and Terrorism, [Online]. Available at: http://www.direct.gov.uk/en/CrimeJusticeAndTheLaw/Counterterrorism/DG_183993 [accessed: 25 May 2011].

Empowering Local Partners to Prevent Violent Extremism in the United States. 2011. [Online]. Available at: http://www.whitehouse.gov/sites/default/files/empowering_local_partners.pdf [accessed: 21 April 2012].

Fenwick, H., and Choudhury, T. 2011. The impact of counter-terrorism measures on Muslim communities, *Equality and Human Rights Commission Research Report 72,* [Online]. Available at: http://www.equalityhumanrights.com/uploaded_files/research/counter-terrorism_research_report_72.pdf [accessed: 20 June 2011].

Ferguson, C., and Hussey, D. 2010. *2008–2009 Citizenship Survey: Race, Religion and Equalities Topic Report.* London: Department for Communities and Local Government.

Githens-Mazer, J. and Lambert, R. 2010. Islamophobia and Anti Muslim Hate Crimes: a London case study, *European Muslim Research Centre*, [Online]. Available at: http://centres.exeter.ac.uk/emrc/publications/IAMHC_revised_11Feb11.pdf [accessed: 19 June 2011].

Gregory, F. 2010. Policing the 'New Extremism' in 21st Century Britain. In M.J. Goodwin and R. Eatwell (eds), *The 'New' Extremism in 21st Century Britain,* 85–102.

Guardian Press Association. 2012. Neo-Nazi killers: German intelligence chief steps down.[Online]. Available at: http://www.guardian.co.uk/world/2012/jul/02/german-intelligence-chief-neonazi-murders [accessed: 25 July 2012].

The Guardian. 2009. Outrage over Muslim woman killed in court. Tuesday 7 July. [Online]. Available at: http://www.guardian.co.uk/world/2009/jul/07/muslim-woman-shot-germany-court [accessed: 10 May 2012].

Hillyard, P. (1993) *Suspect Community: People's Experiences of the Prevention of Terrorism Acts in Britain.* London: Pluto Press.

HM Government. 2011. *Prevent Strategy* Presented to Parliament by the Prime Minister and the Secretary of State for the Home Department by Command of Her Majesty, [Online]. Available at: http://www.homeoffice.gov.uk/publications/counter-terrorism/prevent/prevent-strategy/prevent-strategy-review?view=Binary [accessed: 12 March 2011].

HM Government. 2006. *Countering International Terrorism: The United Kingdom's Strategy,* Presented to Parliament by the Prime Minister and the

Secretary of State for the Home Department by Command of Her Majesty, [Online]. Available at: http://www.fco.gov.uk/resources/en/pdf/contest-report [accessed: 10 March 2010].

House of Commons Communities and Local Government Committee. 2010. *Preventing Violent Extremism, Sixth Report of Session 2009–10*, London: The Stationery Office, [Online]. Available at: www.publications.parliament.uk/pa/cm200910/cmselect/cmcomloc/65/65.pdf [accessed: 10 March 2010].

House of Commons Hansard Debate. 2011. *Parliamentary Debate on Prevent Strategy,* [Online]. Available at: http://www.publications.parliament.uk/pa/cm201011/cmhansrd/cm110706/debtext/110706-0002.htm [accessed: 3 July 2011].

Innes, M., Roberts, C., Innes, H., Lowe, T., and Lakhani, S. 2011. *Assessing the Effects of Prevent Policing: A Report to the Association of Chief Police Officers*, Cardiff: Universities' Police Studies Institute.

Ipsos MORI. 2011. *Race, Faith and Cohesion*, [Online]. Available at: http://www.ipsosmori-com/researchspecialisms/socialresearch/specareas/racefaithandcohesion.aspx [accessed: 1 June 2011].

Lambert, R. 2008. Salafi and Islamist Londoners: Stigmatised minority faith communities countering al-Qaida, *Crime Law Social Change,* 50: 73–89.

Lambert, R. 2011. Neo Conservative Ideology Trumps Academic Research and Practitioner experience Responding to Prevent 2011, *Muslim Council of Britain,* [Online]. Available at: http://www.mcb.org.uk/comm_details.php?heading_id=121&com_id=2 [accessed: 1 July 2011].

Mahmood, M. 2004. *Good Muslim, Bad Muslim: America, the cold war and the roots of terror.* New York: Three Leaves Press.

May, T. 2011 'CONTEST Speech, *Home Office,* [Online, 12 July] Available at: http://www.homeoffice.gov.uk/media-centre/speeches/contest-speech [accessed: 20 July 2011]; Also see Travis, A 2011 Counter-terrorism strategy driven by 'cyberjihad' threat, *The Guardian* (July). [Online]. Available at: http://www.guardian.co.uk/politics/2011/jul/12/counter-terrorism-strategy-cyberjihad-threat [accessed: 13 July 2011].

National Strategy for Combating Terrorism. 2003. [Online].Available at: https://www.cia.gov/news-information/cia-the-war-on-terrorism/Counter_Terrorism_Strategy.pdf [accessed: 25 April 2012].

National Strategy for Counterterrorism. 2011. [Online]. Available at: http://www.whitehouse.gov/sites/default/files/counterterrorism_strategy.pdf   [accessed: 22 April 2012].

Spalek, B. 2010. Community Policing, Trust, and Muslim Communities in Relation to New Terrorism, *Politics & Policy,* 38(4): 789–815.

Spalek, B., El Awa, S., and McDonald, L. 2008. Police-Muslim Engagement and Partnerships for the Purposes of Counter-Terrorism: An Examination, *Arts and Humanities Research Council,* [Online]. Available at: http://www.religionandsociety.org.uk/uploads/docs/2009_11/1258555474_Spalek_Summary_Report_2008.pdf [accessed: 10 April 2010.]

Spalek, B., and Lambert, R. 2008. Muslim Communities, Counter- Terrorism and De-Radicalisation: A Reflective Approach to Engagement, *International Journal of Law, Crime and Justice.* 36(4): 257–270.

Thornton, S. 2010. *Project Champion Review,* [Online]. Available at: www.west-midlands.police.uk/ latest-news/docs/Champion_Review_FINAL_30_09_10.pdf [accessed: 10 March 2010].

Townsend, M. 2011. Nottingham University films students suspected of extremism, *The Guardian,* [Online]. Available at: http://www.guardian.co.uk/uk/2011/jun/11/nottingham-university-secret-films-students [accessed: 8 July 2011].

Chapter 6

Extremist Groups and Organisations

Brian Blakemore

Extremism may be in the mind of the individual and although there are lone wolf extremists, generally the extremism that comprises a significant and continuing threat to society comes from organised groups of extremists. The protest by Trenton Oldfield that stopped the 2012 Oxford and Cambridge boat race appears to be an individual action to highlight anti-capitalist feeling and economic anxieties. The history of extremism includes those wanting to improve conditions for the underdog, whether people or animals: In 1913 suffragette Emily Wilding Davidson disrupted the Epsom Derby horse race and died in the process; feminist protesters disrupted the Miss World Competition in 1970 and People for the Ethical Treatment of Animals (PETA) have disrupted designer fashion shows more recently. Extremism may breed counter extremism, for example in a backlash to proposed animal rights legislation, pro-hunting campaigners entered and disrupted the House of Commons during the debate on the Fox Hunting Bill in 2004 (Pukas 2012).

Boynes and Ballard (2004: 117) make the point that 'social movements and organisations are dependent upon the availability of resources.' To be an effective group, extremists need members who can offer the skills and knowledge needed to develop the group's strategy, implement plans and manage the group and the individual members within the group. The group will require financial backing which may be beyond the contributions of its inner membership. In order to commit extremist activities the group will need to acquire access to materials that may be difficult to obtain e.g. chemicals for improvised explosive devices. The group may need to generate propaganda to grow membership, raise funds and ensure the group's message and coherence continues. Davis and Cragin (2009) add that there needs to be at least tolerance of any insurgent activities if the group is to be successful. Different groups may employ different strategies to both increase their resources and achieve their objectives. Success will require the group to continue to be seen as relevant, legitimate and effective by members within the group; those outside the group who support it less directly and those outside the group who may be attracted to the group and its objectives in the future. In short, the extremist group needs to develop a supportive social base from which to draw resources and if successful may become like Al-Qaeda, not just a group nor even a cult but also a social movement that is all the more threatening because of its wider appeal and because it does not depend singularly on cultic control of a core group (Lifton 1999). While the difference between a group and a movement may be one of scale and control both are organisations and recognising the activities that the organisation uses, for example crime such as drug dealing or money laundering, can be used to police extremist activities. The report 'Roots of Violent Radicalisation' for the British Government suggests that, in some cases, the threat of becoming a proscribed organisation may be sufficient to compel the organisation to disassociate itself from extremist activities (Home Affairs Committee 2012).

Fitzgerald (2011) considers the problem of identifying extremism and states that each recruit's characteristics may vary. It is a mistake to only profile young men with few educational qualifications and poor employment prospects as there are many examples of educated, female and wealthy extremists and terrorists. The report 'Behavioural Science Unit operational briefing note: Understanding Radicalisation and Violent Extremism in the UK' from the British Security Service (MI5) in 2008 concluded that extremists and terrorists were widely distributed within the population and that they could not be profiled on the basis of nationality and demographics. The report found that they were mostly British citizens, not immigrants or foreign nationals, the majority were not regularly practicing their religion, they were not disproportionately suffering from mental illness or pathological personality traits and that many have steady relationships and families (Travis 2008). However, more recent studies of far right movements support these characteristics as being disproportionately present. Ethnicity and religion may be important in some cases of extremism but some may be extremists within their particular ethnicity and religion, especially where there are a number of schisms within the religion in question. The argument made by Fitzgerald (2011) that Muslims and Buddhists are the most diverse from an ethnicity perspective, is based upon a very limited use of the term ethnicity which might better be called nationality. The definition of the word ethnic is:

1 sharing distinctive cultural traits as a group in society
2 relating to a group or groups in society with distinctive cultural traits
3 relating to a person or to a large group of people who share a national, racial, linguistic, or religious heritage, whether or not they reside in their countries of origin
4 belonging to or associated with the traditional culture of a social group.
Encarta dictionary online (nd: 1)

So nationality is only a small part of ethnicity. Fitzgerald (2011) does indeed identify the social and demographic variation within the religious groups and these are important features and an important first step in looking for sub groups within a community that may be more likely to be, or produce, extremists. The British government notes that potential extremists come from widely diverse backgrounds and that the 7/7 bombings in London were carried out by home-grown extremists (Commons Select Committee 2012) while Security sources claim up to 50 British Jihadist terrorists are active in Somalia fighting for Al-Shabaab who are associated with Al-Qaeda: they were recruited on the streets of Britain to an 'honourable cause' that they could identify with (Dixon C 2012a) (see Chapter 9).

Far Right Extremism: New Right and Populist Organisations

Right wing hate crimes are likely to involve crimes against minorities in society such as; migrants, homosexuals and anti-racist activists. Right wing groups are based upon nationalism or separatism built upon an excessive pride in their own traditions and the perception of an ever-present threat of losing their identity due to immigration, economic recession and globalisation. The report 'Roots of Violent Radicalisation' for the British Government presents the view that the major threat from far right extremism comes from lone wolves who are disillusioned with the views of society (Home Affairs Committee 2012).

The image of a masked German police officer giving the Nazi salute was posted on Facebook on a remembrance day in 2012 for ten people killed by a neo-Nazi organisation (the National Socialist Underground) during the new millennium. Nine of the victims were immigrant businessman and the tenth was a police woman. The accompanying text stated that 'you call it freedom and tolerance. I call it a death dance for Europe. You talk of multi-cultural state. For me it is only white betrayal' (Dixon C 2012b: 24). A study for the think-tank Demos (Bartlett et al. 2011) found that a new kind of movement is gaining ground in Europe that is critical of globalisation, is anti-establishment and supports workers' rights (conventional left wing politics) but also is concerned with protecting national culture and opposition to immigration (conventional far right policy) and so they do not fit into an existing political category and have been named 'Populist' extremist parties or 'the New Right'. The term 'New Right' was coined to capture the philosophy behind the policies of the Reagan and Thatcher governments operating in the US and UK respectively in the 1980s (Merkl and Weinberg 2003). These extremist parties make good use of online social media and their online followers far outnumber the physical activists in these parties, 'This mélange of virtual and real-world political activity is the way millions of people – especially young people – relate to politics in the 21st century. This nascent, messy and more ephemeral form of politics is becoming the norm for a younger, digital generation' (Bartlett et al. 2011: 15). The Demos study canvassed over 10,000 respondents across Europe using an online survey and found that these digital populists are disproportionately young men (63 per cent under the age of 30 and 75 percent males), have double the unemployment rate in their ranks, with 30 per cent claiming further or higher education achievements and another 20 per cent still in education. However, using an online survey may attract a disproportionally higher response rate from younger age groups. The respondents' perceptions included pessimism about their country's future and being highly critical of the European Union, especially regarding a loss of control over borders and the erosion of cultural identity.

Goodwin and Evans (2012) define five stages of increasing activism from potential support for extremism; peripheral voters for extremist parties; those that identify with the extremist group and former members who are now less active and finally core members. Table 6.1 overleaf shows the drivers that turn the Digital Populist into a member and party activist.

Table 6.1   Routes to activism for Digital Populists

From	To	Drivers	Stage of support
Online activism	Voting	Concerns over immigration, and Islamic extremism	Potential supporter Peripheral voter
Online activism	Party membership	Concerns over multiculturalism and the belief that politics is an effective way to respond to their concerns	Identification with group Former core members
Online activism	Active extremism such as street protesting	Concerns over corruption, correlated with male gender, and strong views on politics and violence	Core members

Source: Adapted from Bartlett et al. (2011) and Goodwin and Evans (2012).

Goodwin and Evans (2012) found that for both the British National Party (BNP) and United Kingdom Independence Party (UKIP) supporters, immigration was the most important concern, followed by the economy then thirdly the perceived influences that Muslims living in Britain may have on their way of life. Bartlett et al. (2011) conclude that the way forward is to restore confidence in government institutions and mainstream political processes as Digital Populist activists who are also involved in physical activism appear to be more democratic, have more faith in politics and are more likely to recant violence. This would seem to be more likely to hold for UKIP members than for BNP members according to Goodwin and Evans (2012) who found that there was a much higher anticipation of inevitable inter-group violence amongst BNP members (60 per cent) compared to UKIP members (30 per cent); UKIP members were much more likely to read newspapers with almost half of BNP members not reading any newspaper; very few BNP members said they had friends from minority ethnic groups even though they tended to live in areas with large populations of minority ethnic groups present.

Bartlett et al. (2011) found that the English Defence League (EDL) is mainly a Facebook group comprising around 30,000 supporters and sympathisers but within this body are a core of activists numbering 500 or so and only these are to be found demonstrating on the street. The EDL allows free access via social media and does not require a membership fee; this removes the normal barriers to entry to joining a movement. However, this may greatly reduce the power, control and internal discipline that can be exercised by the core activists and leaders. The study concluded that the main focus of their extremism is driven by major concerns regarding an uncertain future, especially the lack of employment, high rates of immigration and the loss of traditional British identity. These concerns are common across the Western world and are part of a globalised postmodern trend (see Chapter 9): 'As anti-Semitism was a unifying factor for far-right parties in the 1910s, 20s and 30s, Islamophobia has become the unifying factor in the early decades of the 21st century', according to Thomas Klau a member of the European Council on Foreign Relations (*Daily Telegraph* 2011: 1).

Goodwin and Evans (2012) note that only 17 members of far right groups have been convicted of terrorism-related offences in the UK in recent years despite the Commons Select Committee (2012) expressing concern regarding the trend of growing support for both non-violent extremism and for more extreme and violent forms of far-right ideology. Across Europe the scale of the problem in the year 2010 is shown in Table 6.2 below.

Table 6.2   Terrorist activity across Europe in 2010

Terrorist	Attacks	Arrests for planning
Islamist	3	89
Separist	160	349
Right wing	0	0

Source: Europol (2010).

The report postulated that the lack of threat from far right groups might be due to factors such as poor internal cohesion and coordination within these groups, a lack of public support and effective law enforcement which in part may be due to the relative ease of infiltrating such groups. The study for Demos revealed that far-right parties based upon promoting anti-Muslim ideas have gained some popularity in countries where such views were not previously thought to have any form of popular support, such as the Netherlands and Scandinavia. It is argued by anti-extremist organisation 'Hope not hate' that this global rise of far right extremism has evolved into an international network of far right/counter-jihadist groups and that this network is increasing in size, with 190 different counter-jihadist groups identified (Townsend 2012). 'Hope not hate' also claims that the lone wolf Anders Behring Breivik was an online supporter of the Norwegian Defence League. Their report suggests that Breivik's attack has catalysed the development of these far right groups.

These networks may operate at different levels and in different ways; the 'Hope not hate' report cites examples such as the EDL and BNP collaborating regarding standing for election in Britain to avoid splitting their vote (two BNP Members of the European Parliament were elected in Britain in the 2009 European Elections (Communities and Local Government 2009)) and a well-funded US group, the International Civil Liberties Alliance, reportedly co-ordinated individuals and groups in 20 countries online and also held a counter-jihad conference in London (Townsend 2012).

Far Left Extremism and Single Issue Groups

Political extremism is on the rise not just within populist far right parties but in anti-globalisation movements such as 'Occupy London' and in more extreme far left groups. 'Occupy London' may be considered to be a single issue group in that they seek 'global democracy', however, this single issue has many facets such as replacing the dominant governments' global powers with a global representation of all people and that corporate and government institutions must not be allowed to make decisions that shape people's lives without the democratic participation and consent of the world's population. They require institutions to be fair to all irrespective of faith, religion, race, location, politics or wealth. However, this group claim to be a non-violent organisation, with a remit to change on a global scale both corporate and governmental processes covering the whole range of activities from wars to economics, social policy to intellectual copyright.

Left wing extremist activity in Germany increased by 53 per cent (to 1,822 acts of violence) during 2009, after many years of low levels of activity. This is considerably more attacks than those committed by right-wing extremists (Berg et al. 2010). The attacks have included targets such as public service buildings, for example a police station and paint-bombing new upmarket apartment complexes. Berg et al. (2010) argue that the start of this resurgence coincided with the G-8 summit in 2007 and estimate the scale of Left wing extremist members to be 6,600 based on data from the German Federal Police. Berg et al. (2010) attribute the reasons for the upsurge to be reduction in welfare benefits for the long term unemployed, the economic crisis exacerbated by several banking scandals and the gentrification of poorer neighbourhoods displacing the existing community by generating unaffordable rents for the less affluent members of the community. Although the authorities only know a small fraction of the extremists' identities they believe that generally the extremists are disproportionately young. The policing response in Germany has been a mix of traditional tactics relying on physical surveillance, Information Communication Technology (ICT) surveillance and the use of both informants and 'virtual agents' to infiltrate the organisation via websites and identify the extremists. This use of informants and or agents (both physical and virtual) can have damaging results in the community as found previously in the UK during the Irish 'troubles' and today within Islamic communities (see Chapter 9).

The policing response may also be to move further along the route to an electronic police state. Englund (2011) notes that Russia is likely to move further towards this state and the Arab Spring has demonstrated the utility of cyber space, from organising demonstrations to managing a revolutionary army and Russia has already begun monitoring social media to detect, disrupt and deter those who might engage in any aspect of extremism. Media organisations that have reported on extremism have been prosecuted for advocating the extremism reported. Englund (2011) also notes that Russia, China and Tajikistan are suspicious of the Western countries' support of 'extremists' (referred to as freedom fighters by the

Western countries) within their countries and fear that this support may include Western state-sponsored cyber-terrorism within their borders. Consequently, these three countries in particular are proponents of an international treaty to tighten state control on information security.

National Identity, Cohesion and the Radicalisation Process

Common values or norms within a community are products of informal social control which is characterised by the lack of stated rules; these common values are obtained from diffuse sources and experiences as the individual is shaped by the everyday customs and practices within their society. This socialisation is supported by rewards for conforming and deterrents for deviance. Each religion has rules and norms that are extremely important for its followers and so provides strong informal social control. The media has always played a part in social control and with the prevalence of mass media and social network communications the influence on public opinion is significant. Historically it has been argued that knowledge is power and as such can be used to shape society, including its values. Today much information is accessible to the many that are connected online. Moreover, hackers and organisations such as WikiLeaks aim to publish unseen information to all, as a form of democratic extremism. Authoritarian governments are more likely to tightly control access to both government and general information and communication systems to maintain their power and are more likely to engage in mass surveillance and other elements of an electronic police state to enforce strong, formal social control over their constituents.

Hawkins (2011) terms mechanisms of control emanating from the criminal justice system 'back loaded' social control and drawing upon experiences in the USA cites two specific forms of this control 1) profiling of individuals based upon a category (their ethnicity, race or class) for policing interventions and 2) the differentiation in the way such groups are treated after an incident within the criminal justice system. Hawkins argues that in the USA, crime increased due to such back loaded social control:

> I contend that perhaps one set of factors, namely, the social control response was the causal lynchpin. That is, without the mass incarceration of adult drug dealers and other older community residents, the violence explosion may not have occurred or its effects may have been much more muted ... They [the CJS] further undermined the already tenuous "trust" between law enforcement/ courts and citizens needed to foster the kind of social cohesion that is conducive to indigenous social control and its interface with the law. Hawkins (2011: 28)

Hawkins further contends that this over-policing is also exacerbated by 'under policing' of crimes within the Black and Hispanic communities:

that interracial killings among Blacks and Latinos have tended to draw much less attention from the police, prosecutors, and the courts than interracial acts of violence and property crime. Further, despite the inextricable link between violence and drug sales during the 1980s upsurge in crime, authorities may have actually been more attentive to the brazen, open-air marketing of drugs than the taking of the life of a fellow dealer. Hawkins (2011: 30)

The experiences recounted by ethnic minorities in Britain support Hawkins's thesis of over- and under-policing and its effect on reducing community cohesion. British examples of such were posted on the Guardian website and relate to the misuse of stop and search powers; use of excessive force; of being arrested for assault when stopped by plain clothes police who did not disclose their identity; of brothers being accused of being a gang and of these individuals' hate of police and distrust of society in general (Guardian 2012).

British Policy and Jihadist Extremism

The UK Government identified the most serious threats to the country as emanating from international terrorism and in particular, the threat posed by the lose network centred around Al-Qaeda; terrorism from still-troubled Northern Ireland and from extreme right-wing groups (Her Majesty's Government 2011). This report also highlighted animal rights extremism and anti-capitalist extremism as potential threats. Hasan (2011) suggests that the new United Kingdom counter-terror strategy is based on the 'conveyor belt' theory of radicalisation and cites David Cameron's (the British Prime Minister) speech introducing this strategy:

> As evidence emerges about … those convicted of terrorist offences, it is clear that many of them were initially influenced by what some have called 'non-violent extremists', and they then took those radical beliefs to the next level by embracing violence. Hasan (2011: np)

In his speech, David Cameron argued that multiculturalism had failed as a strategy in the UK and that this approach had not supported the Christian faith whilst positively supporting other religions. Several individuals are taking the British Government to the European Court of Human Rights (ECHR) to argue that under Article 9 they have the right to manifest their religion at work:

- Mrs Eweida was prevented from wearing the cross by British Airways who later relaxed their employee dress code, the ECHR did not find for MRs Eweida,
- Mrs Chapin, a nurse, was excluded from work by her National Health Trust for wearing the cross (Dixon, S 2012).

The feeling of losing this particular aspect of 'Britishness' was voiced by TV personality and chef Delia Smith who posted a statement on the web: 'Militant neo-atheists and devout secularists are busting a gut to drive us off the radar and try to convince us that we hardly exist' (Dixon, 2012: 5). David Cameron defined non-negotiable 'British Values' for any who wanted to belong in Britain as including recognising equal rights regardless of sexuality or race; a belief in democracy and the integration of different ethnic, religious and cultural groups within society. He stated that any organisations not positively supporting these values will not be funded by the government regardless of whether they are otherwise beneficial, let alone extremist or violent (Wintour 2011). This new policy is very much in line with the British government's definition of extremism given in Chapter 1:

> Extremism is vocal or active opposition to fundamental British values ... and mutual respect and tolerance of different faiths and beliefs (Home Office 2011: 107)

David Cameron claimed that many young men have been drawn to extremism due to the lack of a single, shared and strong British cultural identity:

> Under the doctrine of state multiculturalism we have encouraged different cultures to live separate lives, apart from each other and the mainstream. We have failed to provide a vision of society to which they feel they want to belong ... We have even tolerated these segregated communities behaving in ways that run counter to our values. So when a white person holds objectionable views – racism, for example – we rightly condemn them. But when equally unacceptable views or practices have come from someone who isn't white, we've been too cautious, frankly even fearful, to stand up to them ... Europe needs to wake up to what is happening in our own countries. We need to be absolutely clear on where the origins of these terrorist attacks lie – and that is the existence of an ideology, Islamist extremism. (Wintour 2011: 1)

This identifies that 'under-policing' of minority ethnic groups with regard to racist actions has occurred and that this also creates rifts within wider society. David Cameron recognises that there is a spectrum of association with Islamist extremism from terrorists driven by this ideology, from general anti-Western feelings, to neutrality, to outright renouncement of such an extremist interpretation of Islam (see Chapter 1). The new strategy will formally recognise that Muslims are not a homogeneous group, with one monolithic culture, a single way of living and just one voice that the government should listen to. For example, Muslims4UK, responding to Mr Cameron's speech, argued that his argument was 'ill-judged and deeply patronising. The overwhelming majority of UK Muslims are proud to be British and are appalled by the antics of a tiny group of extremists and so will hardly be pleased with his lecture on integration' (Wintour 2011: 1).

The conveyor belt theory of radicalisation which describes a linear process whereby individuals who are initially disillusioned and aggrieved with society become simultaneously more religious and extreme, and ultimately become involved in violence and terror has been called into question (Hasan 2011). The British Security Service's 'Behavioural Sciences Unit Operational Briefing Note: Understanding Radicalisation and Extremism in the UK', is reported to have found that extremists and terrorists are a diverse group and do not follow any one path into radicalisation and extremism (Travis 2008).The British Government received a further classified report in July 2010 that also called into question the validity of conveyor belt theory, it found that the influence of extreme groups such as al-Muhajiroun or Hizb ut Tahrir and ideological factors were not the main actors within the radicalisation process (Gilligan, 2010). The report recommends that countering extremism should be removed from the security context to prevent adverse reactions from within communities as was found in the Birmingham 'safety' project (see Chapter 9).

Silber and Blatt (2007) argue there are four distinct phases, rather than a continuum, involved in the Muslim radicalisation process: pre-radicalisation; self-identification; indoctrination and jihadisation. They recognise that an individual may start the process but may not necessarily progress through to the final stage and they may remain at any stage in the process.

The British Government is concerned that extremism is being promoted and inculcated on university campuses and it has called for more active resistance from universities and from organisations such as the Federation of Student Islamic Societies. Gardham et al. (2010) give examples of extremists who have studied at British universities such as Abdulmutallab who had trained in Yemen but had become increasingly radical during his time in Britain and Taimur Abdulwahab al-Abdaly who had studied at Bedfordshire University in Luton.

Given the diversity of extremist backgrounds and the variety of routes to extremism and terrorism how can security, police and community safety organisations prevent violent extremism? These organisations need to recognise this diversity and uniqueness and develop responses that are both tailored and targeted. This requires excellent community intelligence that will only be garnered from a coherent community in a trusting relationship between that community and the policing organisations. The challenges in maintaining community links and support and delivering counter extremism strategies are enormous with a persistent dilemma to balance human rights against security concerns:

> The UK, like other democracies, is faced with the problem of devising counter-terrorist policies and legislation that can deal with the terrorist threat without demeaning the civil liberties that democratic states seek to uphold – such as the rule of law and respect for human rights. Makarenko (2007: 42)

Can the British Government diminish extremism by creating 'Britishness' and encouraging all to adopt this common set of values? Will diverse groups from diverse backgrounds 'buy in' to this concept, or will they see it as another attack on their identity, their mores and their culture? One part of the British Government

PREVENT strategy is to identify extremist behaviour in the young and to attempt to counter it at this early stage in the belief that such extremism might be 'nipped in the bud' more easily than changing views in adults. This approach appears to be based upon the conveyor belt theory of radicalisation. As part of this approach schools are required to report any extremist pupils to the Preventing Extremism Unit within the Department of Education. Kundnani (2009) found that this practice was identifying naughty or angry pupils rather than extremists and that the consequences for the pupil were increased likelihood of bullying or being ostracised following this labelling. Kundnani (2009) recommended that teachers need to facilitate pupil debate in schools about the issues of society and faith to develop an appreciation of and respect for the views of others. This view echoes that of Sunstein (2009) who proposes that a key antidote to extremism and group polarisation is information exchange.

The British Government's policy to counter extremism does not seem to consider the effects of British foreign policy generating feelings of injustice that can lead to radicalisation. Baroness Manningham-Buller, former head of MI5 (British security service), stated to the Chilcot inquiry that the British involvement in the war in Iraq in 2003 may well have resulted in increased radicalisation, extremism, support for Al-Qaeda and terrorism within the UK from British subjects:

> Our involvement in Iraq, for want of a better word, radicalised a whole generation of young people, some of them British citizens who saw our involvement in Iraq, on top of our involvement in Afghanistan, as being an attack on Islam, … not a whole generation, a few among a generation [and that] The Iraq war heightened the extremist view that the West was trying to bring down Islam. We gave Bin Laden his jihad. (BBC News 2010: np)

This frank admission demonstrates the importance of making foreign policy sympathetic to home policy regarding community cohesion and encouraging a British identity.

'Britishness' and the English Riots

The extremists taking part in the English riots were 'part of a feckless criminal underclass' according to Wilson in the *Sun* (2011) whose analysis was based upon the first 1,984 rioters to be processed by the criminal justice system most of whom (76 per cent) had a criminal record and the majority were young, having poor school attendance and level of education and low income were also prevalent factors. Newburn (2011) exposes the weakness in the data used by Wilson, as those first appearing in court are more likely to be those who are known to the police as their identification can be aided by the use of police intelligence systems. Newburn (2011) supports social deprivation as a significant risk factor in becoming involved in criminality.

The Government's response to the English riots and the growing concern over gang violence includes prevention requiring the police to target gang leaders, the creation of an Ending Gang Violence Team to implement the government response and more emphasis on partnership work at local level developing innovative ways to prevent youth violence, involving teachers, the National Health Service and social workers in this preventative work (Newton Dunn 2011). A further response has been the tough punishment given to those convicted of rioting, for example arsonist Gordon Thomas who received an 11-year sentence, taking into consideration that families living in the building were imperilled by the blaze (Pilditch 2011). The Government is also discussing issuing mandatory jail sentences for those 16 years old and over who threaten with knives and increased time in jail for the use of firearms. The final part of the Government's strategy involves pathways out of gang membership, where members will be helped to develop alternative, acceptable world views and lifestyles.

Policing Extremism in Cyber Space and Private Spaces

The Commons Select Committee (2012) cited a recent conviction of four British men from London and Cardiff, for plotting to attack the London Stock Exchange, as evidence of the use of both cyber and private space as part of the radicalisation and planning terror process. Hence the report called for more resources and powers to police these threats and to prevent radicalisation through these spaces. An alternative to increasing the powers of the police and tending towards becoming a Police State is to encourage informal social control in cyber space and in social media generally. Cyber bulling borders on extremism (see definition above) and is termed 'trolling'.

As Ann Widdecombe (2012) points out, these trolls are to be found throughout society and may seem normal in their everyday social interactions. Liam Stacy is an example of expressing extremist views online; he posted hate/racist remarks about Fabrice Muamba, a footballer who 'died' on pitch following coronary arrest but was saved by medical intervention. Stacy pleaded guilty to inciting racial hatred on Twitter; he posted 'LOL [laugh out loud] **** Muamba. He's Dead!!! haha.' (Reynolds 2012: 7). Stacy was then reported to the police by others online. An example of more direct action is that of a celebrity (Noel Edmunds) who used 'web Sheriff' to find out who had created a site called 'will somebody kill Noel Edmunds' (Reynolds 2012: 7).

Innes and Roberts (2011) considered the relationship between formal and informal social control and found that full involvement and resources of the community were not being tapped into. In one case study, in a wealthy area with a relatively low crime rate, the community was asked what its problems were but then the police and local council marshalled and analysed the response to form their interpretation of community intelligence and implemented their solutions (horizontal co-production). In a second case study Innes and Roberts (2011) found a strong sense of community and that informal social control was used to ensure conformity to the norms of that community but that the community was very closed and so would not report intelligence to the police. They defined two categories of co-production that they found to be effective:

> Type 1 Co-production – in some situations the police act to deal with issues brought to their attention by the community ... As part of prevent, this mode is engaged for two main reasons. First, because a problem is sufficiently troubling that it is beyond the scope of purely community led interventions to impact upon it. Second, on some occasions police can fashion a response in order to build community trust and confidence.
>
> Type 2 Co-production as the ideal model for social control is where police identify a problematic issue, but enable or encourage community based actors to deal with it. This can either be through material / practical support, or more tacit forms of backing. Engaging this style of collaboration in prevent work tends to reflect the fact that some of the problems encountered are complex and cannot be effectively treated through application of the criminal law. To the best of our knowledge, this style of working has not been previously identified by researchers. ... It remains the case though, reflecting a key finding of the earlier UPSI report, that Muslim communities appear to continue to express a preference for using their own informal social control resources to solve a problem when this is feasible. Innes and Roberts (201:1 14)

Innes and Roberts (2011) give an example of successful Type 2 co-production social control when local Muslim groups organised both public meetings to counter extremist propaganda and diversionary activities to keep their youth away from a planned visit by a radical cleric and an English Defence League protest march.

Conclusion

Extremism may take many forms from lone wolf discontents, extremist groups, to full social movements, however, the basic drivers for extremism are similar irrespective of the focus of the extremism from left wing to far right wing and including digital populist movements. There needs to be a full recognition of the failings of the recent attempt at multiculturalism in the UK. To counter extremism, truly integrated communities are needed, with encouragement and freedom to discuss contentious issues to give better knowledge and allow the building of relationships between different groups holding different belief systems, while allowing all to maintain their identity and prevent the fear of their group identity being under siege. Community policing that generates co-production of solutions to the community's disparate problems, coupled with both national and foreign policy to support cosmopolitan views is required. Policing must maintain a balanced approach to policing the internet without abusing human rights and drifting into an electronic police state and policing communities without alienating groups, especially avoiding over- and under-policing as part of back-loaded social control.

Further Reading

20th Century Right Wing Groups in Europe (TTSRL, 2008) available at the Transnational Terrorism, Security and the Rule of Law Publications/Contextual papers website http://www.transnationalterrorism.eu/publications.php (click Right-wing terrorism)

Chakraborti, N., and Garland, J. 2009. *Hate Crime: Impact, Causes and Responses.* London: Sage Publications.

Davies, L. 2008. *Educating Against Extremism*. Stoke on Trent: Trentham Books.

Eatwell, R. 2006. Community Cohesion and Cumulative Extremism in Contemporary Britain. *The Political Quarterly*, 77(2): 204–16.

Eatwell, R., and Goodwin, M.J. (eds) 2010. *The New Extremism in 21st Century Britain.* London: Routledge.

Grayling, A.C. 2009. *Liberty in the Age of Terror: A Defence of Civil Liberties and Enlightenment Values*. London: Bloomsbury.

Hussain, E. 2007. *The Islamist.* London: Penguin.

Pantazis, C., and Pemberton, S. 2009. From the 'Old' to the 'New' Suspect Community. Examining the Impacts of Recent UK Counter-Terrorist Legislation. *British Journal of Criminology*, 49(5), 646–6.

References

Bartlett, J., Birdwell, J., and Littler, M. 2011. The New Face of Digital Populism. Demos. [online]. Available at: http://www.demos.co.uk/publications/thenewfaceofdigitalpopulism. [accessed: 5 June 2012].

BBC News. 2010. Iraq inquiry: Ex-MI5 boss says war raised terror threat, 20 July [Online]. Available at: http://www.bbc.co.uk/news/uk-politics-10693001. [accessed: 8 June 2012].

Berg, S., Hollersen, W., Stark, H. and Ulrich, A. 2010. Crisis Fuels Rise in Left-Wing Extremist Violence. *Spiegel,* 20 May. [Online]. Available at: http://www.spiegel. de/international/germany/0,1518,695415,00.html. [accessed: 15 May 2012].

Boynes, D., and Ballard, J.D. 2004. Developing a sociological theory for the empirical understanding of terrorism. *The American Sociologist*, 35(2): 5–25.

Commons Select Committee. 2012. MPs urge internet providers to tackle on-line extremism. 6 February [Online] available at: http://www.parliament. uk/business/committees/committees-a-z/commons-select/home-affairs-committee/news/120206-rvr-rpt-publication/. [accessed: 9 May 2012].

Davies, P.K., and Cragin, K. 2009. *Social Science for Counter terrorism: Putting the Pieces Together*. Santa Monica: RAND.

Dixon, C. 2012a. Jihadis recruited from gangs in Britain, *Daily Express,* 24 February, 15.

Dixon, C. 2012b. Nazi salute by a policeman that shocks Germany, *Daily Express,* 24 February, 17.

Dixon, S. 2012. Church Fury as Government denies right to wear cross *Daily Express,* 12 March, 5.

Englund, W. 2011. Russia hears an argument for Web freedom, *Washington Post,* 28 October. [Online]. Available at: http://www.washingtonpost.com/world/europe/russia-hears-an-argument-for-web-freedom/2011/10/28/gIQAFybZPM_story.html. [accessed: 30 March 2012].

Europol. 2011. TE-Sat 2011: EU Terrorism Situation and Trend Report, European Police Office.

Fitzgerald, M. 2011. Identifying Extremism. *Police Professional,* 21 July 18–21.

Gardham, D., Oscarsson, M., and Hutchison, P. 2011. Sweden suicide bomber: Taimur Abdulwahab al-Abdaly was living in Britain. *The Telegraph* 12 December. [Online]. Available at: http://www.telegraph.co.uk/news/uknews/terrorism-in-the-uk/8198043/Sweden-suicide-bomber-Taimur-Abdulwahab-al-Abdaly-was-living-in-Britain.html. [accessed: 14 February 2012].

Gilligan, A. 2010. Hizb ut Tahrir is not a gateway to terrorism, claims Whitehall report. *The Telegraph,* 25 July. [Online]. Available at: http://www.telegraph.co.uk/journalists/andrew-gilligan/7908262/Hizb-ut-Tahrir-is-not-a-gateway-to-terrorism-claims-Whitehall-report.html#. [accessed: 8 June 2012].

Goodwin, M., and Evans, J. 2012. HOPE not hate: voting to violence? Far right extremism in Britain, Searchlight Educational Trust, London. [Online]. Available at: www.hopenot hate.org.uk. [accessed: 18 June 2012].

Guardian. 2012. The people's panel, 8 January. [Online] Available at: http://www.guardian.co.uk/commentisfree/2012/jan/08/peoples-panel-stop-and-search. [accessed: 20 January 2012].

Hasan, M. 2011. So, prime minister, are we to call you an extremist now? *The Guardian,* 9 June. [Online]. Available at: http://www.guardian.co.uk/theguardian/2011/jun/09/cameron-counter-terror-muslims?INTCMP=SRCH [accessed: 1 November 2011].

Hawkins, D.F. 2011. Things Fall Apart: Revisiting Race and Ethnic Differences in Criminal Violence amidst a Crime Drop. *Race and Justice* 2011 1: 3 [Online]. Available at DOI: 10.1177/2153368710392791. [accessed: 15 May 2012].

Her Majesty's Government 2011b. *CONTEST: The United Kingdom's Strategy for Countering Terrorism.* Cmnd. 8123. Norwich: TSO.

Home Affairs Committee. 2012, *Roots of violent radicalisation.* [Online] Available at: http://www.publications.parliament.uk/pa/cm201012/cmselect/cmhaff/1446/144605.htm#a10. [accessed: 14 June 2012].

Home Office. 2011. PREVENT strategy review, June. [Online]. Available at: http://www.homeoffice.gov.uk/publications/counter-terrorism/prevent/prevent-strategy/prevent-strategy-review?view=Binary. [accessed: 18 April 2012].

Innes, M., and Roberts, C. 2011. *Field Studies on the Co-Production of Social Control: A Backing Paper for the UPSI ESRC Expert Seminar*, Universities' Police Science Institute, Cardiff University 17–18 March 2011 [Online]. Available at: http://www.upsi.org.uk/storage/CoPro%20Empirics%20D1.pdf. [accessed: 24 April 2012].

Kundnani A. (2009) *Spooked! How not to prevent violent extremism*, London: Institute of Race Relations. Available at http://www.irr.org.uk/pdf2/spooked. pdf. [accessed: 14 June 2012].

Lifton, R.J. 1999. *Destroying the World to Save It: Aum Shinrikyo, Apocalyptic Violence and the New Global Terrorism*. New York: Metropolitan Books – Henry Holt and Company.

Makarenko, T. 2007. 'International Terrorism and the UK'. In Wilkinson P (ed.), *Homeland Security in The UK: Future preparedness for terrorist attack since 9/11*. Abingdon: Routledge.

Merkl, P.H., and Weinberg L. 2003. *Right-Wing Extremism in the Twenty-First Century*. London: Frank Cass.

Newburn, T. 2011. A riot born in deprivation. *Guardian.* [Online]. Available at: http://www.guardian.co.uk/commentisfree/2011/oct/25/uk-riot-born-in-deprivation, 25 October. [accessed: 12 April 2012].

Newton Dunn, T. 2011. War on gangs Theresa May unveils battle plan, *The Sun*. [Online]. Available at: http://www.thesun.co.uk/sol/homepage/news/politics/3906330/War-on-gangs.html. 1 November. [accessed: 12 April 2012].

Pilditch, D. 2012. 11 years for £3m riot thug. *Daily Express,* 12 April, 7.

Pukas, A. (2012) Invasion of the Protesters, *Daily Express*, 9 April, 20–21.

Reynolds, M. 2012. The Miracle of Muamba, *Daily Express*, 31 March, 7.

Silber M.D., and Blatt, A. 2007. *Radicalization in the West: The Homegrown Threat,* New York: New York City Police Department.

Sunstein, C. 2009. *Going to Extremes: How Like Minds Unite and Divide*. Oxford: Oxford University Press.

The Telegraph. 2011. Far-Right groups in Europe 'on the rise' [Online]. Available at: http://www.telegraph.co.uk/news/worldnews/europe/8873158/Far-Right-groups-in-Europe-on-the-rise.html 6 November. [accessed: 7 June 2012].

Townsend, M. 2102. Far-right anti-Muslim network on rise globally as Breivik trial opens. *Guardian*. [Online]. Available at: Guardian.co.uk, 14 April. [accessed: 16 April 2012].

Travis, A. 2008. MI5 report challenges views on terrorism in Britain. *The Guardian*, Wednesday 20 August [Online]. Available at: http://www.guardian. co.uk/uk/2008/aug/20/uksecurity.terrorism1. [accessed: 8 June 2012].

Widdecombe, A. 2012. Internet trolls are, sadly all too Human, *Daily Express*, 4 April, 13.

Wintour, P. 2011.David Cameron tells Muslim Britain: stop tolerating extremists PM says those who don't hold 'British' values will be shunned by government *The Guardian*, Saturday 5 February [Online]. Available at: http://www. guardian.co.uk/politics/2011/feb/05/david-cameron-muslim-extremism. [accessed: 8 June 2012].

Chapter 7

An Identity Crisis: Creating Extreme Identities in an Era of Counter-Terrorism

Angharad Saunders

On 22 July 2011, 69 people were massacred on the Norwegian island of Utøya and a further eight were killed in a car bomb that exploded in the city of Oslo. It was the worst terrorist attack ever carried out on Norwegian soil. According to the perpetrator, Anders Behring Breivik, his actions that day were 'preventative attacks to defend the indigenous Norwegian people' (*The Guardian*, 22 June 2012). In Breivik's mind Norwegian identity had been under assault from a combination of Muslim immigration and rampant multiculturalism and his actions were merely a way of preventing Norway from destroying itself from within. Wider social discourse has, of course, been quick to condemn Breivik's actions and the ideas that underpin these, labelling him an extremist; an individual whose beliefs, values and ideology are outside and beyond the norm.

The delineation of Breivik as an extremist is part of a larger discourse of terror, which has become a powerful organising narrative in many Western states since the events of 9/11 and 7/7 (Jackson, 2007). Discourse, Foucault (1977) argues, is the way we come to know the world through the manner in which we discursively construct and ascribe significance to it. Thus, we understand and give meaning to terrorism through such terminology as the 'War on Terror', religious fundamentalism, Islamic jihad and increasingly White supremacy. A discourse, however, is not merely an objective registering or representation of events; rather, it is an active intervention in the world, which shapes the identities of both self and other (Fairclough, 2002). The shaping of identity, therefore, is a powerful outcome of any discourse and in many Western states the prevailing discourse of terror has been complicit in the drawing of ideological boundaries within and between different social groups. At times these boundaries can be self-imposed as individuals and groups seek to preserve distinctive ways of life in the face of globalisation, at others they can be forged through the delineation of what Pantazis and Pemberton (2009) term 'suspect communities'; groups whose beliefs, ideas, appearance or ideology is singled out as problematic and threatening.

If we return to Anders Breivik, what this suggests is that his extremism was neither natural nor given, rather, it grew and evolved in and through wider social processes. As Giddens (1991) suggests, identity is reflexive and relational, it is continually being made and re-made through the relationships we have with other people, places and cultures. Consequently, as Hopkins and Kahani-Hopkins (2009) intimate, it is more productive to explore the idea of extreme identities as categories of practice rather than analysis, for extreme identities are brought into being; they are fabricated and spun across time and space by different combinations of self and other. This chapter explores the bringing into being, or creation, of 'extreme' identities, doing so against the back-drop of counter-terrorism policy. It begins by re-visiting the contours of identity politics to offer some indication of why identity has become so central to the prevailing discourse of terrorism. From this it moves on to explore the ambiguous role that policy and politics play in the construction of 'extreme' identities.

The Giving and Making of Identity

The modern world, Giddens (1991) argues, is a post-traditional order. It is an order characterised by time-space compression, the dis-embedding of social life and the development of reflexive thinking, which together are upturning traditional and established ways of knowing and understanding the world: social relations now take place across wider spans of space and time, face-to-face and locally-based interactions are in decline and there is greater uncertainty over what we know and hold as true. One very profound result of all this is a fundamental challenge to our sense of self and self-identity. Where self-identity was traditionally something that was given – one was born into a social class or culture and changes in this identity were shaped solely through such rites of passage as puberty or marriage – in the modern world self-identity has come to be seen as a much more reflexive project; it is not given but is made by the individual through the connections they make between their biographical self, their society and social change. This shift is often seen as a process of emancipation, for the self has been freed from the bonds of tradition and expectation and is able to forge its own identity: identity becomes a process of achievement not ascription (Bauman, 1997).

There is, however, a darker side to this process of 'achievement', for as we seek to make our self the uncertainty and discontinuity of the modern world can cause us to pursue what Beck (1997) calls, counter-modern forms of identity-creation. As traditional sources of meaning break down or lose their significance – kinship, locality, social collectivity and nationhood – some individuals seek to reinvigorate these categories of meaning but do so in ways that are rigid, regressive and highly exclusionary. Counter-modernism is a process of identity creation that redraws and re-solidifies the boundaries of class, culture, ethnicity and locality that modernisation undid. Thus, where modern society seeks to escape a social order based on pre-given and established differences, its darker, counter-modern side seeks to reinstate and re-articulate these differences in what often appear to be quite aggressive ways. The construction of a counter-modern form of identity is not, of course, a purely defensive or new process. In *Orientalism*, Said (1978) argues that Western identities have long been premised on a vision of the 'East' as exotic, traditional, uncivilised and regressive. Although 'West' and 'East' are broadly and fluidly defined, Said suggests that it is the 'West' that makes and ascribes the East as counter-modern; it is an appellation that comes from without and not from within.

Post-traditional and counter-modern forms of identification are often seen as mutually exclusive, but Said's work hints at the indivisibility of one from the other. If we turn to the 'West's' discourse of terrorism we can see that it is premised on counter-modern representations of non-Western states; these states are depicted as traditional and tribal, in order to emphasise the West's liberalism, individualism and freedom (Lazar and Lazar, 2004). This suggests that any practice of identity is a tussle between achievement and ascription; we seek to make ourselves but our making is always controlled by those outside our self. Thus, identity remains a relational concept but it is relational not only in terms of the self and its biography but equally in terms of the self and its other. It is here that identity formation begins to prove problematic, for in the tussle between achievement and ascription some actors have greater agency and power than others. In terms of understanding how extreme identities arise this reading of identity is instructive, for it challenges, what Githens-Mazer and Lambert (2010) term, the conventional wisdom of radicalisation: the popular assumption that difference, disassociation and a dissonance in lifestyles are casual to the transformation of fundamental beliefs in to extreme ideologies, actions and identities. Instead, it suggests that extremism is more likely to arise through differentials in relative levels of social power, which hinder and impede processes of self-making (Bauman, 1997; Philips, 2006).

Of course, the motivations for and the causes of extremism are far more convoluted and discontinuous (Jackson et al. 2012). In part this is due to the lazy parlance that has come to characterise the discourse of terrorism, wherein fundamentalism, extremism and radicalisation are used somewhat interchangeably and uncritically, making it difficult to unravel cause and effect (Briggs et al. 2006). Yet it also owes to the broader instability of the term in time and space. Take, for instance, Ghandi and Martin Luther King. Today they are often seen as inspirational figures but in their own time and place they were considered extremist. This likewise demonstrates the difficulty of conflating extremism with violence and wrongdoing. Perhaps all we can say about extremism is that it is the holding of a world view that is at odds with, outside of, or not considered the norm (Barkun, 2004; Wintrobe, 2006). The irony though, as Hopkins and Kahani-Hopkins (2009) observe, is that any designation of someone or something as extreme is to normalise one's own identity and point of view as moderate.

Thus, extremism tends to be applied from outside as a pejorative and controlling term. It is used to hold identities in place, with Briggs et al. (2006) observing that in the wake of 9/11 and 7/7 many British Muslims feel unable to express themselves in ways that are anything other than supportive of government for fear of being labelled an extremist. At the same time, in a country that has embraced what Giddens (1991) terms reflexive modernisation, it could also be argued that a vocabulary of extremism serves its own political purpose. Through its implicit articulation of what is moderate – that which is unemotional, dispassionate and undemonstrative – it creates a narrative around which a British identity can be forged. Thus, ascribing others as extremist gives greater clarity to one's own process of self-achievement.

Extremism could, therefore, arise from and be considered a tool of government part, perhaps, of what Foucault (1977) might term its disciplinary regime; its strategies for maintaining social and political control. In some respects extremism may well be too lithe a tool for political control, for it can potentially encompasses too much, hence, we have seen a multiplicity of extremisms emerge in the wake of 9/11: violent extremism, non-violent extremism, religious extremism and ideological extremism (Wintrobe, 2006). In theory these terms are tools that allow the government to differentiate between threats and to distance themselves from accusations that they are turning whole communities or ways of life into 'suspects', yet these appellations inescapably ascribe communities and ways of life as qualitatively different from the 'norm'. In this era of counter-terrorism therefore, extreme identities are not achieved *de novo*. Instead, they are bound up with the generation of ideological support, political allegiance and state power.

To examine the making of extremism from outside it is useful to return to the work of Hopkins and Kahani-Hopkins (2009) who, in emphasising the problematic nature of extremism as a category of analysis (as something that exists absolutely), urge us to understand it as a category of practice; as something made differently across space and time. Consequently, this chapter explores how governments, in reacting and responding to extremism, participate in its creation. At its focus are the discursive practices of government and the manner in which policy discourse and political rhetoric are part of extremism's making. It begins by examining the relationship between the PREVENT strategies, extremism and British national identity. From this it moves on to address the relationship between community and identity, which has been so central to contemporary debates about belonging. In all this it does not take extremism as given or singular, but rather suggests how extreme identities or the reading and construal of identities as extreme could well arise from the current practice of counter-terrorism policy within Britain.

PREVENT I and PREVENT II: Old Wine in New Bottles?

One of the most strident criticisms of New Labour's counter-terrorism strategy–CONTEST, and in particular the PREVENT strand, designed to stop people supporting or getting involved with terrorism – was that it criminalised and made 'suspect' large swathes of the country's Muslim population (Kundnani, 2009; Pantazis and Pemberton, 2009). Although it begins benignly enough, discussing the general threat from terrorism and the need for communities to work together to counter this threat, as the strategy progresses the subject (and suspect) of PREVENT is made quickly unambiguous:

> This is not about a clash of civilisations or a struggle between Islam and "the West". It is about standing up to a small fringe of terrorists and their extremist supporters. Indeed, Government is committed to working in partnership with the vast majority of Muslims who reject violence and who share core British values in doing this. (DCLG 2007: 4)

PREVENT was modelled as a tool for identifying 'at risk' groups but in its clear focus on Muslim communities it was complicit in producing these communities not as 'at risk' but as 'risky' and therefore, in need of policing (Mythen et al. 2009; Pantazis and Pemberton, 2009; Heath-Kelly, 2012). At a discursive level Muslims were produced as 'risky' through the manner in which being Muslim was differentiated from being British; Muslims were not straightforwardly British, they were Muslim first and British second. The last line is particularly inflammatory for it aligns Muslims with violence, while distancing violence as something un-British. At the same time, despite positioning itself as a soft approach to preventing terrorism, PREVENT was accused of subjecting Muslim communities to heightened (and disproportionate) regulation and surveillance under the guise of community cohesion initiatives (Khan, 2009; Kundnani, 2009).

In 2011 the Coalition Government unveiled a renewed PREVENT Strategy. It was a document that was intended to respond to the criticism of its predecessor, namely that it was alienating Muslims through its creation of them as a suspect community. Perhaps one of the most symbolic aspects of PREVENT II was its separation of prevention from community cohesion initiatives. It was believed that moving cohesion initiatives to the Department for Communities and Local Government would circumvent the indiscriminate assumption that all (and only) Muslims were alienated from British society and therefore 'at risk' of radicalisation. At a discursive level there is, compared to its predecessor, little mention of Muslim communities or the Islamic faith, instead, the strategy is rooted in a broader discourse of terrorism:

> we will respond to the ideological challenge of terrorism and the threat from those who promote it. In doing so, we must be clear: the ideology of extremism and terrorism is the problem; legitimate religious belief emphatically is not. (Home Office, 2011: 1)

Yet, despite paying lip service to a broader conception of extremism, PREVENT II remains problematic, principally because it is the creature of its predecessor. This is more than the sharing of nomenclature, it is an inability to escape the symbolic legacy of PREVENT. When the Coalition Government came to office in 2010 they had an opportunity to fundamentally change the nature and conduct of counter-terrorism policing. Instead, they reinvented –albeit with some tinkering round the edges – what they recognised as a highly flawed strategy. The result is a strategy that will always be associated with and understood through the lens of its predecessor, as such it becomes very difficult for the 'new' PREVENT strategy to shake off the negative connotations and 'othering' of Muslim groups that was so central to the New Labour PREVENT strategy. This is particularly worrying for Britain's Muslim communities, for the 'new' PREVENT strategy sends them very muddled messages of change and continuity; the practice of the 'new' PREVENT may be different, it will for instance work through institutions not communities, but at a symbolic level it suggests that the Government is not entirely committed to altering the interpretative framework of counter-terrorism policing. As such, while the 'new' PREVENT strategy may not criminalise Muslim groups *per se*, it does little to actively recover or regenerate Muslim identities in more positive ways. What we see therefore, is a subtle ascription of identity that draws its power from the enduring legacy of previous policy discourse.

This ambiguity is evident elsewhere within the 'new' PREVENT strategy, for despite participating in a broader discourse of terrorism and eschewing explicit reference to the Islamic faith or Muslim communities it is rooted within and empowered by a very specific drawing of Britishness:

> There is evidence to indicate that support for terrorism is associated with rejection of a cohesive, integrated, multi-faith society and of parliamentary democracy. Work to deal with radicalisation will depend on developing a sense of belonging to this country and support for our core values. (Home Office, 2011: 13)

In the first instance, there is a subtle presumption that extremists come from outside '*this country*' and in this very act of coming from outside they have different values. This is problematic not only because it loses sight of the manner in which extremism is 'home-grown' and can develop among seemingly integrated individuals but more significantly, it does little to resolve anxieties among Muslim groups over the role counter-terror strategies play in turning them in to 'suspect communities'. Secondly, the 'new' PREVENT strategy assumes that a British identity exists as something given and enduring. Yet national identity is a construct, or what Anderson (1983) calls a collective representation – a set of images, symbols and myths through and around which people develop a shared sense of belonging. These images, symbols and myths and the meanings that accrue around them are not stable, rather they transform and evolve over time and, as Jarvis and Lister (2011) observe, herein lies the problem with PREVENT. In entertaining a vision of national identity as something stable and permanent there is no scope for new, more fluid or, what Spivak (1988) might term, subaltern forms of Britishness to emerge.

This tension goes to the very heart of the practice of the 'new' PREVENT strategy for it is designed to work through Britain's established, national institutions – its education systems, its health system, local government, prisons and religious organisations. Not only are these institutions part of Britain's established myth about itself, what Billig (1995) might call its spaces of banal nationalism, but they are part of the apparatus of state power (Foucault, 1977). Consequently, they are unlikely to be spaces for thinking progressively and transformatively about Britishness.

Thus, where the 'new' PREVENT strategy emphasises the separation of community cohesion and integration initiatives from preventative actions and practices, its reliance on a strong narrative of British values and belonging suggests that this separation is more semantic than real; like its predecessor the 'new' PREVENT is construed as an agent of social change. In some respects, however, the focus on national identity is more worrying than its predecessor's concern with community cohesion, for where the former recognised differences within and between communities, a narrative of belonging is a little more intransigent, for it has a tendency to look backwards not forwards. Despite its practical limitations at a conceptual level, New Labour's PREVENT strategy was rooted within a narrative of cosmopolitan citizenship. This was an insistence on building dialogue between different groups wherein privilege and inheritance are 'unlearnt' in the creation of new cultural norms, values and associations (Young, 2003; Stevenson, 2003). Although this project has been somewhat discredited, both for its assumption that cultural divestment will be unproblematic and for the ease with which society-wide projects can become focussed on particular minority groups, it does acknowledge that our narrative of belonging must transform in the face of progressive, social change (McGhee, 2005). The 'new' PREVENT in its reification of particular British values is at risk of reducing difference to sameness (Young, 1990); of discouraging diversity of thought, belief and practice. The danger of this is that expressions of difference, such as the wearing of the veil or headscarf, may well be conflated with extremism or at least seen as 'non-British'. Thus, to insist on a relatively intransigent narrative of Britishness as a way of countering extremism is to risk breeding new forms of extremism, or of endorsing existing intolerance and xenophobia.

Beyond Policy: Practising Identity in the Community

Although the separation of community cohesion and preventative practice may be more imagined than real, the Coalition government has stressed that responsibility for cohesion will now rest with the Department for Communities and Local Government. In part this reflects their belief that extreme identities are the result of complex social, economic and cultural processes that need to be addressed both earlier and in a more holistic manner than through their submergence in PREVENT. It similarly recognises that by disassociating community cohesion from the Home Office there is more scope to build trust among those communities previously made 'suspect' by it. Yet there is also an ideological driver for, as the author of The Big Society, the Coalition believes that 'building a more integrated society is not just a job for government. It requires collective action across a wide range of issues, at national and local levels, by public bodies, private companies and, above all, civic society at large' (DCLG, 2012:6). By devolving responsibility to civic society the government recognises the difference that place makes to the constitution of identity – where one is, shapes who one is. Thus, rather than initiate a one-size-fits-all approach to integration the Coalition is keen to present itself as a 'listening' government that is building local capacity. There is, however, a darker side to this, for it enables the Government to distance itself from integration failures, for responsibility lies not with them but with the locality.

This 'responsibilisation'strategy, as Raco (2009) terms it, characterised much social policy under New Labour and it has now been mainstreamed through the Coalition's 'Big Society'. The Coalition work from the assumption that extremism can be countered from within civic society, for it is those who are inside and who know their 'community' who are best placed to initiate appropriate and effective responses. Yet this rests on a very bucolic and situated notion of community that conflates it with democracy, empowerment and localism, while presuming it to be geographically located or identifiable through particular spaces. This raises two inter-related points. Firstly, empowering communities can be exclusionary in its inclusiveness; giving power to communities often means giving power to dominant social groups and voices. Thus, rather than providing an arena for dialogue between different views, cultures and ways of life, it can perpetuate and reinforce existing power relationships, marginalising those voices that do not chime with that of the 'community' and isolating those without the social capital to enable them to participate (Rose, 1996; Kisby, 2010). Within this it is very easy to lose sight of the disaffected, for troubling views are more likely to be denied or ignored rather than challenged. Meanwhile, disaffection can be created and inscribed on individuals through the 'vigilantism' of more powerful community voices. Secondly, the Coalition presumes that integration arises where 'people come together through day-to-day activities' (DCLG 2012:8) and this rests on a vision of community as a cohesive entity that is located and delineated in space. In a highly globalised society this is not always the case, for everyday life is characterised by flexibility and discontinuity; social media, online shopping, remote working and international travel all combine to disaggregate real-time, face-to-face interactions (Beck, 2002). As a result, our identities have become dislocated; not only are they less likely to be tied to particular people and places but there is less inclination and fewer opportunities for coming together and building collective, social forms.

This returns us to the case of Anders Breivik for, while a Norwegian rather than British example, it highlights the limits of responsibilisation that underpin the role that community plays in counter-terrorist policing. If we recognise, as Blakemore does (Chapter 6), that terrorist organisations are characterised more by networks than by situated places, Breivik was operating beyond and outside the reach of community as something situated and based on spatial proximity. A lone terrorist, his views reflected not those of one group but rather the hewing together of the ideological messages of various far-right networks operating across Europe and the United States of America (Lowles, 2012). Breivik did not associate with people, he associated with ideas and this underlines the limitations of premising integration on community: community is not something fixed or located, it is not based purely on face-to-face interaction and the challenge and compromise this brings with it, and where communities are seen to exist their capacity to act is circumscribed by the nature of their 'gaze'. Consequently, community is a difficult concept to co-opt into counter-terrorism strategies, yet this is what the Government's 'Creating the Conditions for Integration' strategy seeks to do. In devolving power in this way the Government may well create conditions in which extreme identities can thrive, for in mobilising community they obscure and evade their own responsibility for alleviating the social injustices that can be causal to inequality, marginalisation and alienation (Jackson et al. 2012; Kisby, 2010).

The very policy of community integration, therefore, may well be crucial to the development of extreme identities, not merely in terms of demanding that communities 'police' themselves and engage in self-surveillance, but in the way community is relied upon as a stand-in for government. This is made particularly manifest when communities react to 'government through community'. In explaining the summer riots of 2011 David Cameron argued that:

> This is not about poverty, it's about culture. A culture that glorifies violence, shows disrespect to authority, and says everything about rights but nothing about responsibilities. In too many cases, the parents of these children – if they are still around – don't care where their children are or who they are with, let alone what they are doing. The potential consequences of neglect and immorality on this scale have been clear for too long, without enough action being taken. (Cameron 2011)

In line with the responsibilisation agenda the intimation is that the riots occurred because community did not exist. Cameron's explanation seeks refuge in a theory of social deviance that attempts to exceptionalise the rioters and make them appear as outside community – immoral, self-interested, uncivilised and 'extreme'. Wallace (2012), however, offers a more critical and provocative reading of the riots, arguing that they were not an expression of an absence of community, but were rather, an expression of a self-authored community. At a time when urban space is increasingly being remade through the neoliberal strategies of community politics and responsibilisation, it is possible to read the riots as a way for local people, particularly the young, to regain, albeit momentarily, control of their lives. Thus, rather than have community constructed for them and imposed from outside they were able to make and express it as an act of resistance (Wallace, 2012). Somewhat ironically therefore, the summer riots can be seen as a situated working (or re-working) of the 'Big Society': an expression of local empowerment that seeks to prevent 'community' being arbitrarily imposed from outside as a force for surveillance and instead activates local agency in the shaping of its own future.

This returns us to place – to the government's belief that it matters – but also to the paradox on which this is built, for while the government talk of community response, their understanding of it is singular and formulaic. In part this reflects their own community of praxis and what Haraway terms its positionality – the social norms, values and beliefs it encompasses – for this affects how they construe and understand their 'others'. We tend to understand those who come from outside our community of praxis in objective, observational and de-personalised ways, whereas in understanding those who come from inside our community we tend to seek meaning in strategies of similarity and association (Buttimer, 1977). This has broader implications for counter-terrorism, for it indicates the manner in which our own place – whether social or physical – gets intertwined with how we understanding and rationalise terrorist threats. Take, for instance, the threats posed by Anders Breivik and Al-Qaida. Where we see terrorists coming from outside our communities, as in the case of Al-Qaida, we objectify and stress their difference, yet when they come from within we are more likely to try and empathise with them in order to understand where their views diverge from our own. This was evident in the case of Breivik, Freedland (2012) argues, for where there was broad condemnation of his actions there was also a certain empathy with his hatred of multiculturalism and an attempt to contextualise his action not as rooted in fanaticism but in insanity. What this intimates is that we understand and give meaning to extremism not in absolute but in relative terms, which depend upon how we view our position *vis-á-vis* our other.

Conclusion

The events of 9/11, 7/7 and more recently 22/7, as the Norwegian massacres have become known, have revealed a growing ontological insecurity over the nature and value of belonging and identity within the world. At a political level this is manifesting itself in concerns over the rise of extremist ideologies and identities. Within Britain PREVENT (2007; 2011) has been central to attempts to try and ameliorate these anxieties, through preventing 'at risk' groups from becoming 'risky' groups. PREVENT under both New Labour and the Coalition has been subject to much contention, with accusations that under the former it made communities 'suspect' and under the latter that it is a strategy conceived in very intransigent terms. Thus, rather than seeing PREVENT as a preventative strategy, this chapter has sought to understand how the various iterations of PREVENT, and the counter-terrorism discourse these are a part of, have been complicit in discursively making extreme identities.

Extremism is a weighted term, for it straightaway implies a certain positionality; to term something extreme indicates that one is outside it and that one considers one's own position the norm. As such, any examination of extreme identities will always tend to be from outside, for it is a term we apply to others but rarely to ourselves. It is, therefore, a term of our making and our meaning and if, like Foucault (1977), we understand language as a form of power, then using and applying the term 'extreme' to certain groups or individuals suggests that identities are ascribed perhaps more than they are achieved. This is not to deny or downgrade extremism but rather to differentiate between the making of extremism and the actions of 'extremists'. PREVENT, while seeking to intervene in and disrupt this 'making', is simultaneously complicit in it. It is a discursive strategy that delineates lines of belonging and responsibility in a very tight and unyielding manner – traditional British values are employed to work through established British institutions, with little acknowledgement of internal heterogeneity. At the same time, the associated turn to community rests upon very fixed ideas of geography, which fail to recognise the power of place in the making and ascription of meanings.

Suggesting that PREVENT and its associated ideas of community empowerment is part of extremism's 'making' makes us question, as O'Toole et al. (2012) do, the efficacy of such counter-terrorism policy. In separating prevention from integration the 'new' PREVENT strategy resolved an inherent tension but it also made its purpose more ambiguous. To prevent is to hinder or intervene in order to stop something from happening but for this to work in the long-term it must address causes and not just effects. It is difficult, therefore, to divorce prevention from integration and doing so makes us ask how useful PREVENT is to our future security. Thus, to do away with PREVENT might be the most powerful and symbolic way in which the Coalition Government can begin to distance itself from the 'making' of extremism.

Further Reading

Jackson, R. (2007). Constructing Enemies: 'Islamic Terrorism' in Political and Academic Discourse, *Government and Opposition*, 42(3): 394–426.

Hopkins, N., and Kahani-Hopkins, V. (2009). Recoceceptualising Extremism and Moderation: from Categories of Analysis to Categories of Practice in the Construction of Collective Identities. *British Journal of Social Psychology*, 48(1): 99–113.

Said, E. (1978). *Orientalism*. London: Routledge and Kegan Paul.

Wallace, A. (2012). The 2011 'Riots': Reflections on the Fall and Rise of Community, *Sociological Research Online*, 17(2), http://www.socresonline.org.uk/17/2/15.html.

Young, I.M. (1990). *Justice and the Politics of Difference*. Princeton: Princeton University Press.

References

Anderson, B. (1983). *Imagined Communities*. London: Verso.

Barkun, R. (2004) Religious Violence and the Myth of Fundamentalism. In L. Weinberg and A. Pedahzur (eds), *Religious Fundamentalism and Political Extremism*. London: Frank Cass.

Bauman, Z. (1997). *Postmodernity and its Discontents*. Oxford: Polity Press

Beck, U. (1997). *The Reinvention of Politics: Rethinking Modernity in the Global Social Order*. Oxford: Polity Press.

Beck, U. (2002). The Cosmopolitan Society and its Enemies, *Theory, Culture and Society*, 19(1–2): 17–44.

Billig, M. (1995). *Banal Nationalism*. London: Sage.

Briggs, R., Fieschi, C.,, and Lownsbrough, H. (2006), *Bringing it Home: Community-based Approaches to Counter-terrorism*. London: Demos.

Buttimer, A. (1977), 'Insiders,' 'Outsiders,' and the Geography of Regional Life. In A. Kulinski, O. Kultalahti, and B. Koshioho (eds), *Regional Dynamics of Socioeconomic Change*.Tampera: Finn Publishers, 155–78.

Cameron, D. (2011).*Riot Statement to the House of Commons*, http://www.politics.co.uk/comment-analysis/2011/08/11/david-cameron-riot-statement-in-full (accessed: 9 August 2012).

Department of Communities and Local Government. (2007). *Preventing Violent Extremism: Winning Hearts and Minds*, London: HMSO.

Department of Communities and Local Government. (2012). *Creating the Conditions for Integration*. London: HMSO.

Fairclough, N. (2002). Language in New Capitalism, *Discourse and Society*, 13(2): 163–6.

Foucault, M. (1977). *Discipline and Punish: the Birth of the Modern Prison*, trans. A. Sheridan. London: Penguin

Freedland, J. (2012). Anders Breivik is a terrorist, so we should treat him like one. *The Guardian* 20 April 2012.

Giddens, A. (1991). *Modernity and Self-Identity: Self and Society in the late Modern Age*. Oxford: Polity Press.

Githens-Mazer, J., and Lambert, R. (2010), Why Conventional Wisdom on Radicalisation Fails: the Persistence of a Failed Discourse, *International Affairs*, 86(4): 889–902.

Haraway, D. (1988). Situated Knowledges: the Science Question in Feminism and the Privilege of Partial Perspective, *Feminist Studies*, 14(3): 575–99.

Heath-Kelly, C. (2012). Counter-terrorism and the Counterfactual: Producing the 'Radicalisation' Discourse and the UK Prevent Strategy, *The British Journal of Politics and International Relations*, doi: 10.1111/j.1467-856X.2011.00489.x

Home Office. (2011) *PREVENT Strategy*, London: HMSO.

Hopkins, N., and Kahani-Hopkins, V. (2009). Recocenceptualising Extremism and Moderation: from Categories of Analysis to Categories of Practice in the Construction of Collective Identities, *British Journal of Social Psychology*, 48(1): 99–113.

Jackson, R. (2007). Constructing Enemies: 'Islamic Terrorism' in Political and Academic Discourse, *Government and Opposition*, 42(3): 394–426.

Jackson, R., Jarvis, L., Gunning, J., and Smyth, M. (2012), The Causes of Terrorism: Deconstructing the Myth, *Arches Quarterly*, 5(9): 68–72.

Jarvis, L., and Lister, M. (2011). Values and Stakeholders in the 2011 Prevent Strategy, *Soundings,* available from http://soundings.mcb.org.uk/?p=31 (accessed: 3 August 2012).

Khan, K. (2009). *Preventing Violent Extremism: a Response from the Muslim Community*, London: An-nisa.

Kisby, B. (2010), The Big Society: Power to the People? *The Political Quarterly*, 81(4): 484–91.

Kundnani, A. (2009). *Spooked! How not to Prevent Violent Extremism*. London: Institute of Race Relations.

Lazar, A., and Lazar, M. (2004). The Discourse of the New World Order: 'Outcasting' the Double Face of Threat, *Discourse and Society*, 15(2–3): 223–42.

Lowles, N. 2012. Anders Behring Breivik reflects changing face of modern far right, http://www.guardian.co.uk/world/2012/apr/18/anders-behring-breivik-modern-far-right (accessed: 6 August 2012)

McGhee, D. (2005). *Intolerant Britain? Hate, Citizenship and Difference*. Maidenhead: Open University Press.

Martin, R. (2004). Geography: Making a Difference in a Globalizing World, *Transactions of the Institute of British Geographers*, 29(2): 147–50.

Mythen, G., Walklate, S., and Khan, F. (2009), 'I'm a Muslim, but I'm not a terrorist': Victimisation, Risky Identities and the Performance of Safety, *British Journal of Criminology*, 49(6):736–54.

O'Toole, T., Jones, S., and Nilsson DeHanas, D. (2012). The New Prevent: Can it Work? Will it Work? *Arches Quarterly,* 5(9): 56–62.

Pantazis, C., and Pemberton, S. (2009). From the 'Old' to the 'New' Suspect Community: Examining the Impacts of Recent UK Counter-terrorism Legislation, *British Journal of Criminology*, 49(5): 646–66.

Philips, D. (2006). Parallel Lives? Challenging Discourses of British Muslim Self-segregation, *Environment and Planning D: Society and Space*, 24(1): 25–40.

Raco, M. (2009). From Expectations to Aspirations: State Modernisation, Urban Policy, and the Existential Politics of Welfare in the UK, *Political Geography*, 28(7): 436–44.

Rose, N. (1996). The Death of the Social? Re-figuring the Territory of Government, *Economy and Society*, 25(3): 327–56.

Said, E. (1978). *Orientalism*. London: Routledge and Kegan Paul

Spivak, G.C. (1988). Can the Subaltern Speak?. In C. Nelson and L. Grossberg (eds), *Marxism and the Interpretation of Culture.* Illinois: University of Illinois Press, 271–313.

Stevenson, N. (2003), *Cultural Citizenship: Cosmopolitan Questions*. Basingstoke: Open University Press.

The Guardian. (2012). Anders Behring Breivik: history will exonerate me, *The Guardian*, 22 June 2012, http://www.guardian.co.uk/world/2012/jun/22/anders-behring-breivik-norway (accessed: 25 July 2012)

Wallace, A. (2012). The 2011 'Riots': Reflections on the Fall and Rise of Community, *Sociological Research Online*, 17(2), http://www.socresonline. org.uk/17/2/15.html.

Wintrobe, R. (2006). *Rational Extremism: the Political Economy of Radicalism.* Cambridge: Cambridge University Press.

Young, I.M. (1990). *Justice and the Politics of Difference.* Princeton: Princeton University Press.

Young, J. (2003). To these wet and windy shores: Recent Immigration Policy in the UK, *Punishment and Society*, 5(4): 449–62.

Chapter 8
Countering Global Extremism

Huw Smart

Introduction

Since the coordinated suicide attacks on the United States (on 11 September 2001) and London (on 7 July 2005), the focus of Western law enforcement and intelligence agencies has been to neutralise the terrorist threat posed by Al-Qaeda and its (now dead) leader Osama bin Laden.

A 'one-size-fits-all' approach to dealing with terrorism will almost certainly fail. For example, it is estimated that the 9/11 terrorist attacks in the United States took two years to plan, at a cost of about $500,000. On the other hand, on the night of the 26 November 2008, ten terrorists armed with automatic weapons entered the city of Mumbai in a fishing boat. They shot and killed 166 people and brought the entire city to a standstill for three days.

These two incidents provide an insight into how varied the threat from terrorism can be and the difficulties facing law enforcement and intelligence agencies in their attempts to prevent such attacks. This chapter will explore international responses to the terrorist threat, which can be as extreme as invasions and the assassination of terrorist leaders, or can follow a legislative course. We will examine how effective these measures have been, whether approaches have changed and the impact the strategies have on the human rights of those affected by them.

Invasions and Wars in Pursuit of Terrorists

The Cold War

Western powers have been no strangers to combat on foreign soil. In the immediate aftermath of World War II, from the late 1940s through to the 1970s, Western Governments, with the United States of America as the main protagonists, took part in wars in Vietnam, Korea, Laos and Cambodia.

US troops also participated in invasions closer to home – in the Dominican Republic, in the 1960s, Grenada in the early 1980s and in 1989 the United States invaded Panama in *Operation Just Cause* to resolve the dispute over the transfer of control of the Panama Canal from the United States to Panama by the year 2000.

In what was effectively an offshoot of the Cold War in Europe, successive US governments supported campaigns, either by committing American soldiers to participate in the fighting on the side of the anti-communist regimes in each country, or by assisting directly with material and financial aid.

The 1979 Soviet invasion of Afghanistan saw a new dimension to the Cold War as the Soviet Union fought for nine years on the side of communist government of the Democratic Republic of Afghanistan against the Afghan mujahideen guerrilla movement. The mujahideen, on the other hand, received wide military and financial support from Pakistan and direct and indirect assistance from the United States and China.

The war, which has been described as 'the Soviet Union's Vietnam', was essentially fought over political differences, as opposed to the Islamic fundamentalist ideals which later became synonymous with the region. However, there is no doubt that the tactics subsequently used against the Coalition soldiers attempting to remove the Taliban regime from power and dismantle the Al-Qaeda terrorist organization were similar to those used against the Soviet Army in the 1980s.

The Middle East

The 1980s saw the US Government also turning its attention towards the Middle East. US troops assisted the Lebanese government to restore sovereignty in 1982 but throughout the decade the main focus was on the Iran–Iraq war, with most nations and NATO supporting Saddam Hussein and the Iraqi cause. US military activities were also drawn towards North Africa and the increasing terrorist activities of the Libyan leader Colonel Gaddafi.

The invasion of Kuwait by Iraq in 1991 resulted in Operation Desert Storm being initiated with US and Coalition aircraft attacking Iraqi forces and military targets in Iraq and Kuwait, followed by a ground offensive that drove Iraqi forces out of Kuwait. This was followed by a series of US military exercises in Kuwait, following Iraq's refusal to recognise a new border drawn up by the United Nations and refusal to cooperate with UN inspection teams. The US, the United Kingdom and other Gulf War allies enforced 'no-fly zones' over the majority of Iraqi airspace.

The 2003 Iraq War was triggered by an invasion by the United States and the United Kingdom in March of that year, following the controversial UN Resolution 1441, which called for Iraq to cooperate with UN weapons inspectors relating to its possession of weapons of mass destruction (WMD) and cruise missiles. Whilst no WMD were found, there was also a suspicion that President Saddam Hussein had been harbouring terrorists and supporting Al-Qaeda.

By May 2003, President George Bush announced that the 'mission was accomplished' and that an ally of Al-Qaeda had now been removed. Saddam Hussein was arrested in December 2003 and subsequently executed following his trial. The *New York Times Timeline of Major Events in the Iraq War* published that by September 2004, the loss of US troops had reached over 1,000. A year later the figure reached 2,000 and by March 2008 this figure reached over 4,000. The final figure of US troops killed in the Iraq war was 4,486 (with 179 British soldiers also lost).

The occupation oversaw the first ever democratic elections in Iraq and the election of Prime Minister Nouri al-Maliki and in February 2009, newly elected President Barack Obama announced an 18-month withdrawal plan for combat forces, which would leave approximately 50,000 troops remaining in the country to advise and train Iraqi security forces and to provide intelligence and surveillance. UK forces ended combat operations on 30 April 2009 and in October 2011 President Obama announced that all US troops would leave Iraq by the end of the year. The last US troops eventually left Iraqi territory on 18 December 2011. The occupation of Iraq by peacekeeping soldiers had lasted for nearly ten years

Afghanistan

In October 2001, in the wake of the 9/11 attacks, armed Coalition forces from the United States, the United Kingdom, Australia and the Afghan United Front (Northern Alliance) launched Operation Enduring Freedom with the intention of ending Al-Qaeda's use of Afghanistan as a base and creating a viable democratic state minus the Taliban regime.

In January 2002, the first contingent of foreign peacekeepers was deployed, led by the NATO International Security Assistance Force (ISAF) marking the start of a protracted fight against the Taliban. In its first ever operational commitment outside Europe, NATO took control of security in Kabul in August 2003 (*BBC News* Afghanistan profile, March 2013).

In September 2008, President Bush sent an extra 4,500 US troops to Afghanistan and in February 2009, NATO countries pledged to increase military and other commitments in Afghanistan after the US announced the dispatch of 17,000 extra troops. In March 2009, President Obama unveiled a new strategy for Afghanistan and Pakistan. An extra 4,000 US personnel were committed train and bolster the Afghan army and police.

By December 2009, President Obama again boosted the number of US troops in Afghanistan by 30,000, bringing the total deployed in the country to 100,000. He announced, however, that the US would begin withdrawing its forces by 2011. However, in November 2011, President Karzai negotiated a 10-year military partnership with the US, with the proposal that US troops would remain after 2014, when foreign troops are due to leave the country.

In May 2012, NATO endorsed the plan to withdraw foreign combat troops by the end of 2014, giving security responsibilities to Afghan forces. However, the new French President, François Hollande, stated that France would withdraw its combat mission by the end of 2012, a year earlier than planned. By September 2012, the total number of US soldiers killed in the Afghan war reached 2,125 (with 433 being lost from the UK). The 11-year occupation of Afghanistan has been littered with assassinations of prominent figures, civilians and peacekeeping soldiers. It has also seen Afghan people being able to vote in their first parliamentary elections in more than 30 years.

Africa

While the main focus in this chapter has been on the USA, Western Governments do not have a monopoly over initiating wars and invading foreign countries. In October and November 2011, Coalition forces from Kenya and Ethiopia invaded Somalia to quash the insurgency led by Al-Shabaab, one of Africa's most fearsome militant Islamist groups, which had control of much of southern Somalia since 2006 and which, according to the *New York Times* in November 2011, had pledged allegiance to Al-Qaeda. A year on, a 10,000-strong African Union peacekeeping force remains in the country and while Somalia's government recently selected a new president, the country's future remains uncertain. Al Shabaab has assassinated government officials and several journalists in areas that Somalia's fledging government had claimed were secure. They remain in control in several regions of the country and are seeking to rebuild and strengthen their position.

A Legislative Approach to Combating Terrorism

In December 2001, the United Nations Security Council adopted resolution 1373. This UN resolution sets out the legislative framework which all member states must abide by, in order to combat terrorism (*United Nations Security Council resolution 1373* (2001)). Among its provisions, the resolution obliges all States to criminalise assistance for terrorist activities, deny financial support and safe haven to terrorist and share information about groups planning terrorist attacks.

In summary, the resolution focusses on requiring member states to:

- prevent and supress the financing of terrorist acts;
- deny safe havens to terrorists;
- take necessary steps to prevent the commission of terrorist acts, including suppressing recruitments of terrorists and eliminating the supply of weapons to them;
- provide early warning of terrorist acts to other states by exchange of information;
- bringing offenders who finance, prepare, plan or perpetrate terrorist acts to justice and
- prevent the movement of terrorists through effective border controls.

Legislation in the United Kingdom caters for the above requirements under the Terrorism Act 2000 and in the USA, law enforcement agencies are able to deal with terrorist suspects under the Homeland Security Act 2002. In the document *Uniting against terrorism: Recommendations for a global counter-terrorism strategy* (2006) the then UN Secretary General Kofi Annan outlined the 'five Ds', which are the components that UN member states should focus on to combat terrorism:

- dissuading people from resorting to terrorism or supporting it;
- denying terrorists the means to carry out an attack;
- deterring States from supporting terrorism;
- developing State capacity to defeat terrorism, and;
- defending human rights.

The final bullet point above provides an interesting dilemma for law enforcement agencies when it comes to bringing offenders to justice. Quite rightly, a member state should concentrate on defending the human rights of its citizens, however, what about the human rights of those suspected or accused of terrorist acts? Most democratic countries have legislation which limits the amount of time a person can be held in detention without charge. The Liberty Group paper *Terrorism Pre-charge Detention: Comparative Law Study* (2010) provided an overview of the maximum number of days a person could be held without charge in 12 countries surveyed (see Figure 8.1 below).

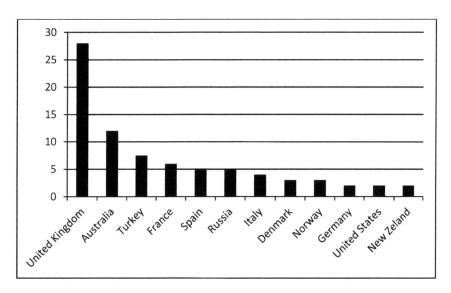

Figure 8.1   How many days can you be held without charge?

Source: *Terrorism Pre-charge Detention: Comparative Law Study* (2010)

With a maximum pre-charge detention time of 28 days, at the time, the UK by far exceeded the other countries surveyed, followed by Australia (12 days) and Turkey (7.5 days). Legislation in the United States, by comparison, limits this time to 48 hours. In the UK, an extended period of detention (compared to the 96 hours allowed for non-terrorist suspects by the Police and Criminal Evidence Act 1984) was provided for under the Terrorism Act 2000, with a maximum detention time of 14 days. However, following the London suicide attacks, it was considered that 14 days was insufficient time to deal with complex cases relating to the detention of terrorist suspects and the maximum period of pre-charge detention was extended from 14 days to 28 days.

In June 2010, the Home Secretary, Theresa May, announced that that the government would review counter-terrorism legislation as a whole and would seek to reduce the 28-day limit.

The Counter-Terrorism Review published by the Home Office in January 2011 concluded that the limit on pre-charge detention for terrorist suspects should be restored to 14 days and subsequently, the Terrorism Act 2000 was amended by s. 57 of the Protection of Freedoms Act 2012, to reflect this change. However, this was not the end of the matter; when the government announced the draft legislation, it indicated that should an emergency situation arise, it would likely replace these procedures and implement draft legislative powers to extend the maximum detention period beyond 14 days, depending on the requirement at the time.

Changes to pre-charge detention time limits mean that law enforcement agencies in the UK have had to re-think how they investigate suspects who are concerned in the commission, preparation or instigation of acts of terrorism. In such an investigation, much of the evidence-gathering must take place *before* a suspect is arrested if their detention time is to be used effectively and significant emphasis is placed on electronic surveillance of individuals during this period. While these tactics are useful in reducing unnecessary pre-charge detention, the pre-arrest phase of an operation can often be lengthy and resource intensive. There is also a genuine danger of the suspect evading surveillance and committing a terrorist act whilst under investigation, thereby undermining confidence in the police service. A balance needs to be met, therefore, between effective evidence-gathering and protecting the public from harm.

Further powers are provided to UK law enforcement agencies under s. 1 of the Terrorism Prevention and Investigation Measures Act 2011. Terrorism Prevention and Investigation Measures (TPIM) replaced the previous system of Control Orders under the Terrorism Act 2005 with a civil preventative measure intended to protect the public from the risk posed by suspected terrorists who can be neither prosecuted nor, in the case of foreign nationals, deported. The Act provides that a TPIM notice may be served on an individual when the Secretary of State reasonably believes that the individual is, or has been, involved in terrorism-related activity and that a notice is necessary to protect members of the public from a risk of terrorism. The measures that may be imposed are set out in Sch. 1 to the Act, have a two year time limit and can include:

- requiring an individual to stay overnight at a specified address;
- requiring an individual to report to a police station on a daily basis;
- excluding an individual from specific places or areas;
- preventing an individual from contacting particular individuals or
- prohibiting travel overseas.

No such legislation is available in the USA and the only other country that grants law enforcement agencies similar powers is Australia, which has a system based on the previous Control Orders in the UK. In a footnote to this section, the courts in the UK also have the power to deport foreign nationals who may be terrorist suspects, if there is insufficient evidence to arrest or charge the individual. However, the lengthy cases of the radical Islamic clerics Abu Hamza al-Masri and Abu Qatada demonstrate that this process is by no means simple. Both have fought extradition from the UK for a number of years and while the former lost his case and was finally extradited to the United States in 2012, the latter continues to fight his deportation to Jordan through the European Court of Human Rights.

Guantánamo Bay, Cuba

When it comes to detention of terrorist suspects without charge, the United States has its own controversial system, which appears to operate outside of US laws. Using a method similar to the internment of Provisional IRA suspects in Northern Ireland by the UK Government in the 1970s, the United States has held prisoners in Guantánamo Bay for a number of years.

In a BBC News article on the subject (*Profile: Guantánamo Bay*, 17 October 2006), it was said that the camp at that time housed about 460 detainees from about 40 countries, including terrorist suspects picked up in Eastern Europe and Africa. Despite allegations of mistreatment of the detainees and a pre-election promise made in 2008 by President Barack Obama to close down the camp, it remains open with approximately 170 prisoners still being detained (see *The Guardian*, 10 September 2012).

The facility was opened in 2002 to hold prisoners suspected of terrorism or links to Al-Qaeda and the Taliban. They include detainees who have been cleared for release but can't find a stable country to accept them and some who have been charged with war crimes and are awaiting either criminal trials or military commissions. The status of the prisoners detained in Guantánamo Bay is uncertain, with the Pentagon stating that the US is 'entitled them to hold 'enemy combatants' who do not enjoy the rights of prisoners of war or US citizens accused of crimes – without charges or trial for the duration of hostilities' and that doing so acts as a deterrent and prevents further attacks on the US.

However, in 2006, the US Supreme Court ruled that the military commission system for Guantánamo violated both US and international law. In the same year, a UN report recommended the closure of the prison. Initially on his election in January 2009, President Obama suspended military commissions and ordered that the facility would close down within one year. Following this, in March 2011, the president lifted the suspension on new military trials (see *The Guardian*, 7 March 2011), which would appear to mean that the Guantánamo Bay facility is to remain open.

Securing Borders against Terrorists

Following the release of its counter-terrorism strategy, *Uniting against terrorism: Recommendations for a global counter-terrorism strategy* (April 2006), the UN set up the Working Group on Border Management Related to Counter-Terrorism to help Member States strengthen their border-control systems. The Working Group set out the following priorities for border management:

- mobility and processing of people;
- integrity and security of document issuing process;
- movement of cash and other bearer negotiable instruments;
- movement and processing of goods;
- movement of small arms, light weapons, ammunition, explosives and CBRN;
- maritime security;
- aviation security;
- early warning and alert systems;
- control of the open border and
- the overarching need for respect for human rights

Whist the Working Group list of priorities set out above appear to provide sound advice for member States, the UN appears to have no measurement of successful outcomes. For example, in the United Kingdom, the UK Border Agency reports on the number of arrests it makes but these mostly relate to people who have committed offences under the Immigration Act 2002. Similarly, the Home Office gathers statistics relating to the arrest and prosecution of terrorist suspects but these are not categorised and it is impossible to establish whether the people were arrested in the UK, or entering or leaving the country.

In the US, the Department for Homeland Security does report on successful border arrests but again, these statistics relate mainly to Immigration drug-related arrests on the Mexican border. The situation is similar relating to the list of proscribed organisations (or Foreign Terrorist Organisations (FTOs) in the USA). Along with the UN, the Governments in these countries state publically which organisations are proscribed, or banned, within their borders. The lists contain the groups you would expect to see, such as Al-Qaeda, Al Shabaab and even the IRA, however, it is impossible to measure whether having such a list actually contributes to the outcome of preventing terrorist activities.

Measuring the Cost of the War on Terror

Is it possible to evaluate the cost of the war on terror in the past 11 years? If so, what measurement should be used? There is of course a direct financial cost for deploying troops in Iraq and Afghanistan but there are other, economic costs that need to be taken into consideration. There is also the human cost relating to the number of lives that have been and will continue to be lost. Nearly 3,000 people were killed in the coordinated suicide attacks on 11 September 2001 and more than 6,000 wounded. In the London bombings on 7 July 2005, 52 people were killed and 700 injured and in the Madrid bombings on 11 March 2004, 191 people were killed and 2,051 injured.

Official figures show that 4,803 coalition soldiers were killed during the Iraq war between 2003 and 2011. The Congressional Research Service Report *Afghanistan Casualties: Military Forces and Civilians*, December 2012 contains the most up-to-date statistics and outlines that in Afghanistan, 3,214 coalition soldiers have been killed to date. However, while accurate figures are kept on casualties from the armed forces, the data on the number of civilians who have been killed is less precise. For example, reporting on Afghan casualties did not begin until 2007 and the above report shows that approximately 17,000 have died in the past five years (including police officers, members of the Afghan National Army and private security guards). The report outlines that in 2012, the number of civilian casualties fell for the first time – some 3,099 non-combatants were killed or injured between January and July, about 15 per cent fewer than in the same period of 2011.

However, the figures for the number of civilian casualties in the Iraq war are hotly disputed, as reported in the *New York Times*, 10 January 2008. The article quotes a study conducted by the World Health Organisation, which estimated that the number of deaths from the start of the war until June 2006 was at least twice as high as the figures released by the Iraq Body Count, a nongovernmental group based in Britain.

The estimates varied widely. The Iraq Body Count based its numbers on news media accounts and estimated the number of civilian fatalities as 47,668 during the period, whereas the World Health Organisation said its study, based on interviews with families, indicated with a 95 per cent degree of statistical certainty that between 104,000 and 223,000 civilians had died. Whatever the true figures turn out to be, it would seem that at least 100,000 people have died in the 11 years since American Airlines Flight 11 crashed into the North Tower of the World Trade Centre in New York City on 11 September 2001, an astronomically high price to pay in human terms.

From a purely financial perspective, another report released by the Congressional Research Service (*Troop Levels in the Afghan and Iraq Wars, FY2001-FY2012: Cost and Other Potential Issues*, July 2009) estimated that the cost to the US in the Financial Year 2008–2009 would be approximately $133.1 billion. This figure is based on a total of 186,300 troops divided between both countries. Taking into account adjustments for the numbers of troops in each location over the whole 11 years, a conservative estimate is that the wars in Iran and Afghanistan have cost the US Government about $1,100 billion dollars so far.

In his paper, *Evaluating the Costs and Benefits of the US War on Terror* (2007), David Gold looks at the cost of war from a different perspective. For example, the above figures do not take into account the cost of replacing military equipment that may be destroyed in battle, or producing larger quantities of equipment for more troops. Other hidden costs might be the projected health-related outlays based upon injuries sustained by members of the armed forces – either mental or physical – who served in combat zones.

In an attempt to measure the economic cost to the war, the author quotes Bilmes and Stiglitz (2006) who suggest that 20 to 40 per cent of the increase in world oil prices since early 2003 has been the result of an increase in perceived risk due to the war in Iraq, combined with a reduction in anticipated production from Iraq's oil fields. Whatever the eventual cost of the wars in Iraq and Afghanistan, as we will discuss below, it is highly unlikely that the US or any other Western democracy will enter into such protracted wars in the future, given the experiences of the past 11 years.

Different Approaches to Combating Terrorism

Targeted Pressure on Terrorist Groups

In his speech at the launch of the United States' newly released *National Strategy Counterterrorism*, John Brennan, President Obama's counter-terrorism advisor, stated that the administration had concluded that precision strikes and raids, rather than large land wars, are the most effective way to defeat Al-Qaeda (*Los Angeles Times*, June 2011). He said:

> Al-Qaeda seeks to bleed us financially by drawing us into long, costly wars that also inflame anti-American sentiment. Going forward, we will be mindful that if our nation is threatened, our best offense won't always be deploying large armies abroad but delivering targeted, surgical pressure to the groups that threaten us.

At the core of the strategy is a change in the thinking that sent large numbers of American troops to Iraq and Afghanistan. Brennan said that Al-Qaeda's leadership has been decimated, thanks not to the wars but to 'unyielding pressure' from operations to kill the group's leaders one by one in the Afghanistan–Pakistan border region. The United States intends pursuing a war that relies heavily on missile strikes from unmanned aerial drones, raids by elite special operations troops, and quiet training of local forces to pursue terrorists. This would continue even after troop numbers have been reduced in Afghanistan and there would be no impact on US counter-terrorism activities in that country or Pakistan, where they will deliver a 'precise and overwhelming force' against militants.

The article reported a significant increase in drone strikes undertaken by US forces in Pakistan between January and June 2009, although this was not confirmed by the US Government. Operations on the Afghanistan–Pakistan border will be conducted largely in secret, as will any targeted killing by the CIA or clandestine special operations units.

Whilst this more targeted approach to eliminating Al-Qaeda followers might seem more effective than large scale wars, the US administration will also be mindful that the activities will stretch Western relations with Pakistan to the limit. As reported in *The Guardian* on Friday 3 August 2012, Wajid Shamsul Hasan, the High Commissioner to London and one of Pakistan's top ambassadors, stated that the use of drones by the US was weakening democracy and pushing people *towards* extremist groups.

PREVENT Strategies

In her Foreword to the UK Government's PREVENT Strategy in June 2011, the Home Secretary, Theresa May, stated:

> Intelligence indicates that a terrorist attack in our country is 'highly likely'. Experience tells us that the threat comes not just from foreign nationals but also from terrorists born and bred in Britain. It is therefore vital that our counter-terrorism strategy contains a plan to prevent radicalisation and stop would-be terrorists from committing mass murder. Osama bin Laden may be dead, but the threat from al Qaeda inspired terrorism is not.

There is much emphasis in the new Strategy on trust in the community and building a society which is cohesive and integrated, which will become resistant to radicalisation by terrorist groups. In an almost mirror image of the UK Strategy, the US equivalent, *Empowering Local Partners to Prevent Violent Extremism in the United States* (2011) (see Chapter 5), concentrates on a community-based approach to combating terrorism, which sets out not to blame communities for being vulnerable to radicalisation but to help them overcome the threat. Moving forward in dealing with the terrorist threat, both the UK and US Governments recognise that even though the battle against Al-Qaeda followers takes place mostly abroad, those determined to pursue the radicalisation of people at home prey on the disenchanted, vulnerable people who need the most assistance to resist it.

Conclusion

In over 60 years of conflicts since the end of World War II very few wars or invasions have resulted in an outright successful outcome. Whether it was the US Troops in Vietnam, the Soviet troops in Afghanistan or the coalition troops in Iraq, each campaign has seen the loss of huge numbers of lives, at great financial cost, with very little changed in the host country when the troops return home. To illustrate this point, since 2005 a United States think-tank, Fund for Peace, has produced an annual Failed States Index. Whilst this Index is not an official report for the US Government, it is said to be a useful guide for determining foreign policy and aid.

There is no official definition of a failed state but according to Fund for Peace, common indicators include a state whose central government is so weak or ineffective that it has little practical control over much of its territory; non-provision of public services; widespread corruption and criminality; refugees and involuntary movement of populations; sharp economic decline. The report uses 12 factors to determine the rating for each nation including security threats, economic implosion, human rights violations and refugee flows.

Unsurprisingly, Afghanistan, Iraq and Somalia have been in the top ten failed states every year since 2005, despite the intervention in their countries by foreign powers. Whilst the situation in Somalia is relatively new compared to Iraq and Afghanistan, coalition forces and the UN have spent years in those two countries attempting to set up democratic societies in our own image but there remain huge obstacles to overcome.

What does success look like for these countries? Will Al-Qaeda recruit fewer members because Middle Eastern countries are more democratic? Will global terrorism dry up as well? Probably not in both cases. It remains to be seen whether the removal of Colonel Gaddafi, Saddam Hussein and the Taliban from their respective power bases will create peace in their countries, or whether we are simply trying to push round pegs into square holes.

Further Reading

Awan, I. 2012. 'The Impact of Policing British Muslims: A Qualitative Exploration', *Journal of Policing, Intelligence and Counter-terrorism,* 7(1): 22–35.
HM Governemnt. 2006. 'Countering International Terrorism: The United Kingdom's Strategy'. *Foreign & Commonwealth Office.* Accessed on 12 September 2012. Available online at http://www.fco.gov.uk/resources/en/pdf/contest-report.
May, T. 2011 'CONTEST Speech'. *Home Office.* Accessed on 12 September 2012. Available online at http://www.homeoffice.gov.uk/media-centre/speeches/contest-speech.

References

BBC News Online, 17 October 2006. *Profile: Guantánamo Bay.*
BBC News Online, 31 March 2013. *Afghanistan Profile.*
Belasco, A. 2009. *Troop Levels in the Afghan and Iraq Wars, FY2001-FY2012: Cost and Other Potential Issues.* Congressional Research Service: Washington.
Bilmes, L., and Stiglitz, J. 2006. *The Economic Costs of the Iraq War: An Appraisal Three Years after the Beginning of the Conflict.* National Bureau of Economic Research Working Paper 12054: Cambridge, Massachusetts.

Chesser, S. 2013. *Afghanistan Casualties: Military Forces and Civilians.* Congressional Research Service: Washington.

Dilanian. K. *Los Angeles Times*, June 2011. *U.S. counter-terrorism strategy to rely on surgical strikes, unmanned drones.*

Empowering Local Partners to Prevent Violent Extremism in the United States. White House Strategy, Washington, August 2011.

Gold, D. 2007. *Evaluating the Costs and Benefits of the US War on Terror.* Graduate Program in International Affairs, The New School, New York.

Her Majesty's Government 2011a. Prevent Strategy. Cmnd. 8092. Norwich: TSO.

National Strategy Counterterrorism. White House Strategy, Washington, June 2011.

Review of counter-terrorism and security powers. Home Office, London, 26 January 2011.

Terrorism Pre-charge Detention: Comparative Law Study (July 2010). The Liberty Group. London.

The Guardian, 7 March 2011. (Staff and agencies). *Barack Obama restarts Guantánamo trials.*

The Guardian, 3 August 2012. (Woods, C.) *CIA drone strikes violate Pakistan's sovereignty, says senior diplomat.*

The Guardian, 10 September 2012. (Associated Press in San Juan.) *Guantánamo inmate becomes ninth detainee to die at prison camp.*

The New York Times, 10 January 2008. (Altman, L.K. and Oppel Jr, R.A.) *W.H.O. Says Iraq Civilian Death Toll Higher Than Cited.*

The New York Times, 21 October 2011. (Crichton, K, Lamb, G and Jacquette, R.F.) *Timeline of Major Events in the Iraq War.*

The New York Times, 28 November 2011. (Ibrahim, M. and Gettleman, J.) *Rebels Resume a Crackdown on Somali Aid.*

Uniting against terrorism: Recommendations for a global counter-terrorism strategy, Report by the United Nations Secretary General, United Nations General Assembly, 27 April 2006.

United Nations Security Council resolution 1373: 28 September 2001.

Chapter 9

Trends and the Postmodernist Extremist

Brian Blakemore

Introduction

The more recent changes in society, technology, economics and politics are often described by terms such as postmodernism and globalisation. This chapter will consider these trends and this terminology and apply it to the threat of extremism. Peters (2004) suggests that the factors driving postmodern extremism are based less on ideological concerns and more upon religious and ethnic/separatist causes than previously. Comparisons will be made in this chapter between older patterns of extremism and violence, for example the IRA in the 1970s and more recent extremism from within the jihadist movement.

Postmodern Trends Including Globalisation

Postmodernism represents a paradigm shift from previous views of the world. It acknowledges the rejection of the previously held validity of the concept of universal theories and their apparent ability to model the complexity and dynamics of modern life. However, this is a contested position and the turbulent changes that societies are undergoing may also be termed *late modernity*, arguing that this change is moderated by structural mechanisms such as: the continuity of government, capitalism, nationalism and particular cultures (Giddens 1997; Robins 2002). Gray (2003: 1–2) argues that the Al Qaeda 9/11 attack challenged the concepts of late modernity, that is a homogeneous trend to 'civilisation' as societies develop and that the exploitation of science and technology propels society to become secular, more enlightened and peaceful. Gray (2003) also notes that despite the contradictory evidence these concepts are still believed. This myth of late modernity is exemplified by the British establishment's attitude towards Christianity. For many years the tendency has been to suppress both openly displaying signs of and performing Christian activities in public and by those employed by the state, for example the High Court finding that a council was unlawful in scheduling prayers at commencement of its meetings (Riches 2012). This suppression has resulted in media criticism and with the British Prime Minister publicly welcoming this media attack on political correctness and excessive support for multiculturalism (Hall 2012) which is now beginning to be seen as a failed strategy.

Smith (2011) argues that the USA is no longer the dominant world power and that this is the third time in a century it has fallen from this pinnacle: Each fall followed a prolonged war diverting its resources to waging these wars, in this last case the 'war on terror'. Smith (2011) attributes this to recurring phases of excessive nationalism. The recent losses of world power allowed the overthrow of allies such as the regime in Egypt during the Arab Spring. Nederveen Pieterse (2009) states that during the last 20 years two major trends peaked and started to decline – American hegemony and neo-liberalism – and that 'new forces' are rising around the globe in a multi-polar mode. In America the rise of religious extremism has produced a new emphasis on defence and Homeland Security and the formation of new security alliances. Nederveen Pieterse (2009) also notes that there are increasing levels of inequality found in localised areas, both rural and urban, and that this in turn has increased economic migration between countries, further stressing communities and undermining community coherence. The evolving postmodern Europe is based on transparency, mutual surveillance and economic interdependency (Cooper 2001). In postmodern Europe it is unlikely that Member States would attack each other. However, Cooper (2001) recognises zones of anarchy within Europe, where criminal or extremist powers hold sway and the postmodern state is prompted to intervene. These contentions agree with that of Muir and Wetherell (2010) who argue that the two main trends affecting British society in the last quarter of a century are 'individualisation' and increased 'cultural diversity' and these have profoundly unsettling impacts on identity, belonging and nationality.

In this era, 'Postmodern terrorism seemingly has no limits, no inside or outside: it is transnational, truly global, highly mobile, and cellular. It makes use of new global technologies in communication and information-exchange: cells are 'intelligent networks' able to conduct surveillance, decode and hack into official systems and databases' (Peters 2004). This is demonstrated by the actions of extremist supporters of Palestinian rights who are suspected of a cyber-attack on websites of the First International Bank of Israel, Massad bank, Otzar Hahayalhigh bank, El Al airlines and the Tel Aviv stock exchange (*Guardian* 2012). The offensive was welcomed by Hamas 'This is a new field of resistance against the occupation and we urge Arab youth to develop their methods in electronic warfare in the face of (Israel's) crimes' (Guardian 2012: 1). Mazzetti (2010) notes the intermixing of civilian and military services in the war on terror with the CIA becoming the vanguard in military operations such as planning and executing extra-judicial killings – drone attacks on those identified as terrorist leaders in the Afpak (Afghanistan and Pakistan) arena. For example, the CIA was recently credited with the drone air strike in the Yemen that killed Fahad al-Quso who was located after extended surveillance activity in the area (Flanagan 2012).

Lee (2002: 45) describes globalisation as a culture formed by 'convergence of cultural hedonism and uniform expectations' coupled with 'immediate access to information and increased creativity in multicultural settings'. The individual is connected to and influenced by large-scale systems and information is, more than ever, a source of power, wealth and control. Turbulent change is unevenly distributed with unpredictable outcomes that make redundant and outdated once-universal rules. Although globalisation is also a contested concept it includes many factors that are of importance in terms of understanding postmodern extremism. Nederveen Pieterse (2004) views polarisation as an important consequence of globalisation where disaffiliated and disconnected individuals are more likely to take up extremist viewpoints and that this extremism is likely to be based upon either ethnic or religious criteria.

Hickman et al. (2011) noted that extremist Islamic violence is perceived to be rational and based upon ideology and driven by religion, whilst that of the IRA was reported to be irrational and of a political rather than a religious nature. However, an example of postmodern, anti-globalisation extremism that is neither religious nor ethnic in its origin is the Occupy London group who state:

> We are losing control over our lives. This must stop. This will stop. The citizens of the world must get control over the decisions that influence them in all levels – from global to local. That is global democracy. That is what we demand today.
>
> Today, like the Mexican Zapatistas, we say "¡Ya basta! Aquí el pueblo manda y el gobierno obedece": Enough! Here the people command and global institutions obey! Like the Spanish Tomalaplaza we say "Democracia Real Ya": True global democracy now!" Today we call the citizens of the world: let us globalise Tahrir Square! Let us globalise Puerta del Sol! (Occupy London website, nd:1)

Postmodern extremism in any guise aims to maximise the telegenic characterisation of its activities (Peters 2004), from peaceful demonstrations such as the occupying of St Paul's Cathedral in London by Occupy London, to atrocities such as 9/11 by Al Qaeda, which attempt to use all the modes of the media to their full potential to gain attention and support for their organisation and to threaten, intimidate and attack the opposition.

The Individual, the Community and Community Cohesion

Greater cultural diversity, brought about by the trends above, changes the fundamental structure of society. As new groups arrive and others depart, inter-racial, ethnic and religious relationship patterns change these may then change intra- and inter-group dynamics. Such changes ultimately question the concept of a single national identity. In this increasingly fractured and dynamic environment society experiences frequent uncertainty and the need to be alert against attacks from unknown foes in unknown forms resulting in an emphasis on 'Homeland Security' and the development of the technology of mass surveillance and other defensive security systems (Peters 2004). Neumann (2009: 11) also cites two similar key factors, the 'tools of globalization' (ICT, improved weapons for example IED or dirty bombs), coupled with uncertainty and argues that these may be exploited by extremists to spread violence and hatred. The challenge for the forces of law and order therefore remains to keep pace with change, to innovate and use technology to achieve socially positive goals.

The UK Government currently assess community cohesion levels by determining what proportion of the local community feel that 'in this area people from different backgrounds get along well together'. In the eight London community areas that registered less than 60 per cent agreement with this statement, there has tended to be an increase in electoral support for the British National Party (BNP) (Your Lancashire 2009). In other areas of the country, especially in North West England, Cantle (2001) found that there were communities within the community that lived 'parallel lives' where both groups were highly suspicious of each other and community cohesion was minimal. Muir and Wetherell (2010) consider identity not to be fixed at any point in each person's life but rather a continual process as one continues to evolve, interpret new narratives and labels throughout our lives, they cite Butler's concept of 'performativity as a practice of improvisation within a scene of constraint' (Butler 2004: 1).

Within this state of flux the relationship between the individual, the community and the state will also be in a state of flux. These relationships may become stronger or weaker, individuals may become more closely associated with their community, or more alienated from it and communities may be aligned and integrated within the state, or may be isolated and antagonistic to the national culture and its politics. Within this increasingly fragmented landscape multiple paths exist for radicalisation and extremism. Social Identity Theory (Tajfel 1978, cited in Malim 1997) suggests that the various social groups that an individual belongs to represent an integral part of their own self-concept. This social identity determines how individuals are perceived by others within and without their groups and provides a framework for the individual in terms of the roles they perceive they should occupy and the appropriate behaviours attached to such roles. Members of a group, viewed from the outside, by others, appear relatively homogeneous. However, when viewed from inside the group, the same level of homogeneity does not exist (see Chapter 4, Cults, in Awan and Blakemore 2012).

Cooper and Innes (2009: 3) note that community cohesion is increasingly viewed in government circles as an attribute possessed by 'strong, healthy and vibrant communities'. However, for both groups involved in the physical intermixing of cultural/ethnic/religious backgrounds as a part of mass migration Merton's (1938) strain theory, also called '*anomie*', may be an appropriate concept. Anomie contends that if sections of society are alienated, that is community cohesion is poor, the individuals in this grouping will be unaware of or unable to conform to the culture, that is the expectations and aspirations that create a coherent community. Merton (1938) argued that anomie is more relevant if the alienated individuals recognise that society places a strong emphasis on particular goals but does not clearly define the norms associated with acceptable and unacceptable ways of achieving such goals. It has been stated that in the world of virtual reality, anomie is both 'a condition and a pleasure' (Osborne 2002: 29) suggesting that cyber space allows the individual the freedom to be themselves whilst recognising their differences and their disaffiliation with mainstream society.

The large scale migrations associated with globalisation will produce different impacts in different host nations and host communities, ranging from full integration and acceptance to parallel cultures and identities which can produce ghettoes of isolated communities. Woodward (1999) uses the phrase 'imagined community', for a constructed imaginary combination of individual identity and relationships needed to support the individual's need to maintain their identity and to feel at home within a community. Does creating such an imagined community reduce the likelihood of disaffiliation from the actual community and if so will it in turn reduce the tendency to extremism? This reluctance to change may allow reassuring ideologies to be promoted that superficially, at least, resolve the discord caused by the failure to adapt to the reality of change for example the narratives of the Salafi jihadist or Far Right supremacist. Even moderate right wing media such as the *Daily Express* raise the negative effects of multiculturalism and mass immigration frequently with titles such as 'Mass immigration is destroying this once great nation' (McKinstry 2012: 12) which includes references to 'the scandal of the 50-strong gang of Romanian beggars' and 'Muslim sex gangs'.

Jones (2011) notes the recent postmodern idea that human rights only apply to citizens and not 'illegals' and foreign migrants can be found in the USA, Israel and India all of which would claim to be democratic civilisations. Jones (2011) identifies Gandhi who, jailed in 2009 for inciting communal violence against Muslims as part of election, gained a large majority and was not only accepted by the populace but by the party machine that also appointed him national secretary of the Bharatiya Janata Party. Similarly Jones (2011) cites Israel's prime minister stating that he appreciated the positive contribution made to Israel by foreign workers but that he would not give them citizenship in order to prevent a flood of illegal migrants that would be expected to follow such a move.

These examples are part of the 'Janus face' or 'othering' or 'groupism' (Brubacker et al. 2004) world view of us and them which is continually changing due to experiencing ever-evolving narratives of life in an unpredictable world. Globalisation has not homogenised communities around the world nor has it reduced 'groupism' (Jones 2011). The war on terror exemplifies this description of good *vs* evil and has resulted in an acute emphasis on borders – Jones (2011) again cites the USA, India and Israel as examples of countries which have spent large sums on miles of fencing along their borders to protect the civilised society within from the barbaric evil lurking without.

Research in Northern Ireland (Schmidt et al. 2009) found that all-Protestant or all-Catholic neighbourhoods had strong community cohesion but higher levels of prejudice and even hatred of the other faction, whereas in mixed neighbourhoods, although the overall community (area) cohesion was lower, there was also less evidence of prejudice and hatred directed against the other religious group. They conclude that there is a trade-off between community cohesion based upon homogeneity and prejudice and hate against the other group. Contrasting this situation is the finding that in some cosmopolitan cities in the UK race and ethnicity is not an issue. For example, in Birmingham there is a Roman Catholic school where 90 per cent of the students are of the Muslim religion and their parents are tolerant of the Christian religious teaching they receive as they are more concerned with their children going to a good school (Pickard 2012). Gilroy (2006) terms this a 'convivial culture' where factors other than ethnicity underpin interpersonal perceptions and behaviours. Hickman et al. (2011) reported that many Irish and Muslim respondents identified strongly with these areas of convivial culture and that for Muslims these areas were seen as safer than other parts Britain.

The Irish participants recalled eventually resuming normal relations within their culturally and socially diverse cities and emerging from the labelling of being a 'suspect community'. A further example of this convivial culture is illustrated in the news headline 'Muslim cabbie kicks out family for carrying wine' (Broster 2012). At first sight this appears to be a religious or ethnic dispute between a white family and a Muslim taxi driver but on further reading the episode shows multiculturalism at its best. The Cartwright family were taking alcohol to an unlicensed Indian restaurant serving Halal food when the driver said he was sorry but his faith did not allow him to have alcohol in his taxi, the co-operative company of taxi drivers (predominantly Muslim) provided alternative transport and sacked the driver involved as they were concerned with providing good customer service across the entire community.

A case review of the arrest at gunpoint of six Muslim street cleaners prior to the Papal visit to London, found that the police had lawfully used the powers afforded to them under the Terrorism Act 2000 (Sherwin, 2011). However, the arrests were based upon weak and general information, in this case the suspects had been observed looking at a newspaper featuring the visit and were overheard saying they intended to kill the Pope in revenge for a recent burning of their holy book, the Qur'an. It later emerged that this, the only piece of evidence found despite a full investigation including searching ten premises, had been no more than a joke. The independent reviewer cautioned the police to avoid 'future temptations' to use their anti-terrorism powers unless there is sufficient real evidence to justify arrests and the consequential distress to the individuals involved and potential damage to police–community relationships.

For Great Britain over the year ending 30 September 2011 there was a rise in the number of individuals arrested for terrorism-related offences compared to the previous year – up from 133 to 153 – and this increase was also recorded for individuals arrested using the Terrorism Act 2000 – up to 70 from 53 in the previous year (HMSO 2011). Of these 45 per cent were prosecuted compared to 36 per cent of the 2,050 arrested since 11 September 2001. The report (HMSO 2011) also shows that there were 121 convicted terrorists in prison in Great Britain on 30 September 2011, including 22 classified as domestic extremists. In this context a domestic extremist is one who follows a cause that originated in the United Kingdom; this includes 'single-issue' activists who may follow one of a wide range of causes from extreme left- to extreme right-wing political factions, animal rights groups and 'lone wolf' activists. The report notes that the majority belong to either far-right political groups or are animal rights extremists (HMSO 2011).

Social Control and Social Media

The term 'hyperreality' has been coined to describe the situation where media informs (misinforms) or influences perceptions to such an extent that there is little distinction between fact and fiction (Baudrillard 1981, 1983). The post-modernisation assertion that there has been a collapse of belief in theory and analysis coupled with a culture centred on immediate consumption and sensationalized impact but with little depth of analysis or contextualization (Osborne 2002) facilitates the likelihood of individuals occupying the world of 'hyperreality'. Ameli et al. (2007) studied the effects of contemporary media representations of 'Muslims' and 'Islam' in and by the British media. They found that the language and discourse employed to depict Muslims and Islam was broadly negative. This work is supported by Moore et al. (2008) who found over a four year period in the national press that 36 per cent of articles about British Muslims were about extremism/terrorism and some 26 per cent of the articles depicted Islam as dangerous, backward or irrational, with only 2 per cent of the stories giving a positive message regarding the followers of this religion.

However, the UK Home Office (2011) statistics show a decrease of racist incidents reported to the police in England and Wales from 54,872 in 2009–10 to 51,187 in 2010–11 suggesting that although the media can influence perception and attitude it is more difficult to change behaviour. In the UK the National Police Improvement Agency best practice for managing critical incidents is to include a tactical advisor for social media, acknowledging the power and potential for misinformation fuelling community anxiety and unrest (NPIA 2012).

Informal social control may be exercised to a greater or lesser degree by society and can support or compete with modes of formal social control. Examples of the power of social control include villagers in Poland who used a mobile crane to perch a car belonging to a youth known for driving recklessly in a tree (*Daily Express*, 2012), while the use of social media to police is demonstrated by a campaign launched by several international cricketers in different countries appealing for help to find the items stolen from the family of a deceased cricketer in Australia (Tahir 2012).

The factors that underpin an electronic police state include mass surveillance, excessive data-gathering by the state, the removal or prevention of a user's anonymity, infringing the Human Rights of the individual and excessive sharing of data by state security and policing organisations. Using these criteria Privacy International considered that Britain is the worst western democracy at protecting individual privacy. Globally the two worst countries according to Privacy International's survey were Malaysia and China, with Britain in fifth position (BBC News 2006).

The global trend towards mass surveillance is demonstrated by the commercial opportunities it has spawned such as IBM launching the IBM i2 Intelligence Analysis Portfolio, in May 2012. This is a first-generation analytics software package for law enforcement and government agencies to sift the exceedingly large amounts of data they routinely collect to help them discern, disrupt and prevent criminal, extremist and fraudulent activities (Cooney 2012). This software is designed to search unstructured data, enable inter- and intra-organisational communication and to provide various types of analysis to discern relationships, patterns and trends in data that reveal how various parties are interconnected. Britain in particular shows a continuing intensification of this trend.

The UK has become a surveillance society (dataveillance) according to the UK's Information Commissioner and the Surveillance Studies Network has also argued that the United Kingdom is an advanced electronic police state (BBC news 2006). CCTV cameras continue to be deployed in the UK since 2006, when there were 4.2m CCTV cameras in Britain, with some £515 million being spent on CCTV by local authorities over the four-year period ending March 2011 (Brown 2012). The government intends to further enforce data retention by both internet service providers and telephone service providers, requiring them to capture, store and allow access to all customer usage on their systems as proposed by the British Coalition government in April 2012 (Westcott 2012). Commenting on this proposal, included in the June 2012 Queen's Speech, David Davis (a Conservative Member of Parliament) claimed that 'it is not focusing on terrorists or on criminals. It is absolutely everybody. Historically governments have been kept out of our private lives' and he further points out that in specific cases where there is reasonable suspicion the British courts already have adequate powers to grant powers to intercept and monitor communications (Westcott 2012:4).

The UK has laws regulating the use of cryptography and/or privacy-enhancing technologies, combating attempts by users to remain anonymous as demonstrated by the conviction of Oliver Drage for failing to reveal his password to the police (Radenedge 2010). Further reductions of constitutional protections within the criminal justice system have been suggested by the British Justice Secretary aiming to introduce closed trials where only judges would hear evidence from security agents which might be considered too sensitive to put into the public domain (Naughton 2012). The excessive and according to some unnecessary sharing of data between various government agencies in the intelligence and policing sphere is part of evolving national (and international) strategies to combat terrorism.

Morozov cites the United States government using social media for its own purposes, to support demonstrators in another country (in Pilkington 2011), and that the United States Government requested that Twitter postpone maintenance work that would have taken Twitter off air in Iran during June 2009 and impacted adversely on the ability of anti-government protesters to organise their activities. Twitter complied, demonstrating government influence over an internet provider. A more overt example is that of Amazon and Paypal who denied access for supporters of WikiLeaks to further fund this organisation following its publication of sensitive United States Government data online. Consequentially, Morozov believes that many authoritarian regimes now realise that cyber space is a control mechanism (in Pilkington 2011).

He further argues that such tools are now more sophisticated than simple denial of services to all at an unwanted website, as exercised by the Chinese government for 10 months in 2009, to specifically denying access to those believed to be anti-government activists or extremists based upon their 'dataveillance' history (Pilkington 2011). Gregory (2011) supports the central position surveillance and communications strategy play in fighting extremist network-centric warfare but points out that the outsourcing of cyber attacks masks the source of the attacker and blurs the boundaries between civilian and military action, also the United States cyber command, initiated in 2010, stated a fortress mentality will not succeed in cyber space as it is an offence-dominated environment.

Bartlett et al. (2011) found that police monitoring of the English Defence League social network was ineffective in that the police could not discern the activists and real threats on the streets as opposed to the members that join in online discussion but are not active in their extremism and may post hypothetical and confusing material on the site. Better ways of analysing the data such as IBM's i2 Intelligence Analysis Portfolio software are needed to provide useful intelligence in advance of action taking place. This social media based activism, also known as 'clicktivism', is here to stay and more understanding of its dynamics, power and weaknesses is urgently needed.

The report 'Roots of Violent Radicalisation' found that personal contact with radicals is, in many cases, a significant factor in the radicalisation process but concludes that the internet is one of the most significant vehicles for promoting violent radicalism featuring in most, if not all, of the routes of radicalisation – and was found to be more prevalent than any specific physical location such as prisons, universities or places of worship. The report also found that cyber space is one of the few unregulated spaces where radicalisation is able to take place despite Britain being regarded as a high surveillance state. These finding were seen to be equally valid for both Jihadist and for far right organisations (Commons Select Committee 2012).

A further concern regarding cyber extremism is the process of self-radicalisation that occurs in isolation and how the messages and manipulation that can be found online may cause such predisposed individuals to initiate or progress their own self-radicalisation (Home Affairs Committee 2012). The Terrorism Act 2006 enables law enforcement agencies to order unlawful material to be removed from the internet, however, the Commons Select Committee recommends that this power be assisted by internet service providers self-regulating and controlling the material they host and by empowering civil society groups to challenge online extremist material. This would require a code of practice for the removal of material which promotes violent extremism to be developed and agreed by the stakeholders concerned. However, many of those who created the internet are currently opposed to state control or corporate control of cyber space, for example Sir Tim Berners-Lee (2010).

Comparison of Different Extremist Case Studies

McGovern and Tobin (2010) orchestrated a symposium of those who were, or had been, political prisoners or human rights activists and were from Irish and British Muslim backgrounds. They found that many of the counter-terrorism activities in Northern Ireland were counter-productive, reducing both confidence in the establishment and state–community relations and so delivered a poorer quality of intelligence to the police and security services.

Hickman et al. (2011) found that in the time of the Troubles in Northern Ireland and in the present postmodernist era both the media and the government frequently referred to 'Britishness' to portray a homogeneous, constant culture as prevalent throughout the nation and that these British were a group strongly opposed to the 'other', whether it be the Irish extremists of yesterday or Muslim extremists today. The Government, its agents and the media use or used terms that created a Janus face (see Chapter 10 in Awan and Blakemore 2012) for the relevant communities, they could be labelled as innocent or as extremist leading to the creation of the suspect community or as Hickman et al. (2011:3) argue: 'It is in these ambiguous representations of Irish and Muslim communities, and in their construction as separate, bounded communities (with varying degrees of "integration into British society"), that public discourse has most impact on the lives of people identifying as Muslim and Irish and living in multiethnic Britain.' This is exemplified by the recent debate about Muslim women wearing the veil where they may be seen as victims of male oppression, merely following their religion and culture, to practitioners of extremist propaganda. McGovern and Tobin (2010) also found a regular detrimental use of language and 'othering' to be a common factor and one that damages intergroup engagement.

Hickman et al. (2011) also found some respondents felt that Muslims were more forceful than Irish people had been in response to being treated as suspect and that a greater inclusion in policy-making processes and the development of anti-discrimination policies may account for some of this empowerment. This assertiveness included demonstrating their 'Britishness', whereas for many Irish respondents the need and action was to be more Irish so as to avoid being mistaken as being English.

Hickman et al. (2011) also found that surveillance of specific community areas, especially mosques, Catholic churches and Irish pubs was detrimental to community cohesion. This is similar to the response experienced to a community safety project (Project Champion) in Birmingham which used anti-terrorism funding for surveillance of the area's inhabitants (Awan 2011). The use of informers is also detrimental to building trust and cohesion within the community according to McGovern and Tobin (2010).

For Irish respondents the negative events included the arrests of friends and family, while for Muslim respondents, being subjected to 'stop-and-search' was a more prevalent negative experience. 'High' policing (Brodeur, 2007) refers to activities relating to national security and intelligence agencies while 'low' policing reflects everyday policing conducted by uniformed police officers. The possible tensions between different components of the state apparatus and the challenges presented by competing objectives and different methods which might exist between the different levels are highlighted by several authors, as is the need to integrate these activities both vertically and horizontally (see Chapter 10 Awan and Blakemore 2012). McGovern and Tobin (2010) noted that temporary anti-terrorism measures were extended regularly during the Troubles in Northern Ireland and since the British Counter Terrorism Act 2000 such extension of wider state powers for control has similarly developed in the present 'war on terror'. The symposium found that this amounted to counterproductive legislation and ineffective British Government campaigns. Especially noted were actions such as extending detention from seven to 28 days under the British Terrorism Act 2006 and wide use of stop-and-search powers and that this extended state control was seen as signs of a new dual track system of justice for extremists, separating them from the everyday criminal justice system. Furthermore, the meaning and application of recent laws such a 'glorification of terrorism' and criminalising accessing certain information are unclear in the community and this promotes fear of and vulnerability to being a potential suspect.

These negative examples of state surveillance down to street level stop-and-search produced feelings of fear and resulted in respondents keeping a low profile and avoiding certain locations. This in turn resulted in varied reactions from a reduced feeling of belonging to and trust in the wider British community and its governance, to increased political activism (Hickman et al. 2011). The British Government's involvement in rendition to areas where torture allegedly took place is also seen as similar to claims of torture used by security forces in Northern Ireland and were most strongly opposed by the communities concerned. Moreover, families of those held under extraordinary powers and the prisoners themselves may experience isolation and alienation (McGovern and Tobin 2010).

The British Government is attempting to treat community cohesion as a distinct and separate dimension from counter-terrorism but their focus on defeating extremist ideas and violence from within and by Muslim communities remains. While visiting Thailand and hailing the country for its transition to democracy and religious freedom, 'PM urges Muslims to defeat Al Qaeda' (Little 2012: 34), David Cameron chose to make this appeal to the world in the country with the largest Muslim population. According to Briggs et al. (2006) the reasons for such a strategy are that communities offer the best sources of intelligence; they are more able to divert young Muslims from becoming extremist (social control); communities must articulate and proactively engage in solving problems that either create grievances or disable the community to act in the ways suggested above and finally that policing must be based upon the informed consent of the communities involved. However, Hickman et al. (2011) found that this strategy was tried and found to be inadequate in Northern Ireland. It is counter-productive in that it reinforces the 'us and them', 'in and out', or 'other group' attitudes demonstrated above and continues to generate further anxiety over extremist violence in the community at large.

Briggs et al. (2006) recognised the practical problems in implementing the prevention of violent extremism using this approach. Defining who or what is a community and who speaks for a community is a difficult problem; it is difficult to build trust and confidence, for example, Project Champion was created to tackle all forms of crime but the association with and labelling of the community as extremist further alienated and reduced cohesion within the local community (Awan 2011) and communities need to feel secure to tackle such behaviour and sufficient resources may be lacking. The community cohesion strategy attempts to integrate supposedly separate communities but surely the cosmopolitanism that promotes the 'convivial culture' found in cities such as London and Birmingham is the dimension to be supported for effective cohesion. The UK Government's Contest strategy is seen as too negative by McGovern and Tobin (2010) hence a recent government suggestion to use the phrase 'engagement' instead of 'prevent' within the 'contest' strategy but will this merely mire another positive word?

Perhaps the most useful findings from McGovern and Tobin (2010) are that protecting human rights and civil liberties and the need for nurturing an inclusive and bespoke community infrastructure are paramount in order to facilitate a long-term working solution; both of these finding are based upon experiences in the Northern Ireland.

Conclusion

Much can be learned from previous experiences such as the Troubles in Northern Ireland, especially the counterproductive effects of some policing activities and government policies. Today we live in more dynamic and interconnected societies subject to the forces of globalisation. The task of achieving and maintaining community cohesion is made more difficult given the contemporary global trends discussed in this chapter. 'Convivial culture' can be found within Britain and lessons must be learned from these communities. Government policy and policing must beware of the positive and negative effects of social media and the dangers inherent in a drift in to a surveillance society.

Further Reading

Innes, M., Abbott, L., Lowe, T. and Roberts, C. 2007. *Hearts and Minds and Eyes and Ears: Reducing Radicalisation Risks through Reassurance-Oriented Policing*. London: ACPO.

References

Ameli, S.R., Marandi, S.M., Ahmed, S., Kara, S., and Merali, A. 2007. *British Muslims' Expectations of the Government. The British Media and Muslim Representation: The Ideology of Demonisation.* London: Islamic Human Rights Commission. [online]. Available at: http://www.ihrc.org.uk/file/1903718317. pdf on 29/3/10). [accessed: 15 December 2011].

Awan, I. 2011. A lesson in how not to spy upon your community, *Criminal Justice Matters, Special Issue, Myths and Criminal Justice,* 83(1): 10–11.

Awan, I., and Blakemore, B. (eds) 2012. *Policing Cyber Hate, Cyber Threat and Cyber Terror.* Farnham: Ashgate.

Bartlett, J., Birdwell, J., and Littler, M. 2011. 'The rise of populism in Europe can be traced through online behaviour' The New Face of Digital Populism, Demos. [Online]. Available at: http://www.demos.co.uk/publications/ thenewfaceofdigitalpopulism. [accessed: 5 April 2012].

Baudrillard, J. 1981. *Simulacres et Simulation,* Paris: Edition Galilee. (English translation Ann Arbor 1994. *Simulacra and Simulation,* Michigan: University of Michigan Press.)

Baudrillard, J. 1983. The Orders of Simulacra, *Simulations.* New York: Semiotext, 81–159.

BBC News. 2006. Britain is 'surveillance society'. [Online]. Available at: http:// news.bbc.co.uk/1/hi/uk/6108496.stm. [accessed: 31 March 2012].

Berners-Lee, T. 2010. Long live the web. *Scientific American,* December, 56–61.

Boyns, D., and Ballard, J.D. 2004. 'Developing a sociological theory for the empirical understanding of terrorism'. *The American Sociologist,* 35(2): 5–25.

Briggs, R., Fieschi, C., and Lownsbrough, H. 2006. *Bringing it Home: Community-based approaches to counter-terrorism.* London: Demos. [Online]. Available at http://www.demos.co.uk/publications?end_year=2009&page=8&start_ year=2005&tab=publications pp.58–83. [accessed: 14 November 2011].

Brodeur, P. 2007. 'High and Low Policing in Post-9/11 Times', *Policing,* 1(1): 25–37.

Broster, P. 2012. Muslim cabbie kicks out family for carrying wine. *Daily Express,* 14 April, 34.

Brown, M. 2012. Councils waste £515 on CCTV in crime war. *Daily Express,* 21 February, 24.

Brubacker, R., Loveman, M., and Stanatov, R. 2004. Ethnicity and cognition, theory and society, *The Geographical Journal,* September 177(3): 213–17.

Butler, J. 2004. *Undoing Gender.* London: Routledge.

Cantle, T. 2005. *Community Cohesion: a new framework for race and diversity.* Basingstoke: Palgrave Macmillan.

Commons Select Committee. 2012. MPs urge internet providers to tackle on-line extremism. [Online]. available at:http://www.parliament.uk/business/ committees/committees-a-z/commons-select/home-affairs-committee/ news/120206-rvr-rpt-publication/. [accessed: 9 May 2012].

Cooney, M. 2012. *IBM Melds Crime-Fighting, Big Data Analytics in One Security Package.* CIO.IN. [Online] available at: http://www.cio.in/news/ibm-melds-crime-fighting-big-data-analytics-one-security-package-256572012. [accessed: 3 May 2012].

Cooper, H., and Innes, M. 2009. *The Causes and Consequences of Community Cohesion in Wales: A Secondary Analysis.* Cardiff University: Universities' Police Science Institute.

Daily Express. 2012. Car up a tree? Looks like a job for special branch. *Daily Express*, 10 May, 19.

Flanagan, P. 2012. CIA Drone missile kills Al Qaeda chief. *Daily Express*, 8 May, 15.

Giddens, A. 1997. (3rd edition). *Sociology.* Cambridge: Polity Press.

Gilroy, P. 2006. After Empire: Multiculture or Postcolonial Melancholia. London: Routledge.

Gray, J. 2003. *Al Qaeda and What It Means to be Modern.* London: Faber & Faber.

Gregory, D. 2011. The everywhere war. *The Geographical Journal*, September, 177(3): 238–50.

Guardian. 2012. Israel hit by cyber-attacks on stock exchange, airline and banks. [Online]. available at: http://www.guardian.co.uk/world/2012/jan/16/israel-cyber-attacks-banks-airline. [accessed: 17 April 2012].

Hall, M. 2012. Cameron Backs Christian fightback. *Daily Express,* 4 April, 2.

Hickman, M.J., Thomas, L., Silvestri, S., and Nickels, H. 2011. Suspect communities? Counterterrorism Policy, the Press, and the impact on Irish and Muslim Communities in Britain, Institute for the Study of European Transformations, London Metropolitan University. [Online]. Available at: http://www.londonmet.ac.uk/fms/MRSite/Research/iset/Suspect%20 Communities%20Findings%20July2011.pdf . [accessed: 13 April 2012].

Home Affairs Committee. 2012. *Roots of violent radicalisation.* para 33 [Online]. Available at: http://www.publications.parliament.uk/pa/cm201012/cmselect/cmhaff/1446/144605.htm#a10. [accessed: 9 May 2012].

HMSO. 2011. *Operation of police powers under the Terrorism Act 2000 and subsequent legislation: Arrests, outcomes and stops and searches*, Home Office Statistical Bulletin Quarterly update to September 2011. [Online]. Available at: http://www.homeoffice.gov.uk/publications/science-research-statistics/research-statistics/counter-terrorism-statistics/hosb0412/?view=Stan dard&pubID=1013468. [accessed: 17 April 2012].

Home Office. 2011. *Statistical News Release: Racist Incidents, England and Wales, 2010/11 Racist Incidents fall by seven per cent in 2010/1.* Home Office 18 September 2011. [online]. Available at: http://www.homeoffice.gov.uk/publications/science-research-statistics/research-statistics/crime-research/hosf0111/. [accessed: 1 November 2011].

Jones, R. 2011. Border security 9/11 and the enclosure of civilisation, *The Geographical Journal*, September 177(3): 213–17.

Laqueur, W. 1996. 'Postmodern Terrorism: New Rules for an Old Game', *Foreign Affairs*, September/October. [Online]. Available at: http://www.fas.org/irp/news/1996/pomo-terror.htm. [Accessed: 20 October 2003].

Lee, R.L.M. 2002. Globalization and Mass Society Theory, *International Review of Sociology: Revue Internationale de Sociologie*, 12(1): 45–60. [Online]. Available at: DOI: 10.1080/03906700220135318. [accessed: 13 March 2012].

Little, A. 2012. 'PM urges Muslims to defeat Al Qaeda' *Daily Express,* Thursday 12 April, 2.

McGovern, M., and Tobin, A. 2010. Counter terror or counter productive: Comparing Irish and British Muslim experiences of counter-insurgency law and policy. Edge Hill University. [Online]. Available at: http://www.edgehill.ac.uk/documents/news/CounteringTerror.pdf. [accessed: 23 May 2012].

McKinstry, L. 2012. Mass immigration is destroying this once great nation, *Daily Express*, 17 May 12.

Mazzetti, M. 2010. CIA takes on bigger and riskier role on front lines, *New York Times*, 1 January.

Moore, K., Mason, P., and Lewis, J. 2012. *Images of Islam in the UK: The representation of British Muslims in the national print media 2000-2008*, Cardiff University. [Online]. Available at: http://www.cardiff.ac.uk/jomec/resources/08channel4-dispatches.pdf. [accessed: 18 May 2012].

Muir, R., and Wetherell M. 2010. *Identity, Politics and Public Policy,* The Institute for Public Policy Research. [online]. Available at: http://www.ippr.org/publications/55/1765/identity-politics-and-public-policy. [accessed: 5 April 2012].

Naughton, P. 2012. We need secret courts for spies Clarke says, *The Times.* [Online]. Available at: http://www.thetimes.co.uk/tto/news/. [accessed 4 April 2012].

Nederveen Pieterse, J. 2009. 21st Century Globalization: Sociological Perspectives *Sociological Analysis*, 3(2), Autumn: 49–74.

Newburn, T. 2011. A riot born in deprivation. *Guardian.* [Online]. Available at: http://www.guardian.co.uk/commentisfree/2011/oct/25/uk-riot-born-in-deprivation, 25 October. [accessed: 12 April 2012].

Newton Dunn, T. 2011. War on gangs Theresa May unveils battle plan, *The Sun.* [Online]. Available at: http://www.thesun.co.uk/sol/homepage/news/politics/3906330/War-on-gangs.html. 1 November. [accessed: 12 April 2012].

NPIA. 2012. Gold Commanders Course, NPIA, University of Glamorgan, April 2012.

Occupy London (nd) *United for Global Democracy.* [Online]. Available at: http://occupylsx.org/?page_id=2958. [accessed: 14 April 2012].

Osborne, R. 2002. *Megawords.* London: Sage.

Peters, M.A. 2004. *Globalization 2004: Postmodern Terror in a Globalized World.* [Online]. Available at: http://globalization.icaap.org/content/v4.1/peters.html. [accessed: 3 April 2012].

Pickard, M. 2012. The Catholic school that's 90% Muslim. *Daily Express*, 16 July, 18.

Pilkington, E. 2011. Evgeny Morozov: How democracy slipped through the net. *Guardian*. 13 January. [Online]. Available at: http://www.guardian.co.uk/technology/2011/jan/13/evgeny-morozov-the-net-delusion. [accessed: 5 April 2012].

Radenedge, A. 2010. Jailed for refusing to reveal password. *Metro*, 6 October, 1.

Riches, C. 2012. English way of life is eroded by prayer ban. *Daily Express*, April 3, 6.

Robins, K. 2002. What in the world's going on?. In P. Du Gay (ed), *Production of Culture/Cultures of Production* (pp. 11–66). London: Sage.

Schmid, K., Hewstone, M., Hughes J., Jenkins, R., and Cairns, E. 2009. 'Residential Segregation and Intergroup Contact: Consequences for Intergroup Relations, Social Capital and Social Identity'. In M. Wetherell (ed.), *Theorizing Identities and Social Action, Identity Studies in the Social Sciences* 2009. Basingstoke: Palgrave Macmillan.

Sherwin, A. 2011. Police warned not to misuse anti-terror laws to round up innocent people. *The Independent*. [Online]. Tuesday, 17 May. Available at http://www.independent.co.uk/news/uk/crime/police-warned-not-to-misuse-antiterror-laws-to-round-up-innocent-people-2284994.html# [accessed: 17 April 2012].

Smith, N. 2011. Ten years after. *The Geographical Journal*, September 177(3), 203–207.

Tahir, T. 2012. Stars' Twitter hunt for late England ace's stolen gear, *Metro*, 19 April, 39.

Taylor, M., and Walker, P. 2011. EDL supporters are young, male and anti-immigration, says survey, *Guardian*, 30 October. [Online]. Available at: http://www.guardian.co.uk/uk/2011/oct/30/english-defence-league-membership?INTCMP=SRCH. [accessed: 14 April 2012].

Townsend, M. 2102. Far-right anti-Muslim network on rise globally as Breivik trial opens. *Guardian*. [Online]. Available at: Guardian.co.uk, Saturday 14 April. [accessed: 16 April 2012].

TTSRL. 2008. *20th-Century Right Wing Groups in Europe,* Transnational Terrorism, Security and the Rule of Law. [online]. Available at: http://www.transnationalterrorism.eu/publications.php. [accessed: 13 April 2012].

Westcott, S. 2012. Fury at Big Brother bid to snoop on every e-mail. *Daily Express*, 2 April, 4.

Wilson, G. 2011. I predict a rioter, *The Sun,* 25 October. [online]. Available at: http://www.thesun.co.uk/sol/homepage/news/politics/3891972/August-riot-yobs-and-thugs-revealed.html. [accessed: 12 April 2012].

Woodward, K. (ed.)1999. *Identity and Difference*. London: Sage.

Your Lancashire 2009. *Place Survey 2008/2009*. Lancashire County Council [online]. Available at: http://www.lancashire.gov.uk/office_of_the_chief_executive/lancashireprofile/main/cohesion.asp. [accessed 19 April 2013].

Chapter 10

Extremism, Counter-Terrorism and Policing

Imran Awan and Brian Blakemore

The previous chapters have raised factors that can lead to extremism and terrorism, discussed what extremist groups are seen as risks to society, how to try to prevent the development of extremism and extremist activities and how best to police these groups and their actions. Extremism may take many forms from lone wolf discontents, to extremist groups, to social movements and may be driven by thrill seeking, reactionary protectionism or by those with a mission. The extremist needs support from within the community (see Chapter 6) but that may be from relatively few members of that society and may not reflect the general membership of that community. Furthermore, it is difficult to identify extremists within society as they do not necessarily possess any different characteristics from other moderate and mainstream members of their community. One exception is the recent development of support for the far right movement which is more likely to be from younger, working-class white males (Bartlett et al. 2011, see Chapter 6). The need to create a sense of belonging and acceptance of self-defined positive norms rather than allowing difference, disassociation and dissonance to breed new extremists has featured in several chapters of this book. However, creating a strong sense and agreed norm of 'Britishness' if taken too far, may be counterproductive and produce these effects, resulting in 'othering' and new forms of extremism.

Initially the British Government's CONTEST Strategy was more concerned with the protection of infrastructure than with recognising and defusing the ideological driving forces of extremism and terrorism. Although the latest strategy has focused upon this important aspect, there is still much to be learned and used to enable cohesive communities to enjoy the Queen's peace and to contribute fully to help preserve that peace. One especially important learning point is the risk of increasing alienation by using covert policing surveillance, informants and undercover agents both online or in society. So called 'supergrasses' were used by British security organisations to identify IRA members in Northern Ireland resulting in over 100 convictions but were still seen as counterproductive due to the distrust and fragmentation it produced (Hewitt 2008 25). More recently (in 2007) the Deputy Commissioner of the Metropolitan Police Service stated that much more intelligence is needed from the Muslim community than the limited amount gained by these traditional methods (Hewitt 2008). The conveyor belt theory of radicalisation has also been discredited (Chapter 6) as the only path to extremism and measures to counter extremism should not be solely based upon this theory but should recognise that there are many routes to and causes of extremism. Community policing that generates co-production of solutions to the community's disparate problems coupled with both national and foreign policy positions that consistently support the maintenance and development of cosmopolitan views is required.

Many writers agree that the heavy-handed responses to extremism and terrorist activities including introducing new laws that curtail liberty are counterproductive and constitute the greatest threat to society as a whole (Awan 2012; Blake et al. 2012, Townshend 2002 and English 2009) and that over-reaction and military responses such as Bloody Sunday in Northern Ireland damage relationships for many years (Whittaker 2002). The debate over whether to strike back hard and give no ground to extremists and terrorists (Gutteridge 1986), or not to do so in the belief that striking back hard will only cause even more followers to join extremist groups and commit even more atrocities (Thakrah 2004) continues. Policing communities must take place without alienating groups especially avoiding over- and under-policing as part of back loaded social control (see Chapters 2 and 6).

Buckelew (1984) argued that foreign policy is equally important as domestic policy in fuelling extremism and Riedel found that extraordinary rendition was as important as stop-and-search in this respect (2008). Clutterbuck (2010 228) calls upon the establishment to challenge the extremist ideology in a 'battle of ideas'. The Muslim Contact Unit and the Preventing Extremism Unit are British government organs set up to try and win this 'battle of ideas' the former works with radicals who are non-violent to engage with the community (Innes and Thiel 2008). While recent relaxing of the anti-terrorist laws, e.g. reduced detention times before trial, will support this battle, unlawful incidents such as the De Menezes shooting are still recounted and while heavy handed policing continues to take place the 'battle of ideas' will be very difficult to win.

The British government's Home Affairs Select Committee also recommends that the current name of the counter-radicalisation strategy, 'PREVENT', should be changed to 'Engage', to reflect a more supportive, partnership-based approach to working with those at risk of radicalisation: a battle of words is part and parcel of the battle of ideology. The media and government should avoid the use of extreme language and labelling when describing communities and religions that have extremists within them, to help diminish the negative impacts of such representations on communities and in particular, not equate fanaticism with religion (Hickman et al. 2011). Governments face a persistent dilemma to balance human rights against security concerns in framing legislation and in policing extremism. The release of an anti-Muslim film on Youtube in September 2012 has resulted in riots and deaths across the globe. Some governments have taken no action and defend the right to free expression even when that expression is extreme, whilst other governments have blocked the broadcasting of the offending material.

The mass migration as part of globalisation has increased diversity and potentially the process of 'othering' within the mix that forms a community or communities within a location. The tendency to form a polarised view is increased within a postmodern and globalised society producing disaffiliated and disconnected individuals who are more likely to take up extremist viewpoints. Young (2008) emphasises that 'othering' is reinforced by the process of 'self-othering':

> the stigma of being 'a loser' is countered by a hardening, an essentialist self-othering, often of machismo, race, religion, even locality and postal code; internecine splits of spurious identity striating an obscured class structure. (Young 2008: 526)

Briggs et al. (2006) suggest community-based approaches to countering terrorism should be locally based and recognise differences within the Muslim community. The approach must be rooted in an understanding of the faiths and belief systems found within that community. Government must ensure that their policy-making process is as transparent and accountable as possible. Specifically, the British government must also admit and respond to the grievances of the British Muslim community.

However, the globalisation facilitated through cyber space reduces the need for face-to-face interaction and enhances affiliations outside of the local, potentially hindering local efforts to develop cohesive communities (see Chapter 7). Hickman et al. (2011) call for the government to support multiculturalism as a means to promote social cohesion without trying to define specific communities, given the increasingly ethnically, religiously and culturally diverse society found within the UK. However, the British Prime Minister recognises that an attempt at multiculturalism in the UK has produced a negative effect, undermining the sense of British identity needed within society to prevent alienation of the majority group and exacerbating labelling and othering as a consequence (see Chapter 2). In some British minority ethnic communities the sense of 'Britishness' is stronger than that found in the majority ethnic group (see Chapter 3). Following Merton's theory of anomie (1938) community cohesion must place not only a strong emphasis on particular goals, but also must clearly define the norms associated with acceptable and unacceptable ways of achieving such goals. Examples of a convivial culture within British communities are given in Chapter 9 and developing and maintaining this cohesive and tolerant society should be in the forefront of anti-extremist policies.

In the UK regional counter-terrorist units appear to be working effectively to prevent further attacks given that none have occurred on the mainland for some considerable time and the tempting target of the London 2012 Olympic Games was incident free. However, the Home Affairs Select Committee highlights the need to improve liaison and information-sharing following the release of prisoners who have been convicted for extremism or who may have been radicalised whilst in prison. Agencies such as prison authorities, the police and probation services must develop fully integrated processes and systems to ensure that such potential extremists are accepted back into society and that they rehabilitate, including disassociating from extremist ideology and that effective social control continues to prevent their return to their former extremist activities.

The English riots show that extremism may not necessarily be about religion or race as Harding (2012) primarily blames the state for neglecting poor communities and points out the power of the combination of street gangs and social network media. LaGrange states that governments in France and Britain have not learned from previous riots and that no meaningful institutional or policy change has resulted from them (2012). Calvalcanti (2012) cites labelling and over-policing of targeted groups as factors that create a stressed environment for the youth in so called 'crime prone' areas. Awan (2011) argues that Pakistani gang culture may have had an impact, while Treadwell (2012) notes that the EDL has used this disenfranchisement of the white working-class caught in a postmodern global change to expand its powerbase and activism feeding on the anxieties of this group in particular.

UK PREVENT Strategy 2011

Countries have also made legal and political provisions in order to tackle extremist threats (see Chapters 5 and 7). In particular in the UK the new PREVENT Strategy 2011 (HM Government 2011) has been used in order to transform policy in this area. The PREVENT Strategy 2011 will tackle a wide variety of cases of extremism and terrorism; it targets not just violent extremism but also non-violent extremism, ensuring government funding and support cannot reach organisations with extremist views or which do not accept democratic and tolerant values. The strategy challenges the ideology that supports extremism; supports sectors and institutions, including universities and prisons, where there are risks of radicalisation and emphasizes evaluating the effectiveness and value for money of certain projects.

As noted in Chapter 5 the PREVENT Strategy 2011 contains three main objectives. Firstly, tackling the ideological causes and challenges of terrorism; secondly to prevent people from being drawn into terrorist-related acts by ensuring advice and support measures are provided to people who are deemed at risk of extremism and finally promoting partnerships between institutions working together to tackle the risk of radicalisation and extremism. Although in principle this notion of tackling terrorism seems proportionate it is, however, in practice similar to previous PREVENT strategies in that it lacks clarity when it comes to defining key terms and above all fails to distinguish between extremists and Muslims.

Policing extremism requires excellent community intelligence that will only be garnered from an open, tolerant and coherent community having a trusting relationship with policing organisations. McGovern and Tobin (2010) found that protecting human rights and civil liberties and the need for nurturing an inclusive and bespoke community infrastructure are paramount in order to facilitate a long-term working solution, based upon experiences in Northern Ireland. Fenwick and Choudhury (2011) explored the impact of counter-terrorism laws and policy with both Muslims and non-Muslims across Britain. Their study revealed that British Muslims felt that there was a lack of accountability regarding the policing of PREVENT and were concerned that government counter-terrorism strategies had undermined the Government's central focus of community cohesion. Indeed, the PREVENT Strategy 2011 has the potential of making Muslim communities more suspicious of law enforcement agencies leading into a growing sense of fear and a lack of trust in the British political system and policing. Furthermore, PREVENT policies have led to a perception by Muslim communities that they have been unfairly targeted and treated as a 'suspect' community due to the nature in which counter-terrorism policy has solely focussed on identifying Muslim citizens as extremists.

Overall, the PREVENT Strategy 2011 aims to eradicate and prevent extremism through the identification of extremists by tackling the 'root' causes of that ideology (that is the radicalisation process which is where people support extremism and, in some cases, join terrorist groups). According to the British Home Secretary, Theresa May, the previous PREVENT policy was flawed because it failed to identify the threat of extremism (May 2011). However, the Home Secretary does fail to identify what the terms 'extremism' and 'radicalisation' actually mean, or provide any robust research or insights as to who might be an 'extremist' or how to identify characteristics of someone that has been 'radicalised'. The problem with this lack of detail is the potential to profile activities and people as extremists or terrorists without evidence, for example the police could use their powers of investigation to arrest innocent Muslims purely because of their ethnicity, name and religion.

Clearly, Muslim communities reject terrorism but are increasingly, in political discourse, being asked questions about their patriotism and stance on British values. The only way to prevent extremism is for the state to interfere less and begin to try to understand the causes and drivers for radicalisation. Societal issues such as gang culture, bullying, deprivation and a lack of education would be some examples. Furthermore, there needs to be more dialogue and communication. Political pressures on local police forces have meant a higher level of policing that has further fuelled dissent and alienation (Awan 2011). Moreover, the PREVENT Strategy 2011 acts as a double edged sword; on the one hand it encourages Muslims to integrate and help support community engagement but on the other hand it uses counter-terrorism policies to gather information about Muslim communities. The new PREVENT II strategy uses the same name and so carries the old negative associations engendered by PREVENT I (Chapter 7).

The Internet and Extremism

The internet has also become a safe haven for terrorist groups who wish to remain anonymous and recruit vulnerable individuals. Indeed, US policy on dealing with extremists who use websites and the internet as a tool for extremism has been deemed hard line:

> Toward this end, we will continue to closely monitor the important role the internet and social networking sites play in advancing violent extremist narratives. We protect our communities from a variety of online threats, such as sexual predators, by educating them about safety on the internet, and we are using a similar approach to thwart violent extremists. We will work to empower families and communities to counter online violent extremist propaganda, which is increasingly in English and targeted at American audiences. (Empowering Local Communities to Prevent Violent Extremism 2011: 6)

This has been a particularly acute problem in the US following the hunt to capture Anwar Al-Alawki, described by the US as an extremist preacher who had used his charismatic appeal to lure both US and UK citizens to commit an act of violence. According to the US intelligence service, he had been able to use internet chat rooms and forums to successfully get US citizens to partake in a number of terrorist operations across America. His transnational appeal also led to citizens in Britain being influenced by his online sermons. For example, Rajib Karim, who was a survey analyst at Heathrow airport, was using his inside information to provide Al-Qaeda with information on possible targets at Heathrow airport. Moreover, in 2010 a student, Roshonara Choudhry, attacked her local MP, Stephen Timms in his local surgery after being influenced by Anwar Al-Alawki. In her interview with the British police Choudhry argued that she had been radicalised via the internet through Alawki's sermons and speeches (Seamark et al. 2010).

A global rise of far right extremism has evolved into an international network of far right/counter-jihadist groups (Townsend, 2012) and postmodern terrorism is dynamic and makes use of new global technology; countering these threats will require international cooperation. English (2009) supports coordinated international agreements and action on security, financial and technological counter-measures, however, countries do not know how to defend against cyber-attacks on infrastructure and cyber espionage and they do not care to disclose attacks making cooperation difficult, according to the outgoing director of NATO Cyber Defence Centre of Excellence (D'Arcy 2012). The United States Department of Defence Strategy for Operating in Cyberspace (2011) estimated that the USA alone will need an additional 700,000 cyber security professionals by 2015 (Coleman 2012).

Terrorist groups like Al-Qaeda are using the powers of the internet to radicalise and recruit vulnerable people to an ideology of hate and terror. One of the core issues as regards the UK PREVENT Strategy 2011 is also how the internet has become a tool for extremism. As Lord Carlile (2011) states; 'To protect our society, we must be prepared to use the internet as a tool of good governance: internet radicalisation must face a competing narrative, with the good facing up to the bad on equal terms, using the same or better technology and methods' (Carlile 2011: 7).

Archick et al. (2011) add that:

> individuals may become susceptible to radicalization by extremist Muslim clerics or fundamentalist youth groups. Some analysts also highlight the role that information technology and the Internet now play in increasing the ability of Islamist extremists to communicate their ideology, especially among tech-savvy youth (Archick et al. 2011: 9).

The media and terrorists may benefit from each other's actions; the extremist creates front page news. The more severe and outlandish the act the more coverage obtained for their cause, this in turn increases the public outcry and the fear and 'othering' installed in society and the more likelihood of the government overreacting, reducing individual freedoms producing reactions that feeding further extremism. During the period 1970–90s, the British government tried to starve the terrorist of the oxygen of publicity in a bid to delegitimize the IRA's threats to the integrity of the United Kingdom (Hickman et al. 2011). The Thatcher government in 1988 prohibited the broadcasting of interviews with IRA terrorists the British Broadcasting Corporation (BBC) responded by using actors to voice the terrorists' dialogue (Vieira 1991). This policy recognised that the terrorist discourse shapes identities, behaviour and actions (see Chapter 7).

How far can the right to information be controlled? Organisations such as WikiLeaks exist to publish all information, no matter how sensitive. How moral would a policy to restrict public information about extremist activities be and what support would it have in the population? Without accurate and timely information, rumours will abound and may have a more detrimental effect than receiving the actual news. The power of misinformation is exacerbated in 'hyper reality' and in social networks in cyber space. There needs to be a greater awareness in and by both the media and government of the ambiguous role that policy and politics play in the creation of extreme identities (see Chapters 3 and 7), especially the dangers of characterising a religion as being the cause of extremism rather than an extremist interpretation of that religion; whole communities as supporting extremism rather than having extremist within their midst, and the need to focus on the solution that is community-based but supported by all. Governments must maintain a balanced approach to policing the internet without abusing human rights and drifting into an electronic police state although it has been argued that the UK has already become a surveillance society (BBC 2006). Developing social control within cyber space by the users and suppliers is crucial to policing by consent within cyber space. However, there are many who oppose regulation within the worldwide web (see Chapters 2 and 9).

Moreover, the British Home Secretary, Theresa May, has acknowledged that Al-Qaeda is increasingly using online technology, including popular social networking sites such as Facebook and Twitter, to indoctrinate and recruit would-be extremists for terrorist purposes. She argued that since the Arab Spring in 2010 and the death of Osama bin Laden, the cyber threat from Al-Qaeda has increased because of the risk associated with Al-Qaeda led splinter groups that are based in different countries across the world who are all willing to work in shifting partnerships. She stated that; 'Since the death of Osama bin Laden, al-Qa'ida has explicitly called not only for acts of lone or individual terrorism, but also for cyber-jihad' (May 2011).

Terrorist-related material and websites are increasingly important in the discourse on extremism since both extremist groups at home and those based overseas rely on the internet to spread their message of terror (The Change Institute 2008). Indeed, online terrorist material has included live online beheadings to amplify the act and appeal to a wider international audience (Weimann 2005). Cyber space provides extremist organisations with a psychological platform on which they can transmit their message of terror, or for propaganda, recruitment, training and indoctrination purposes. For example, Pervez Khan who aimed to kill and behead a British Muslim soldier and then use the internet as a tool for posting the beheading online, was arrested and charged for conspiring to commit murder with intent (Guardian Press Association 2008).

The British Terrorism Act 2006 created a number of offences which relate directly to individuals who may be using the internet to incite or glorify a terrorist act. However, although this is a mechanism for prosecution, it does not necessarily provide answers on how to prevent individuals from searching online extremist material or being susceptible to indoctrination through cyber space. For example, Rizwan Sabir was arrested under the Terrorism Act for downloading extremist material that could be used for a terrorist purpose. Rizwan had been studying for a counter-terrorism project on extremism and when he downloaded an Al-Qaeda training manual from the internet he was arrested but later released without charge (BBC News 2009).

Conclusion

Extremism, counter-terrorism and policing are three interrelated areas that require a robust and community-led approach when dealing with the threat from terrorism. As noted in Chapter 1 extremism has a wide range of meanings and interpretations, however, the term will continue to evolve and so too will our understanding of how to tackle extremists. There needs to be a clear understanding that the words 'radicalisation' and 'extremism' are not interchangeable, that neither explicitly imply violence (see Chapter 7) and that the close association of religions with extremists and terrorists is unhelpful. The threat from the far right is also as real as the one from Islamist extremism. Governments are required to show understanding when it comes to making new policy recommendations and this extends to international as well as internal policy. Policy must support the forming and maintenance of convivial cultures. The police, who are there to enforce the law, must be proportionate and not abuse their powers, lessons from previous Troubles in Northern Ireland must be learned, especially in relation to gathering intelligence, stopping and/or arresting suspects based upon poor evidence, or subjective and unfounded suspicions. The policies and politics used to counter extremism from rhetoric such as the 'war on terror', to increased policing powers, must be separate from garnishing votes and must avoid the drift to a police controlled state.

Further Reading

Ameli, S.R., Marandi, S.M., Ahmed, S., Kara, S. and Merali, A. (2007). *Muslims' Expectations of the Government The British Media and Muslim Representation: The Ideology of Demonisation,* London: Islamic Human Rights Commission (Online at http://www.ihrc.org.uk/file/1903718317.pdf on 29/3/10)

Bux, S. 2007. Muslim Youths, Islam and Violent Radicalisation: Addressing Some Myths *Police Journal* 80 3 (267) 1 September 2007

Davies, L. (2008). *Educating Against Extremism,* Stoke on Trent: Trentham Books Ltd.

Deflem, M. (2004) 'Social Control and the Policing of Terrorism: Foundations for a Sociology of Counterterrorism' *The American Sociologist* 35(2): 75–92 (Summer).

Giannasi, P. (2009). *The CJS response to Hate Crime: Race for Justice, ACPO Hate Crime Group, Hate Crime Task Group,* Presentation to the Hate Crime Summit, organised by SCOPE, UK Disabled People's Council and Disability Now in association with the Metropolitan Police Service's Disability Independent Advisory Group (DMAG), 20 January London, accessed at http://www/timetogetequal.org.uk/messages.asp?topicid=368&section=94 on 28 March, 2010.

Fitzgerald, M. (2011) Identifying extremism. *Police Professional.* 263, 21 July, 18–21.

Innes, M., Abbott, L., Lowe, T., and Roberts, C. 2007. *Hearts and Minds and Eyes and Ears: Reducing Radicalisation Risks Through Reassurance-Oriented Policing.* London: ACPO.

Innes et al. 2011. Assessing the Effects of Prevent Policing: A Report to the Association of Chief Police Officers. Innes, Colin Roberts

References

Archick, K., Belkin, P., Blanchard, C., Ek, C., and Mix, D. 2011. Muslims in Europe: Promoting Integration and Countering Extremism, September 7, *Congressional Research Service.* [Online]. Available at: www.crs.gov [accessed: 25 April 2012].

Awan, I. 2011. Terror in the Eye of the Beholder: The Spy cam Saga: Counter-terrorism or Counter-productive, *The Howard Journal of Criminal Justice,* 50(2): 199–202.

Awan, I. 2012. "'I'm a Muslim not an Extremist:' How the Prevent Strategy has constructed a 'Suspect' Community", *Politics & Policy*, 40(6): 1158–85.

Bartlett, J., Birdwell, J., and Littler, M. 2011. The New Face of Digital Populism. Demos. [Online]. Available at: http://www.demos.co.uk/publications/ thenewfaceofdigitalpopulism. [accessed: 5 June 2012].

BBC News. 2006. Britain is 'surveillance society'. [Online]. Available at: http:// news.bbc.co.uk/1/hi/uk/6108496.stm. [accessed: 31 March 2012].

BBC News. 2009. *Student was studying terrorism,* [Online]. Available at: http:// news.bbc.co.uk/1/hi/england/nottinghamshire/7415685.stm [accessed: 12 May 2009].

Blake, C., Sheldon, B, Strezelecki, R, and Williams, P. 2012. *Policing Terrorism, Policing Matters*, London: Sage.

Briggs, R., Fieschi, C., and Lownsbrough, H. 2006. *Bringing it Home: Community-based approaches to counter-terrorism*. London: Demos. [Online]. Available at: http://www.demos.co.uk/publications end_year=2009&page=8&start_ year=2005&tab=publications pp. 58–83. [accessed: 14 November 2011].

Buckelew, A.H. 1984. *Terrorism and the American Response*. San Rafael California: MIRA Academic press.

Carlile, L. 2011. Sixth Report of the Independent Reviewer pursuant to s14(3) of the Prevention of Terrorism Act 2005 [Online] Available at: http://www. statewatch.org/news/2011/feb/uk-counter-terrorism-lord-carlile-sixth-report. pdf [accessed: 3 July 2011].

Carlile, L. 2011. Report to the Home Secretary of Independent Oversight of Prevent Review and Strategy [Online] Available at: http://www.homeoffice. gov.uk/publications/counter-terrorism/prevent/prevent-strategy/lord-carlile-report?view=Binary [accessed 15 July 2011].

Cavalcanti, R., Goldsmith, C., Measor, L., and Squires, P. 2012. Riotous connections? [Online] cjm 87: The August 2011 Riots Available at: http:// www.crimeandjustice.org.uk/cjm/issue87.html. [accessed: 24 July 2012].

Clutterbuck, L. 2010. An overview of Violent Jihad in the UK: Radicalisation and the state response. In M. Ranstorp (ed.), *Understanding Violent Radicalisation: Terrorist and Jihadist Movements in Europe*. New York: Routledge.

Coleman, K. 2012. The Age of Cyber Conflict. *Eye Spy Intelligence Magazine*, 78, 52–3.

D'Arcy, M. 2012. Diplomacy 'burdens' cyber attack responses, *Public Service*, 2 July. [Online] Available at: http://www.publicservice.co.uk/news_story. asp?id=20175. [accessed: 24 July 2012].

Direct Gov. 2011. Reporting Extremism and Terrorism, [Online]. Available at: http://www.direct.gov.uk/en/CrimeJusticeAndTheLaw/Counterterrorism/ DG_183993 [accessed: 25 May 2011].

Empowering Local Partners to Prevent Violent Extremism in the United States. 2011. [Online]. Available at: http://www.whitehouse.gov/sites/default/files/ empowering_local_partners.pdf [accessed: 21 April 2012].

English, R. 2009. *Terrorism: How to Respond*. Oxford: Oxford University Press.

Fenwick, H., and Choudhury, T. 2011. The impact of counter-terrorism measures on Muslim communities, *Equality and Human Rights Commission Research Report 72,* [Online]. Available at: http://www.equalityhumanrights.com/ uploaded_files/research/counter-terrorism_research_report_72.pdf [accessed: 20 June 2011].

Guardian Press Association. 2008. Profile: Perviz Khan, *The Guardian*, [Online]. Available at: www.guardian.co.uk/uk/2008/feb/18/uksecurity3 [accessed: 28 November 2010].

Gutteridge, W. (ed) 1986. *The New Terrorism*. London: Mansell Publishing.

Harding, S. 2012. A reputational extravaganza? The role of the urban street gang in the riots in London. [Online] cjm 87: The August 2011 Riots Available at: http://www.crimeandjustice.org.uk/cjm/issue87.html [accessed: 24 July 2012].

Hewit, S 2008. *The British War on Terror.* London: Continuum.

Hickman, M.J., Thomas, L., Silvestri, S., and Nickels, H. 2011. Suspect communities? Counterterrorism Policy, the Press, and the impact on Irish and Muslim Communities in Britain, Institute for the Study of European Transformations, London Metropolitan University. [Online]. available at: http://www.londonmet.ac.uk/fms/MRSite/Research/iset/Suspect%20 Communities%20Findings%20July2011.pdf. [accessed: 13 April 2012].

HM Government. 2011. *Prevent Strategy* Presented to Parliament by the Prime Minister and the Secretary of State for the Home Department by Command of Her Majesty, [Online]. Available at: http://www.homeoffice.gov.uk/ publications/counter-terrorism/prevent/prevent-strategy/prevent-strategy- review?view=Binary [accessed: March 12 2011].

Home Affairs Committee. 2012. *Roots of violent radicalisation*. para 33 [Online]. Available at: http://www.publications.parliament.uk/pa/cm201012/cmselect/ cmhaff/1446/144605.htm#a10. [accessed: 9 May 2012].

Innes, M., and Thiel, D. 2008. Policing terror. In T. Newburn (ed), *Handbook of Policing*, Collumpton: Willan.

Jarvis, L., and Lister, M. 2011. Values and Stakeholders in the 2011 Prevent Strategy Responding to Prevent 2011, *Muslim Council of Britain,* [Online], Available at: http://www.mcb.org.uk/comm_details.php?heading_id=121&com_id=2 [accessed: 1 July 2011].

Lagrange, H. 2012. Youth unrest and riots in France and the UK. [Online] cjm 87: The August 2011 Riots Available at: http://www.crimeandjustice.org.uk/cjm/ issue87.html . [accessed: 24 July 2012].

McGovern, M., and Tobin, A. 2010. *Counter terror or counter productive: Comparing Irish and British Muslim experiences of counter-insurgency law and policy*. Edge Hill University. [Online]. Available at: http://www.edgehill. ac.uk/documents/news/CounteringTerror.pdf. [accessed: 23 May 2012].

May, T. 2011 'CONTEST Speech, *Home Office*, [Online, 12 July] Available at: http://www.homeoffice.gov.uk/media-centre/speeches/contest-speech [accessed: 20 July 2011]; Also see Travis, A 2011 Counter-terrorism strategy driven by 'cyberjihad' threat, *The Guardian* (July). [Online]. Available at: http://www.guardian.co.uk/politics/2011/jul/12/counter-terrorism-strategy-cyberjihad-threat [accessed: 13 July 2011].

Reidel, B. 2008. *The Search for Al Qaeda: its leadership, ideology and Future*. Washington, DC: Brookings Institution Press.

Seamark, M., Faulkner, F., and Wright, S. 2010. Woman charged with attempted murder over stabbing of Labour MP Stephen Timms. MailOnline. [Online]. Available at: http://www.dailymail.co.uk/news/article-1278459/Woman-charged-stabbing-Labour-MP-Stephen-Timms.html [accessed: 21 April 2011].

Thackrah, R. 2001. Revolutionary Conflicts: Terrorism and unconventional warfare explained. Taunton: Studymates

Townsend, M. 2102. Far-right anti-Muslim network on rise globally as Breivik trial opens. *Guardian*. [online]. Available at: Guardian.co.uk, 14 April. [accessed: 16 April 2012].

Townshend, C. 2002. *Terrorism: A Very Short Introduction*. Oxford: Oxford University press.

Treadwell, J. 2012. White Riot: the English Defence League and the 2011 English riots. [Online] cjm 87: The August 2011 Riots Available at: http://www.crimeandjustice.org.uk/cjm/issue87.html .[accessed: 24 July 2012].

Vieira, J.D. 1991 Terrorism at the BBC: The IRA on British Television. In A.O. Alali, and K.K. Eke, *Media coverage of Terrorism, Methods of Diffusion*. London: Sage 73–85.

Whittaker, D.J. 2002. *Terrorism: Understanding the Global Threat*. London: Longman.

Young, J. 2008. Vertigo and the global Merton. *Theoretical Criminology*, 12(4): 523–3; 1362–4806. DOI: 10.1177/1362480608099771.

Index